I0018889

Shishi - Kerberos 5 Impelementation

A catalogue record for this book is available from the Hong Kong Public Libraries.

Published in Hong Kong by Samurai Media Limited.

Email: info@samuraimedia.org

ISBN 978-988-8381-77-7

Copyright 2002 to 2013 Simon Josefsson.
Permission is granted to copy, distribute and/or modify this document under the terms of the GNU Free Documentation License, Version 1.3 or any later version published by the Free Software Foundation; with no Invariant Sections, no Front-Cover Texts, and no Back-Cover Texts. A copy of the license is included in the section entitled GNU Free Documentation License.

Minor modifications for publication Copyright 2015 Samurai Media Limited.

Background Cover Image by https://www.flickr.com/people/webtreatsetc/

Table of Contents

1 Introduction

Shishi is an implementation of the Kerberos 5 network authentication system, as specified in RFC 4120. Shishi can be used to authenticate users in distributed systems.

Shishi contains a library ('libshishi') that can be used by application developers to add support for Kerberos 5. Shishi contains a command line utility ('shishi') that is used by users to acquire and manage tickets (and more). The server side, a Key Distribution Center, is implemented by 'shishid'. Of course, a manual documenting usage aspects as well as the programming API is included.

Shishi currently supports AS/TGS exchanges for acquiring tickets, pre-authentication, the AP exchange for performing client and server authentication, and SAFE/PRIV for integrity/privacy protected application data exchanges.

Shishi is internationalized; error and status messages can be translated into the users' language; user name and passwords can be converted into any available character set (normally including ISO-8859-1 and UTF-8) and also be processed using an experimental Stringprep profile.

Most, if not all, of the widely used encryption and checksum types are supported, such as 3DES, AES, ARCFOUR and HMAC-SHA1.

Shishi is developed for the GNU/Linux system, but runs on over 20 platforms including most major Unix platforms and Windows, and many kind of devices including iPAQ handhelds and S/390 mainframes.

Shishi is free software licensed under the GNU General Public License version 3.0 or later.

1.1 Getting Started

This manual documents the Shishi application and library programming interface. All commands, functions and data types provided by Shishi are explained.

The reader is assumed to possess basic familiarity with network security and the Kerberos 5 security system.

This manual can be used in several ways. If read from the beginning to the end, it gives a good introduction into the library and how it can be used in an application. Forward references are included where necessary. Later on, the manual can be used as a reference manual to get just the information needed about any particular interface of the library. Experienced programmers might want to start looking at the examples at the end of the manual, and then only read up on those parts of the interface which are unclear.

1.2 Features and Status

Shishi might have a couple of advantages over other packages doing a similar job.

It's Free Software
> Anybody can use, modify, and redistribute it under the terms of the GNU General Public License version 3.0 or later.

It's thread-safe
> The library uses no global variables.

It's internationalized

> It handles non-ASCII username and passwords, and user visible strings used in the library (error messages) can be translated into the users' language.

It's portable

> It should work on all Unix like operating systems, including Windows.

Shishi is far from feature complete, it is not even a full RFC 1510 implementation yet. However, some basic functionality is implemented. A few implemented feature are mentioned below.

- Initial authentication (AS) from raw key or password. This step is typically used to acquire a ticket granting ticket and, less commonly, a server ticket.

- Subsequent authentication (TGS). This step is typically used to acquire a server ticket, by authenticating yourself using the ticket granting ticket.

- Client-Server authentication (AP). This step is used by clients and servers to prove to each other who they are, using negotiated tickets.

- Integrity protected communication (SAFE). This step is used by clients and servers to exchange integrity protected data with each other. The key is typically agreed on using the Client-Server authentication step.

- Ticket cache, supporting multiple principals and realms. As tickets have a life time of typically several hours, they are managed in disk files. There can be multiple ticket caches, and each ticket cache can store tickets for multiple clients (users), servers, encryption types, etc. Functionality is provided for locating the proper ticket for every use.

- Most standard cryptographic primitives. The believed most secure algorithms are supported (see Section 1.4 [Cryptographic Overview], page 5).

- Telnet client and server. This is used to remotely login to other machines, after authenticating yourself with a ticket.

- PAM module. This is used to login locally on a machine.

- KDC addresses located using DNS SRV RRs.

- Modularized low-level crypto interface. Currently Gnulib and Libgcrypt are supported. If you wish to add support for another low-level cryptographic library, you only have to implement a few APIs for DES, AES, MD5, SHA1, HMAC, etc. Look at 'gl/gc-gnulib.c' or 'gl/gc-libgcrypt.c' as a starting pointer.

The following table summarize what the current objectives are (i.e., the todo list) and an estimate on how long it will take to implement the feature, including some reasonable startup-time to get familiar with Shishi in general. If you like to start working on anything, please let me know so work duplication can be avoided.

- Parse '/etc/krb5.keytab' to extract keys to use for telnetd etc (week)

- Cross-realm support (week).

- PKINIT (use libksba, weeks)

- Finish GSSAPI support via GSSLib (weeks) Shishi will not support GSSLib natively, but a separate project "GSSLib" is under way to produce a generic GSS implementation, and it will use Shishi to implement the Kerberos 5 mechanism.

- Port to cyclone (cyclone need to mature first)
- Modularize ASN.1 library so it can be replaced (days). Almost done, all ASN.1 functionality is found in lib/asn1.c, although the interface is rather libtasn1 centric.
- KDC (initiated, weeks)
- LDAP backend for Shisa.
- Set/Change password protocol (weeks?)
- Port applications to use Shishi (indefinite)
- Finish server-realm stuff
- Improve documentation
- Improve internationalization
- Add AP-REQ replay cache (week).
- Study benefits by introducing a PA-TGS-REP. This would provide mutual authentication of the KDC in a way that is easier to analyze. Currently the mutual authentication property is only implicit from successful decryption of the KDC-REP and the 4 byte nonce.
- GUI applet for managing tickets. This is supported via the ticket-applet, of which a Shishi port is published on the Shishi home page.
- Authorization library (months?) The shishi_authorized_p() is not a good solution, better would be to have a generic and flexible authorization library. Possibly based on S-EXP's in tickets? Should support non-Kerberos uses as well, of course.
- Proof read manual.
- X.500 support, including DOMAIN-X500-COMPRESS. I will accept patches that implement this, if it causes minimal changes to the current code.

1.3 Overview

This section describes RFC 1510 from a protocol point of view[1].

Kerberos provides a means of verifying the identities of principals, (e.g., a workstation user or a network server) on an open (unprotected) network. This is accomplished without relying on authentication by the host operating system, without basing trust on host addresses, without requiring physical security of all the hosts on the network, and under the assumption that packets traveling along the network can be read, modified, and inserted at will. (Note, however, that many applications use Kerberos' functions only upon the initiation of a stream-based network connection, and assume the absence of any "hijackers" who might subvert such a connection. Such use implicitly trusts the host addresses involved.) Kerberos performs authentication under these conditions as a trusted third- party authentication service by using conventional cryptography, i.e., shared secret key. (shared secret key - Secret and private are often used interchangeably in the literature. In our usage, it takes two (or more) to share a secret, thus a shared DES key is a secret key. Something is only private when no one but its owner knows it. Thus, in public key cryptosystems, one has a public and a private key.)

---

[1] The text is a lightly adapted version of the introduction section from RFC 1510 by J. Kohl and C. Neuman, September 1993, copyright likely owned by the RFC 1510 authors or some contributor.

The authentication process proceeds as follows: A client sends a request to the authentication server (AS) requesting "credentials" for a given server. The AS responds with these credentials, encrypted in the client's key. The credentials consist of 1) a "ticket" for the server and 2) a temporary encryption key (often called a "session key"). The client transmits the ticket (which contains the client's identity and a copy of the session key, all encrypted in the server's key) to the server. The session key (now shared by the client and server) is used to authenticate the client, and may optionally be used to authenticate the server. It may also be used to encrypt further communication between the two parties or to exchange a separate sub-session key to be used to encrypt further communication.

The implementation consists of one or more authentication servers running on physically secure hosts. The authentication servers maintain a database of principals (i.e., users and servers) and their secret keys. Code libraries provide encryption and implement the Kerberos protocol. In order to add authentication to its transactions, a typical network application adds one or two calls to the Kerberos library, which results in the transmission of the necessary messages to achieve authentication.

The Kerberos protocol consists of several sub-protocols (or exchanges). There are two methods by which a client can ask a Kerberos server for credentials. In the first approach, the client sends a cleartext request for a ticket for the desired server to the AS. The reply is sent encrypted in the client's secret key. Usually this request is for a ticket-granting ticket (TGT) which can later be used with the ticket-granting server (TGS). In the second method, the client sends a request to the TGS. The client sends the TGT to the TGS in the same manner as if it were contacting any other application server which requires Kerberos credentials. The reply is encrypted in the session key from the TGT.

Once obtained, credentials may be used to verify the identity of the principals in a transaction, to ensure the integrity of messages exchanged between them, or to preserve privacy of the messages. The application is free to choose whatever protection may be necessary.

To verify the identities of the principals in a transaction, the client transmits the ticket to the server. Since the ticket is sent "in the clear" (parts of it are encrypted, but this encryption doesn't thwart replay) and might be intercepted and reused by an attacker, additional information is sent to prove that the message was originated by the principal to whom the ticket was issued. This information (called the authenticator) is encrypted in the session key, and includes a timestamp. The timestamp proves that the message was recently generated and is not a replay. Encrypting the authenticator in the session key proves that it was generated by a party possessing the session key. Since no one except the requesting principal and the server know the session key (it is never sent over the network in the clear) this guarantees the identity of the client.

The integrity of the messages exchanged between principals can also be guaranteed using the session key (passed in the ticket and contained in the credentials). This approach provides detection of both replay attacks and message stream modification attacks. It is accomplished by generating and transmitting a collision-proof checksum (elsewhere called a hash or digest function) of the client's message, keyed with the session key. Privacy and integrity of the messages exchanged between principals can be secured by encrypting the data to be passed using the session key passed in the ticket, and contained in the credentials.

1.4 Cryptographic Overview

Shishi implements several of the standard cryptographic primitives. In this section we give the names of the supported encryption suites, and some notes about them, and their associated checksum suite.

Statements such as "it is weak" should be read as meaning that there is no credible security analysis of the mechanism available, and/or that should an attack be published publicly, few people would likely be surprised. Also keep in mind that the key size mentioned is the actual key size, not the effective key space as far as a brute force attack is concerned.

As you may infer from the descriptions, there is currently no encryption algorithm and only one checksum algorithm that inspire great confidence in its design. Hopefully this will change over time.

NULL

> NULL is a dummy encryption suite for debugging. Encryption and decryption are identity functions. No integrity protection. It is weak. It is associated with the NULL checksum.

arcfour-hmac
arcfour-hmac-exp

> arcfour-hmac-* are a proprietary stream cipher with 56 bit (arcfour-hmac-exp) or 128 bit (arcfour-hmac) keys, used in a proprietary way described in an expired IETF draft 'draft-brezak-win2k-krb-rc4-hmac-04.txt'. Deriving keys from passwords is supported, and is done by computing a message digest (MD4) of a 16-bit Unicode representation of the ASCII password, with no salt. Data is integrity protected with a keyed hash (HMAC-MD5), where the key is derived from the base key in a creative way. It is weak. It is associated with the arcfour-hmac-md5 checksum.

des-cbc-none

> des-cbc-none is DES encryption and decryption with 56 bit keys and 8 byte blocks in CBC mode, using a zero IV. The keys can be derived from passwords by an obscure application specific algorithm. It is weak, because it offers no integrity protection. This is typically only used by RFC 1964 GSS-API implementations (which try to protect integrity using an ad-hoc solution). It is associated with the NULL checksum.

des-cbc-crc

> des-cbc-crc is DES encryption and decryption with 56 bit keys and 8 byte blocks in CBC mode, using the key as IV (see Section B.4 [Key as initialization vector], page 245). The keys can be derived from passwords by an obscure application specific algorithm. Data is integrity protected with an unkeyed but encrypted CRC32-like checksum. It is weak. It is associated with the rsa-md5-des checksum.

des-cbc-md4

> des-cbc-md4 is DES encryption and decryption with 56 bit keys and 8 byte blocks in CBC mode, using a zero IV. The keys can be derived from passwords by an obscure application specific algorithm. Data is integrity protected with

an unkeyed but encrypted MD4 hash. It is weak. It is associated with the `rsa-md4-des` checksum.

des-cbc-md5

> `des-cbc-md5` is DES encryption and decryption with 56 bit keys and 8 byte blocks in CBC mode, using a zero IV. The keys can be derived from passwords by an obscure application specific algorithm. Data is integrity protected with an unkeyed but encrypted MD5 hash. It is weak. It is associated with the `rsa-md5 des` checksum. This is the strongest RFC 1510 interoperable encryption mechanism.

des3-cbc-none

> `des3-cbc-none` is DES encryption and decryption with three 56 bit keys (effective key size 112 bits) and 8 byte blocks in CBC mode. The keys can be derived from passwords by the same algorithm as `des3-cbc-sha1-kd`. It is weak, because it offers no integrity protection. This is typically only used by GSS-API implementations (which try to protect integrity using an ad-hoc solution) for interoperability with some existing Kerberos GSS implementations. It is associated with the `NULL` checksum.

des3-cbc-sha1-kd

> `des3-cbc-sha1-kd` is DES encryption and decryption with three 56 bit keys (effective key size 112 bits) and 8 byte blocks in CBC mode. The keys can be derived from passwords by a algorithm based on the paper "A Better Key Schedule For DES-like Ciphers"[2] by Uri Blumenthal and Steven M. Bellovin (it is not clear if the algorithm, and the way it is used, is used by any other protocols, although it seems unlikely). Data is integrity protected with a keyed SHA1 hash in HMAC mode. It has no security proof, but is assumed to provide adequate security in the sense that knowledge on how to crack it is not known to the public. Note that the key derivation function is not widely used outside of Kerberos, hence not widely studied. It is associated with the `hmac-sha1-des3-kd` checksum.

aes128-cts-hmac-sha1-96
aes256-cts-hmac-sha1-96

> `aes128-cts-hmac-sha1-96` and `aes256-cts-hmac-sha1-96` is AES encryption and decryption with 128 bit and 256 bit key, respectively, and 16 byte blocks in CBC mode with Cipher Text Stealing. Cipher Text Stealing means data length of encrypted data is preserved (pure CBC add up to 7 pad characters). The keys can be derived from passwords with RSA Laboratories PKCS#5 Password Based Key Derivation Function 2[3], which is allegedly provably secure in a random oracle model. Data is integrity protected with a keyed SHA1 hash, in HMAC mode, truncated to 96 bits. There is no security proof, but the schemes are assumed to provide adequate security in the sense that knowledge on how to crack them is not known to the public. Note that AES has yet to receive the test of time, and the AES cipher encryption mode (CBC with Ciphertext Stealing, and a non-standard IV output) is not widely standardized

---

[2] http://www.research.att.com/~smb/papers/ides.pdf

[3] http://www.rsasecurity.com/rsalabs/pkcs/pkcs-5/

(hence not widely studied). It is associated with the `hmac-sha1-96-aes128` and `hmac-sha1-96-aes256` checksums, respectively.

The protocol do not include any way to negotiate which checksum mechanisms to use, so in most cases the associated checksum will be used. However, checksum mechanisms can be used with other encryption mechanisms, as long as they are compatible in terms of key format etc. Here are the names of the supported checksum mechanisms, with some notes on their status and the compatible encryption mechanisms. They are ordered by increased security as perceived by the author.

NULL

> NULL is a dummy checksum suite for debugging. It provides no integrity. It is weak. It is compatible with the NULL encryption mechanism.

arcfour-hmac-md5

> `arcfour-hmac-md5` is a keyed HMAC-MD5 checksum computed on a MD5 message digest, in turn computed on a four byte message type indicator concatenated with the application data. (The `arcfour` designation is thus somewhat misleading, but since this checksum mechanism is described in the same document as the `arcfour` encryption mechanisms, it is not a completely unnatural designation.) It is weak. It is compatible with all encryption mechanisms.

rsa-md4

> `rsa-md4` is a unkeyed MD4 hash computed over the message. It is weak, because it is unkeyed. However applications can, with care, use it non-weak ways (e.g., by including the hash in other messages that are protected by other means). It is compatible with all encryption mechanisms.

rsa-md4-des

> `rsa-md4-des` is a DES CBC encryption of one block of random data and a unkeyed MD4 hash computed over the random data and the message to integrity protect. The key used is derived from the base protocol key by XOR with a constant. It is weak. It is compatible with the `des-cbc-crc`, `des-cbc-md4`, `des-cbc-md5` encryption mechanisms.

rsa-md5

> `rsa-md5` is a unkeyed MD5 hash computed over the message. It is weak, because it is unkeyed. However applications can, with care, use it non-weak ways (e.g., by including the hash in other messages that are protected by other means). It is compatible with all encryption mechanisms.

rsa-md5-des

> `rsa-md5-des` is a DES CBC encryption of one block of random data and a unkeyed MD5 hash computed over the random data and the message to integrity protect. The key used is derived from the base protocol key by XOR with a constant. It is weak. It is compatible with the `des-cbc-crc`, `des-cbc-md4`, `des-cbc-md5` encryption mechanisms.

hmac-sha1-des3-kd

> `hmac-sha1-des3-kd` is a keyed SHA1 hash in HMAC mode computed over the message. The key is derived from the base protocol by the simplified key

derivation function (similar to the password key derivation functions of `des3-cbc-sha1-kd`, which does not appear to be widely used outside Kerberos and hence not widely studied). It has no security proof, but is assumed to provide good security. The weakest part is likely the proprietary key derivation function. It is compatible with the `des3-cbc-sha1-kd` encryption mechanism.

`hmac-sha1-96-aes128`
`hmac-sha1-96-aes256`

> `hmac-sha1-96-aes*` are keyed SHA1 hashes in HMAC mode computed over the message and then truncated to 96 bits. The key is derived from the base protocol by the simplified key derivation function (similar to the password key derivation functions of `aes*-cts-hmac-sha1-96`, i.e., PKCS#5). It has no security proof, but is assumed to provide good security. It is compatible with the `aes*-cts-hmac-sha1-96` encryption mechanisms.

Several of the cipher suites have long names that can be hard to memorize. For your convenience, the following short-hand aliases exists. They can be used wherever the full encryption names are used.

`arcfour`

> Alias for `arcfour-hmac`.

`des-crc`

> Alias for `des-cbc-crc`.

`des-md4`

> Alias for `des-cbc-md4`.

`des-md5`
`des`

> Alias for `des-cbc-md5`.

`des3`
`3des`

> Alias for `des3-cbc-sha1-kd`.

`aes128`

> Alias for `aes128-cts-hmac-sha1-96`.

`aes`
`aes256`

> Alias for `aes256-cts-hmac-sha1-96`.

1.5 Supported Platforms

Shishi has at some point in time been tested on the following platforms. Online build reports for each platforms and Shishi version is available at `http://autobuild.josefsson.org/shishi/`.

1. Debian GNU/Linux 3.0 (Woody)

   GCC 2.95.4 and GNU Make. This is the main development platform. `alphaev67-unknown-linux-gnu`, `alphaev6-unknown-linux-gnu`, `arm-unknown-linux-gnu`, armv4l-unknown-linux-gnu, hppa-unknown-linux-gnu, hppa64-unknown-linux-gnu, i686-pc-linux-gnu, ia64-unknown-linux-gnu, m68k-unknown-linux-gnu, mips-unknown-linux-gnu, mipsel-unknown-linux-gnu, powerpc-unknown-linux-gnu, s390-ibm-linux-gnu, sparc-unknown-linux-gnu, sparc64-unknown-linux-gnu.

2. Debian GNU/Linux 2.1

   GCC 2.95.4 and GNU Make. armv4l-unknown-linux-gnu.

3. Tru64 UNIX

   Tru64 UNIX C compiler and Tru64 Make. alphaev67-dec-osf5.1, alphaev68-dec-osf5.1.

4. SuSE Linux 7.1

   GCC 2.96 and GNU Make. alphaev6-unknown-linux-gnu, alphaev67-unknown-linux-gnu.

5. SuSE Linux 7.2a

   GCC 3.0 and GNU Make. ia64-unknown-linux-gnu.

6. SuSE Linux

   GCC 3.2.2 and GNU Make. x86_64-unknown-linux-gnu (AMD64 Opteron "Melody").

7. RedHat Linux 7.2

   GCC 2.96 and GNU Make. alphaev6-unknown-linux-gnu, alphaev67-unknown-linux-gnu, ia64-unknown-linux-gnu.

8. RedHat Linux 8.0

   GCC 3.2 and GNU Make. i686-pc-linux-gnu.

9. RedHat Advanced Server 2.1

   GCC 2.96 and GNU Make. i686-pc-linux-gnu.

10. Slackware Linux 8.0.01

    GCC 2.95.3 and GNU Make. i686-pc-linux-gnu.

11. Mandrake Linux 9.0

    GCC 3.2 and GNU Make. i686-pc-linux-gnu.

12. IRIX 6.5

    MIPS C compiler, IRIX Make. mips-sgi-irix6.5.

13. AIX 4.3.2

    IBM C for AIX compiler, AIX Make. rs6000-ibm-aix4.3.2.0.

14. HP-UX 11

    HP-UX C compiler and HP Make. ia64-hp-hpux11.22, hppa2.0w-hp-hpux11.11.

15. SUN Solaris 2.8

    Sun WorkShop Compiler C 6.0 and SUN Make. sparc-sun-solaris2.8.

16. NetBSD 1.6

    GCC 2.95.3 and GNU Make. alpha-unknown-netbsd1.6, i386-unknown-netbsdelf1.6.

17. OpenBSD 3.1 and 3.2

   GCC 2.95.3 and GNU Make. `alpha-unknown-openbsd3.1`, `i386-unknown-openbsd3.1`.

18. FreeBSD 4.7 and 4.8

   GCC 2.95.4 and GNU Make. `alpha-unknown-freebsd4.7`, `alpha-unknown-freebsd4.8`, `i386-unknown-freebsd4.7`, `i386-unknown-freebsd4.8`.

19. MacOS X 10.2 Server Edition

   GCC 3.1 and GNU Make. `powerpc-apple-darwin6.5`.

20. Cross compiled to uClinux/uClibc on Motorola Coldfire.

   GCC 3.4 and GNU Make `m68k-uclinux-elf`.

If you use Shishi on, or port Shishi to, a new platform please report it to the author (see Section 1.9 [Bug Reports], page 11).

1.6 Getting help

A mailing list where users of Shishi may help each other exists, and you can reach it by sending e-mail to `help-shishi@gnu.org`. Archives of the mailing list discussions, and an interface to manage subscriptions, is available through the World Wide Web at `http://lists.gnu.org/mailman/listinfo/help-shishi`.

1.7 Commercial Support

Commercial support is available for users of Shishi. The kind of support that can be purchased may include:

- Implement new features. Such as support for some optional part of the Kerberos standards, e.g. PKINIT, hardware token authentication.
- Port Shishi to new platforms. This could include porting Shishi to an embedded platforms that may need memory or size optimization.
- Integrate Kerberos 5 support in your existing project.
- System design of components related to Kerberos 5.

If you are interested, please write to:

```
Simon Josefsson Datakonsult
Hagagatan 24
113 47 Stockholm
Sweden

E-mail: simon@josefsson.org
```

If your company provides support related to Shishi and would like to be mentioned here, contact the author (see Section 1.9 [Bug Reports], page 11).

1.8 Downloading and Installing

The package can be downloaded from several places, including:

   `ftp://alpha.gnu.org/pub/gnu/shishi/`

The latest version is stored in a file, e.g., 'shishi-1.0.2.tar.gz' where the '1.0.2' indicate the highest version number.

The package is then extracted, configured and built like many other packages that use Autoconf. For detailed information on configuring and building it, refer to the 'INSTALL' file that is part of the distribution archive.

Here is an example terminal session that download, configure, build and install the package. You will need a few basic tools, such as 'sh', 'make' and 'cc'.

```
$ wget -q ftp://alpha.gnu.org/pub/gnu/shishi/shishi-1.0.2.tar.gz
$ tar xfz shishi-1.0.2.tar.gz
$ cd shishi-1.0.2/
$ ./configure
...
$ make
...
$ make install
...
```

After this you should be prepared to continue with the user, administration or programming manual, depending on how you want to use Shishi.

A few `configure` options may be relevant, summarized in the table.

`--disable-des`
`--disable-3des`
`--disable-aes`
`--disable-md`
`--disable-null`
`--disable-arcfour`

> Disable a cryptographic algorithm at compile time. Usually it is better to disable algorithms during run-time with the configuration file, but this allows you to reduce the code size slightly.

`--disable-starttls`

> Disable the experimental TLS support for KDC connections. If you do not use a Shishi KDC, this support is of no use so you could safely disable it.

`--without-stringprep`

> Disable internationalized string processing.

For the complete list, refer to the output from `configure --help`.

1.9 Bug Reports

If you think you have found a bug in Shishi, please investigate it and report it.

- Please make sure that the bug is really in Shishi, and preferably also check that it hasn't already been fixed in the latest version.

- You have to send us a test case that makes it possible for us to reproduce the bug.

- You also have to explain what is wrong; if you get a crash, or if the results printed are not good and in that case, in what way. Make sure that the bug report includes all information you would need to fix this kind of bug for someone else.

Please make an effort to produce a self-contained report, with something definite that can be tested or debugged. Vague queries or piecemeal messages are difficult to act on and don't help the development effort.

If your bug report is good, we will do our best to help you to get a corrected version of the software; if the bug report is poor, we won't do anything about it (apart from asking you to send better bug reports).

If you think something in this manual is unclear, or downright incorrect, or if the language needs to be improved, please also send a note.

Send your bug report to:

'bug-shishi@josefsson.org'

1.10 Contributing

If you want to submit a patch for inclusion – from solve a typo you discovered, up to adding support for a new feature – you should submit it as a bug report (see Section 1.9 [Bug Reports], page 11). There are some things that you can do to increase the chances for it to be included in the official package.

Unless your patch is very small (say, under 10 lines) we require that you assign the copyright of your work to the Free Software Foundation. This is to protect the freedom of the project. If you have not already signed papers, we will send you the necessary information when you submit your contribution.

For contributions that doesn't consist of actual programming code, the only guidelines are common sense. Use it.

For code contributions, a number of style guides will help you:

- Coding Style. Follow the GNU Standards document (see ⟨undefined⟩ [top], page ⟨undefined⟩).

  If you normally code using another coding standard, there is no problem, but you should use 'indent' to reformat the code (see ⟨undefined⟩ [top], page ⟨undefined⟩) before submitting your work.

- Use the unified diff format 'diff -u'.

- Return errors. The only valid reason for ever aborting the execution of the program is due to memory allocation errors, but for that you should call 'shishi_xalloc_die' to allow the application to recover if it wants to.

- Design with thread safety in mind. Don't use global variables. Don't even write to per-handle global variables unless the documented behaviour of the function you write is to write to the per-handle global variable.

- Avoid using the C math library. It causes problems for embedded implementations, and in most situations it is very easy to avoid using it.

- Document your functions. Use comments before each function headers, that, if properly formatted, are extracted into Texinfo manuals and GTK-DOC web pages.

- Supply a ChangeLog and NEWS entries, where appropriate.

2 User Manual

Usually Shishi interacts with you to get some initial authentication information like a password, and then contacts a server to receive a so called ticket granting ticket. From now on, you rarely interact with Shishi directly. Applications that need security services instruct the Shishi library to use the ticket granting ticket to get new tickets for various servers. An example could be if you log on to a host remotely via 'telnet'. The host usually requires authentication before permitting you in. The 'telnet' client uses the ticket granting ticket to get a ticket for the server, and then uses this ticket to authenticate you against the server (typically the server is also authenticated to you). You perform the initial authentication by typing shishi at the prompt. Sometimes it is necessary to supply options telling Shishi what your principal name (user name in the Kerberos realm) or your realm is. In the example, I specify the client name simon@JOSEFSSON.ORG.

```
$ shishi simon@JOSEFSSON.ORG
Enter password for 'simon@JOSEFSSON.ORG':
simon@JOSEFSSON.ORG:
Authtime:      Fri Aug 15 04:44:49 2003
Endtime:       Fri Aug 15 05:01:29 2003
Server:        krbtgt/JOSEFSSON.ORG key des3-cbc-sha1-kd (16)
Ticket key:    des3-cbc-sha1-kd (16) protected by des3-cbc-sha1-kd (16)
Ticket flags:  INITIAL (512)
$
```

As you can see, Shishi also prints a short description of the ticket received.

A logical next step is to display all tickets you have received. By the way, the tickets are usually stored as text in '~/.shishi/tickets'. This is achieved by typing shishi --list.

```
$ shishi --list
Tickets in '/home/jas/.shishi/tickets':

jas@JOSEFSSON.ORG:
Authtime:      Fri Aug 15 04:49:46 2003
Endtime:       Fri Aug 15 05:06:26 2003
Server:        krbtgt/JOSEFSSON.ORG key des-cbc-md5 (3)
Ticket key:    des-cbc-md5 (3) protected by des-cbc-md5 (3)
Ticket flags:  INITIAL (512)

jas@JOSEFSSON.ORG:
Authtime:      Fri Aug 15 04:49:46 2003
Starttime:     Fri Aug 15 04:49:49 2003
Endtime:       Fri Aug 15 05:06:26 2003
Server:        host/latte.josefsson.org key des-cbc-md5 (3)
Ticket key:    des-cbc-md5 (3) protected by des-cbc-md5 (3)

2 tickets found.
$
```

As you can see, I had a ticket for the server 'host/latte.josefsson.org' which was generated by 'telnet':ing to that host.

If, for some reason, you want to manually get a ticket for a specific server, you can use the `shishi --server-name` command. Normally, however, the application that uses Shishi will take care of getting a ticket for the appropriate server, so you normally wouldn't need to issue this command.

```
$ shishi --server-name=user/billg --encryption-type=des-cbc-md4
jas@JOSEFSSON.ORG:
Authtime:        Fri Aug 15 04:49:46 2003
Starttime:       Fri Aug 15 04:54:33 2003
Endtime:         Fri Aug 15 05:06:26 2003
Server:          user/billg key des-cbc-md4 (2)
Ticket key:      des-cbc-md4 (2) protected by des-cbc-md5 (3)
$
```

As you can see, I acquired a ticket for 'user/billg' with a 'des-cbc-md4' (see Section 1.4 [Cryptographic Overview], page 5) encryption key specified with the '--encryption-type' parameter.

To wrap up this introduction, let us see how you can remove tickets. You may want to do this if you leave your terminal for lunch or similar, and don't want someone to be able to copy the file and then use your credentials. Note that this only destroys the tickets locally, it does not contact any server telling that these credentials are no longer valid. So, if someone stole your ticket file, you must still contact your administrator and have them reset your account. Simply using this switch is not sufficient.

```
$ shishi --server-name=imap/latte.josefsson.org --destroy
1 ticket removed.
$ shishi --server-name=foobar --destroy
No tickets removed.
$ shishi --destroy
3 tickets removed.
$
```

Since the '--server-name' parameter takes a long string to type, it is possible to type the server name directly, after the client name. The following example demonstrates an AS-REQ followed by a TGS-REQ for a specific server (assuming you did not have any tickets to begin with).

```
$ src/shishi simon@latte.josefsson.org imap/latte.josefsson.org
Enter password for 'simon@latte.josefsson.org':
simon@latte.josefsson.org:
Acquired:        Wed Aug 27 17:21:06 2003
Expires:         Wed Aug 27 17:37:46 2003
Server:          imap/latte.josefsson.org key aes256-cts-hmac-sha1-96 (18)
Ticket key:      aes256-cts-hmac-sha1-96 (18) protected by aes256-cts-hmac-sha1-96
Ticket flags:    FORWARDED PROXIABLE (12)
$
```

Refer to the reference manual for all available parameters (see Section 4.6 [Parameters for shishi], page 46). The rest of this section contains descriptions of more specialized usage modes that can be ignored by most users.

2.1 Proxiable and Proxy Tickets

At times it may be necessary for a principal to allow a service to perform an operation on its behalf. The service must be able to take on the identity of the client, but only for a particular purpose. A principal can allow a service to take on the principal's identity for a particular purpose by granting it a proxy.

The process of granting a proxy using the proxy and proxiable flags is used to provide credentials for use with specific services. Though conceptually also a proxy, users wishing to delegate their identity in a form usable for all purpose MUST use the ticket forwarding mechanism described in the next section to forward a ticket-granting ticket.

The PROXIABLE flag in a ticket is normally only interpreted by the ticket-granting service. It can be ignored by application servers. When set, this flag tells the ticket-granting server that it is OK to issue a new ticket (but not a ticket-granting ticket) with a different network address based on this ticket. This flag is set if requested by the client on initial authentication. By default, the client will request that it be set when requesting a ticket-granting ticket, and reset when requesting any other ticket.

This flag allows a client to pass a proxy to a server to perform a remote request on its behalf (e.g. a print service client can give the print server a proxy to access the client's files on a particular file server in order to satisfy a print request).

In order to complicate the use of stolen credentials, Kerberos tickets are usually valid from only those network addresses specifically included in the ticket[4]. When granting a proxy, the client MUST specify the new network address from which the proxy is to be used, or indicate that the proxy is to be issued for use from any address.

The PROXY flag is set in a ticket by the TGS when it issues a proxy ticket. Application servers MAY check this flag and at their option they MAY require additional authentication from the agent presenting the proxy in order to provide an audit trail.

Here is how you would acquire a PROXY ticket for the service 'imap/latte.josefsson.org':

```
$ shishi jas@JOSEFSSON.ORG imap/latte.josefsson.org --proxy
Enter password for 'jas@JOSEFSSON.ORG':
libshishi: warning: KDC bug: Reply encrypted using wrong key.
jas@JOSEFSSON.ORG:
Authtime:       Mon Sep  8 20:02:35 2003
Starttime:      Mon Sep  8 20:02:36 2003
Endtime:        Tue Sep  9 04:02:35 2003
Server:         imap/latte.josefsson.org key des3-cbc-sha1-kd (16)
Ticket key:     des3-cbc-sha1-kd (16) protected by des3-cbc-sha1-kd (16)
Ticket flags:   PROXY (16)
$
```

As you noticed, this asked for your password. The reason is that proxy tickets must be acquired using a proxiable ticket granting ticket, which was not present. If you often need to get proxy tickets, you may acquire a proxiable ticket granting ticket from the start:

```
$ shishi --proxiable
Enter password for 'jas@JOSEFSSON.ORG':
jas@JOSEFSSON.ORG:
Authtime:       Mon Sep  8 20:04:27 2003
```

```
Endtime:        Tue Sep  9 04:04:27 2003
Server:         krbtgt/JOSEFSSON.ORG key des3-cbc-sha1-kd (16)
Ticket key:     des3-cbc-sha1-kd (16) protected by des3-cbc-sha1-kd (16)
Ticket flags:   PROXIABLE INITIAL (520)
```

Then you should be able to acquire proxy tickets based on that ticket granting ticket, as follows:

```
$ shishi jas@JOSEFSSON.ORG imap/latte.josefsson.org --proxy
libshishi: warning: KDC bug: Reply encrypted using wrong key.
jas@JOSEFSSON.ORG:
Authtime:       Mon Sep  8 20:04:27 2003
Starttime:      Mon Sep  8 20:04:32 2003
Endtime:        Tue Sep  9 04:04:27 2003
Server:         imap/latte.josefsson.org key des3-cbc-sha1-kd (16)
Ticket key:     des3-cbc-sha1-kd (16) protected by des3-cbc-sha1-kd (16)
Ticket flags:   PROXY (16)
$
```

2.2 Forwardable and Forwarded Tickets

Authentication forwarding is an instance of a proxy where the service that is granted is complete use of the client's identity. An example where it might be used is when a user logs in to a remote system and wants authentication to work from that system as if the login were local.

The FORWARDABLE flag in a ticket is normally only interpreted by the ticket-granting service. It can be ignored by application servers. The FORWARDABLE flag has an interpretation similar to that of the PROXIABLE flag, except ticket-granting tickets may also be issued with different network addresses. This flag is reset by default, but users MAY request that it be set by setting the FORWARDABLE option in the AS request when they request their initial ticket-granting ticket.

This flag allows for authentication forwarding without requiring the user to enter a password again. If the flag is not set, then authentication forwarding is not permitted, but the same result can still be achieved if the user engages in the AS exchange specifying the requested network addresses and supplies a password.

The FORWARDED flag is set by the TGS when a client presents a ticket with the FORWARDABLE flag set and requests a forwarded ticket by specifying the FORWARDED KDC option and supplying a set of addresses for the new ticket. It is also set in all tickets issued based on tickets with the FORWARDED flag set. Application servers may choose to process FORWARDED tickets differently than non-FORWARDED tickets.

If addressless tickets are forwarded from one system to another, clients SHOULD still use this option to obtain a new TGT in order to have different session keys on the different systems.

Here is how you would acquire a FORWARDED ticket for the service 'host/latte.josefsson.org':

```
$ shishi jas@JOSEFSSON.ORG host/latte.josefsson.org --forwarded
Enter password for 'jas@JOSEFSSON.ORG':
```

```
libshishi: warning: KDC bug: Reply encrypted using wrong key.
jas@JOSEFSSON.ORG:
Authtime:       Mon Sep  8 20:07:11 2003
Starttime:      Mon Sep  8 20:07:12 2003
Endtime:        Tue Sep  9 04:07:11 2003
Server:         host/latte.josefsson.org key des3-cbc-sha1-kd (16)
Ticket key:     des3-cbc-sha1-kd (16) protected by des3-cbc-sha1-kd (16)
Ticket flags:   FORWARDED (4)
$
```

As you noticed, this asked for your password. The reason is that forwarded tickets must be acquired using a forwardable ticket granting ticket, which was not present. If you often need to get forwarded tickets, you may acquire a forwardable ticket granting ticket from the start:

```
$ shishi --forwardable
Enter password for 'jas@JOSEFSSON.ORG':
jas@JOSEFSSON.ORG:
Authtime:       Mon Sep  8 20:08:53 2003
Endtime:        Tue Sep  9 04:08:53 2003
Server:         krbtgt/JOSEFSSON.ORG key des3-cbc-sha1-kd (16)
Ticket key:     des3-cbc-sha1-kd (16) protected by des3-cbc-sha1-kd (16)
Ticket flags:   FORWARDABLE INITIAL (514)
$
```

Then you should be able to acquire forwarded tickets based on that ticket granting ticket, as follows:

```
$ shishi jas@JOSEFSSON.ORG host/latte.josefsson.org --forwarded
libshishi: warning: KDC bug: Reply encrypted using wrong key.
jas@JOSEFSSON.ORG:
Authtime:       Mon Sep  8 20:08:53 2003
Starttime:      Mon Sep  8 20:08:57 2003
Endtime:        Tue Sep  9 04:08:53 2003
Server:         host/latte.josefsson.org key des3-cbc-sha1-kd (16)
Ticket key:     des3-cbc-sha1-kd (16) protected by des3-cbc-sha1-kd (16)
Ticket flags:   FORWARDED (4)
$
```

3 Administration Manual

Here you will learn how to set up, run and maintain the Shishi Kerberos server. Kerberos is incompatible with the standard Unix '/etc/passwd' password database[1], therefore the first step will be to create a Kerberos user database. Shishi's user database system is called Shisa. Once Shisa has been configured, you can then start the server and begin issuing Kerberos tickets to your users. The Shishi server is called 'shishid'. After getting the server up and running, we discuss how you can set up multiple Kerberos servers, to increase availability or offer load-balancing. Finally, we include some information intended for developers, that will enable you to customize Shisa to use an external user database, such as a LDAP server or SQL database.

3.1 Introduction to Shisa

The user database part of Shishi is called Shisa. The Shisa library is independent of the core Shishi library. Shisa is responsible for storing the name of your realms, the name of your principals (users), accounting information for the users (i.e., when each account starts to be valid and when it expires), and the cryptographic keys each user has. Some Kerberos internal data can also be stored, such as the key version number, the last dates for when various ticket requests were made, the cryptographic salt, string-to-key parameters and password for each user. Not all information need to be stored. For example, in some situations it is prudent to leave the password field empty, so that somebody who manages to steal the user database will only be able to compromise your system, and not any other systems were your user may have re-used the same password. On the other hand, you may already be storing the password in your customized database, in which case being able to change it via the Shisa interface can be useful.

Shisa is a small (a few thousand lines of C code) standalone library. Shisa does not depend on the Shishi library. Because a user database with passwords may be useful for other applications as well (e.g., GNU SASL), it might be separated into its own project later on. You should keep this in mind, so that you don't consider writing a Shisa backend for your own database as a purely Shishi specific project. You can, for example, choose to use the Shisa interface in your own applications to have a simple interface to your user database. Your experience and feedback is appreciated if you have chosen to explore this.

Note that the Shisa database does not expose everything you may want to know about a user, such as its full human name, telephone number or even the user's login account name or home directory. It only stores what is needed to authenticate a peer claiming to be an entity. Thus it does not make sense to replace your current user database or '/etc/passwd' with data derived from the Shisa database. Instead, it is intended that you write a Shisa backend that exports *some* of the information stored in your user database. You may be able to replace some existing functionality, such as the password field in '/etc/passwd' with a Kerberos PAM module, but there is no requirement for doing so.

3.2 Configuring Shisa

The configuration file for Shisa is typically stored in '/usr/local/etc/shishi/shisa.conf'. You do not have to modify this file, the defaults should be acceptable to first-time users.

---

[1] And besides, Shishi is intended to work on non-Unix platforms as well.

The file is used to define where your user database resides, and some options such as making the database read-only, or whether errors detected when accessing the database should be ignored. (The latter could be useful if the server is a remote LDAP server that might be unavailable, and then you would want to fall back to a local copy of the database.)

The default will store the user database using directories and files, rooted by default in '/usr/local/var/shishi'. You can use standard file permission settings to control access to the directory hierarchy. It is strongly recommended to restrict access to the directory. Storing the directory on local storage, i.e., hard disk or removable media, is recommended. We discourage placing the database on a network file system, but realize this can be useful in some situations (see Section 3.7 [Multiple servers], page 33).

See the reference manual (see Section 4.5 [Shisa Configuration], page 45) for the details of the configuration file. Again, you are not expected to need to modify anything unless you are an experienced Shishi administrator.

3.3 Using Shisa

There is a command line interface to the Shisa library, aptly named 'shisa'. You will use this tool to add, remove, and change information stored in the database about realms, principals, and keys. The tool can also be used to "dump" all information in the database, for backup or debugging purposes. (Currently the output format cannot be read by any tool, but functionality to do this will be added in the future, possibly as a read-only file-based Shisa database backend.)

The reference manual (see Section 4.8 [Parameters for shisa], page 48) explains all parameters, but here we will give you a walk-through of the typical uses of the tool.

Installing Shishi usually creates a realm with two principals: one ticket granting ticket for the realm, and one host key for the server. This is what you typically need to get started, but it doesn't serve our purposes, so we start by removing the principals and the realm. To do that, we need to figure out the name of the realm. The '--list' or '--dump' parameters can be used for this. (Most "long" parameters, like '--dump', have shorter names as well, in this case '-d', Section 4.8 [Parameters for shisa], page 48).

```
jas@latte:~$ shisa -d
latte
        krbtgt/latte
                Account is enabled.
                Current key version 0 (0x0).
                Key 0 (0x0).
                        Etype aes256-cts-hmac-sha1-96 (0x12, 18).
                        Salt lattekrbtgt/latte.
        host/latte
                Account is enabled.
                Current key version 0 (0x0).
                Key 0 (0x0).
                        Etype aes256-cts-hmac-sha1-96 (0x12, 18).
                        Salt lattehost/latte.
jas@latte:~$
```

The realm names are printed at column 0, the principal names are indented with one 'TAB' character (aka '\t' or ASCII 0x09 Horizontal Tabulation), and the information about each principal is indented with two 'TAB' characters. The above output means that there is one realm 'latte' with two principals: 'krbtgt/latte' (which is used to authenticate Kerberos ticket requests) and 'host/latte' (used to authenticate host-based applications like Telnet). They were created during 'make install' on a host called 'latte'.

If the installation did not create a default database for you, you might get an error similar to the following output.

```
jas@latte:~$ shisa -d
shisa: Cannot initialize 'file' database backend.
Location '/usr/local/var/shishi' and options 'N/A'.
shisa: Initialization failed:
Shisa database could not be opened.
jas@latte:~$
```

This indicates that the database does not exist. For a file database, you can create it simply by creating the directory, as follows. Note the access permission change with 'chmod'. Typically the 'root' user would own the files, but as these examples demonstrate, setting up a Kerberos server does not require root access. Indeed, it may be prudent to run all Shishi applications as a special non-'root' user, and have all Shishi related files owned by that user, so that any security vulnerabilities do not lead to a system compromise. (However, if the user database is ever stolen, system compromises of other systems may be inoccured, should you use, e.g., a kerberized Telnet.)

```
jas@latte:~$ mkdir /usr/local/var/shishi
jas@latte:~$ chmod go-rwx /usr/local/var/shishi
```

Back to the first example, where you have a realm 'latte' with some principals. We want to remove the realm to demonstrate how you create the realm from scratch. (Of course, you can have more than one realm in the database, but for this example we assume you want to set up a realm named the same as Shishi guessed you would name it, so the existing realm need to be removed first.) The '--remove' (short form '-r') parameter is used for this purpose, as follows.

```
jas@latte:~$ shisa -r latte host/latte
Removing principal 'host/latte@latte'...
Removing principal 'host/latte@latte'...done
jas@latte:~$ shisa -r latte krbtgt/latte
Removing principal 'krbtgt/latte@latte'...
Removing principal 'krbtgt/latte@latte'...done
jas@latte:~$ shisa -r latte
Removing realm 'latte'...
Removing realm 'latte'...done
jas@latte:~$
```

You may be asking yourself "What if the realm has many more principals?". If you fear manual labor (or a small 'sed' script, recall the format of '--list'?), don't worry, there is a '--force' (short form '-f') flag. Use it with care. Here is a faster way to do the above:

```
jas@latte:~$ shisa -r latte -f
Removing principal 'krbtgt/latte@latte'...
```

```
Removing principal 'krbtgt/latte@latte'...done
Removing principal 'host/latte@latte'...
Removing principal 'host/latte@latte'...done
Removing realm 'latte'...
Removing realm 'latte'...done
jas@latte:~$
```

You should now have a working, but empty, Shisa database. Let's set up the realm manually, step by step. The first step is to decide on a name for your realm. The full story is explained elsewhere (see Section 4.3 [Realm and Principal Naming], page 38), but the short story is to take your DNS domain name and translate it to upper case. For example, if your organization uses `example.org` it is a good idea to use `EXAMPLE.ORG` as the name of your Kerberos realm. We'll use `EXAMPLE.ORG` as the realm name in these examples. Let's create the realm.

```
jas@latte:~$ shisa -a EXAMPLE.ORG
Adding realm 'EXAMPLE.ORG'...
Adding realm 'EXAMPLE.ORG'...done
jas@latte:~$
```

Currently, there are no properties associated with entire realms. In the future, it may be possible to set a default realm-wide password expiry policy or similar. Each realm normally has one principal that is used for authenticating against the "ticket granting service" on the Kerberos server with a ticket instead of using the password. This is used by the user when she acquire a ticket for a server. The principal must look like 'krbtgt/REALM' (see [Name of the TGS], page 41). Let's create it.

```
jas@latte:~$ shisa -a EXAMPLE.ORG krbtgt/EXAMPLE.ORG
Adding principal 'krbtgt/EXAMPLE.ORG@EXAMPLE.ORG'...
Adding principal 'krbtgt/EXAMPLE.ORG@EXAMPLE.ORG'...done
jas@latte:~$
```

Now that wasn't difficult, although not very satisfying either. What does adding a principal mean? The name is created, obviously, but it also means setting a few values in the database. Let's view the entry to find out which values.

```
jas@latte:~$ shisa -d
EXAMPLE.ORG
        krbtgt/EXAMPLE.ORG
                Account is enabled.
                Current key version 0 (0x0).
                Key 0 (0x0).
                        Etype aes256-cts-hmac-sha1-96 (0x12, 18).
                        Salt EXAMPLE.ORGkrbtgt/EXAMPLE.ORG.
jas@latte:~$
```

To use host based security services like SSH or Telnet with Kerberos, each host must have a key shared between the host and the KDC. The key is typically stored in '/usr/local/etc/shishi/shishi.keys'. We assume your server is called 'mail.example.org' and we create the principal. To illustrate a new parameter, we also set the specific algorithm to use by using the '--encryption-type' (short form '-E') parameter.

```
jas@latte:~$ shisa -a EXAMPLE.ORG host/mail.example.org -E des3
Adding principal 'host/mail.example.org@EXAMPLE.ORG'...
Adding principal 'host/mail.example.org@EXAMPLE.ORG'...done
jas@latte:~$
```

To export the key, there is another Shisa parameter '--keys' that will print the key in a format that is recognized by Shishi. Let's use it to print the host key.

```
jas@latte:~$ shisa -d --keys EXAMPLE.ORG host/mail.example.org
EXAMPLE.ORG
        host/mail.example.org
                Account is enabled.
                Current key version 0 (0x0).
                Key 0 (0x0).
                        Etype des3-cbc-sha1-kd (0x10, 16).
-----BEGIN SHISHI KEY-----
Keytype: 16 (des3-cbc-sha1-kd)
Principal: host/mail.example.org
Realm: EXAMPLE.ORG

iQdA8hxdvOUHZN1iZJv7noMO2rXHV8gq
-----END SHISHI KEY-----
                        Salt EXAMPLE.ORGhost/mail.example.org.
jas@latte:~$
```

So to set up the host, simply redirect output to the host key file.

```
jas@latte:~$ shisa -d --keys EXAMPLE.ORG \
    host/mail.example.org >> /usr/local/etc/shishi/shishi.keys
jas@latte:~$
```

The next logical step is to create a principal for some user, so you can use your password to get a Ticket Granting Ticket via the Authentication Service (AS) from the KDC, and then use the Ticket Granting Service (TGS) from the KDC to get a ticket for a specific host, and then send that ticket to the host to authenticate yourself. Creating this end-user principle is slightly different from the earlier steps, because you want the key to be derived from a password instead of being a random key. The '--password' parameter indicate this. This make the tool ask you for the password.

```
jas@latte:~$ shisa -a EXAMPLE.ORG simon --password
Password for 'simon@EXAMPLE.ORG':
Adding principal 'simon@EXAMPLE.ORG'...
Adding principal 'simon@EXAMPLE.ORG'...done
jas@latte:~$
```

The only special thing about this principal now is that it has a **password** field set in the database.

```
jas@latte:~$ shisa -d EXAMPLE.ORG simon --keys
EXAMPLE.ORG
        simon
                Account is enabled.
                Current key version 0 (0x0).
```

```
                    Key 0 (0x0).
                            Etype aes256-cts-hmac-sha1-96 (0x12, 18).
    -----BEGIN SHISHI KEY-----
    Keytype: 18 (aes256-cts-hmac-sha1-96)
    Principal: simon
    Realm: EXAMPLE.ORG

    Ja7ciNtrAI3gtodLaVDQ5zhcH58ffk0kS5tGAM7ILvM=
    -----END SHISHI KEY-----
                            Salt EXAMPLE.ORGsimon.
                            Password foo.
    jas@latte:~$
```

You should now be ready to start the KDC, which is explained in the next section (see Section 3.4 [Starting Shishid], page 23), and get tickets as explained earlier (see Chapter 2 [User Manual], page 13).

3.4 Starting Shishid

The Shishi server, or Key Distribution Center (KDC), is called Shishid. Shishid is responsible for listening on UDP and TCP ports for Kerberos requests. Currently it can handle initial ticket requests (Authentication Service, or AS), typically authenticated with keys derived from passwords, and subsequent ticket requests (Ticket Granting Service, or TGS), typically authenticated with the key acquired during an AS exchange.

Currently there is very little configuration available, the only variables are which ports the server should listen on and an optional user name to **setuid** into after successfully listening to the ports.

By default, Shishid listens on the 'kerberos' service port (typically translated to 88 via '/etc/services') on the UDP and TCP transports via IPv4 and (if your machine support it) IPv6 on all interfaces on your machine. Here is a typical startup.

```
    latte:/home/jas/src/shishi# /usr/local/sbin/shishid
    Initializing GNUTLS...
    Initializing GNUTLS...done
    Listening on IPv4:*:kerberos/udp...done
    Listening on IPv4:*:kerberos/tcp...done
    Listening on IPv6:*:kerberos/udp...failed
    socket: Address family not supported by protocol
    Listening on IPv6:*:kerberos/tcp...failed
    socket: Address family not supported by protocol
    Listening on 2 ports...
```

Running as root is not recommended. Any security problem in shishid and your host may be compromised. Therefor, we recommend using the '--setuid' parameter, as follows.

```
    latte:/home/jas/src/shishi# /usr/local/sbin/shishid --setuid=jas
    Initializing GNUTLS...
    Initializing GNUTLS...done
    Listening on IPv4:*:kerberos/udp...done
    Listening on IPv4:*:kerberos/tcp...done
```

```
Listening on IPv6:*:kerberos/udp...failed
socket: Address family not supported by protocol
Listening on IPv6:*:kerberos/tcp...failed
socket: Address family not supported by protocol
Listening on 2 ports...
User identity set to 'jas' (22541)...
```

An alternative is to run shishid on an alternative port as a non-privileged user. To continue the example of setting up the EXAMPLE.ORG realm as a non-privileged user from the preceding section, we start the server listen on port 4711 via UDP on IPv4.

```
jas@latte:~$ /usr/local/sbin/shishid -l IPv4:*:4711/udp
Initializing GNUTLS...
Initializing GNUTLS...done
Listening on *:4711/tcp...
Listening on 1 ports...
shishid: Starting (GNUTLS '1.0.4')
shishid: Listening on *:4711/tcp socket 4
```

If you have set up the Shisa database as in the previous example, you can now acquire tickets as follows.

```
jas@latte:~$ shishi -o 'realm-kdc=EXAMPLE.ORG,localhost:4711' \
    simon@EXAMPLE.ORG
Enter password for 'simon@EXAMPLE.ORG':
simon@EXAMPLE.ORG:
Authtime:       Fri Dec 12 01:41:01 2003
Endtime:        Fri Dec 12 01:57:41 2003
Server:         krbtgt/EXAMPLE.ORG key aes256-cts-hmac-sha1-96 (18)
Ticket key:     aes256-cts-hmac-sha1-96 (18) protected by aes256-cts-hmac-sha1-96
Ticket flags:   FORWARDED PROXIABLE RENEWABLE INITIAL (12)
jas@latte:~$
```

The output from Shishid on a successful invocation would look like:

```
shishid: Has 131 bytes from *:4711/udp on socket 4
shishid: Processing 131 from *:4711/udp on socket 4
shishid: Trying AS-REQ
shishid: AS-REQ from simon@EXAMPLE.ORG for krbtgt/EXAMPLE.ORG@EXAMPLE.ORG
shishid: Matching client etype 18 against user key etype 18
shishid: Have 511 bytes for *:4711/udp on socket 4
shishid: Sending 511 bytes to *:4711/udp socket 4 via UDP
shishid: Listening on *:4711/udp socket 4
```

You may use the '-v' parameter for Shishid and Shishi to generate more debugging information.

To illustrate what an application, such as the Shishi patched versions of GNU lsh or Telnet from GNU InetUtils, would do when contacting the host 'mail.example.org' we illustrate using the TGS service as well.

```
jas@latte:~$ shishi -o 'realm-kdc=EXAMPLE.ORG,localhost:4711' \
    simon@EXAMPLE.ORG host/mail.example.org
simon@EXAMPLE.ORG:
```

```
Authtime:          Fri Dec 12 01:46:54 2003
Endtime:           Fri Dec 12 02:03:34 2003
Server:            host/mail.example.org key des3-cbc-sha1-kd (16)
Ticket key:        des3-cbc-sha1-kd (16) protected by aes256-cts-hmac-sha1-96 (18)
Ticket flags:      FORWARDED PROXIABLE (45398796)
jas@latte:~$
```

This conclude our walk-through of setting up a new Kerberos realm using Shishi. It is quite likely that one or more steps failed, and if so we encourage you to debug it and submit a patch, or at least report it as a problem. Heck, even letting us know if you got this far would be of interest. See Section 1.9 [Bug Reports], page 11.

3.5 Configuring DNS for KDC

Making sure the configuration files on all hosts running Shishi clients include the addresses of your server is tedious. If the configuration files do not mention the KDC address for a realm, Shishi will try to look up the information from DNS. In order for Shishi to find that information, you need to add the information to DNS. For this to work well, you need to set up a DNS zone with the same name as your Kerberos realm. The easiest is if you own the publicly visible DNS name, such as 'example.org' if your realm is 'EXAMPLE.ORG', but you can set up an internal DNS server with the information for your realm only. If this is done, you do not need to keep configuration files updated for the KDC addressing information.

3.5.1 DNS vs. Kerberos - Case Sensitivity of Realm Names

In Kerberos, realm names are case sensitive. While it is strongly encouraged that all realm names be all upper case this recommendation has not been adopted by all sites. Some sites use all lower case names and other use mixed case. DNS on the other hand is case insensitive for queries but is case preserving for responses to TXT queries. Since "MYREALM", "myrealm", and "MyRealm" are all different it is necessary that only one of the possible combinations of upper and lower case characters be used. This restriction may be lifted in the future as the DNS naming scheme is expanded to support non-ASCII names.

3.5.2 Overview - KDC location information

KDC location information is to be stored using the DNS SRV RR [RFC 2052]. The format of this RR is as follows:

Service.Proto.Realm TTL Class SRV Priority Weight Port Target

The Service name for Kerberos is always "_kerberos".

The Proto can be either "_udp", "_tcp", or "_tls._tcp". If these SRV records are to be used, a "_udp" record MUST be included. If the Kerberos implementation supports TCP transport, a "_tcp" record MUST be included. When using "_tcp" with "_kerberos", this indicates a "raw" TCP connection without any additional encapsulation. A "_tls._tcp" record MUST be specified for all Kerberos implementations that support communication with the KDC across TCP sockets encapsulated using TLS [RFC2246] (see Section B.1 [STARTTLS protected KDC exchanges], page 236).

The Realm is the Kerberos realm that this record corresponds to.

TTL, Class, SRV, Priority, Weight, and Target have the standard meaning as defined in RFC 2052.

As per RFC 2052 the Port number should be the value assigned to "kerberos" by the Internet Assigned Number Authority (88).

3.5.3 Example - KDC location information

These are DNS records for a Kerberos realm ASDF.COM. It has two Kerberos servers, kdc1.asdf.com and kdc2.asdf.com. Queries should be directed to kdc1.asdf.com first as per the specified priority. Weights are not used in these records.

```
_kerberos._udp.ASDF.COM.        IN      SRV     0 0 88 kdc1.asdf.com.
_kerberos._udp.ASDF.COM.        IN      SRV     1 0 88 kdc2.asdf.com.
_kerberos._tcp.ASDF.COM.        IN      SRV     0 0 88 kdc1.asdf.com.
_kerberos._tcp.ASDF.COM.        IN      SRV     1 0 88 kdc2.asdf.com.
_kerberos._tls._tcp.ASDF.COM.   IN      SRV     0 0 88 kdc1.asdf.com.
_kerberos._tls._tcp.ASDF.COM.   IN      SRV     1 0 88 kdc2.asdf.com.
```

3.5.4 Security considerations

As DNS is deployed today, it is an unsecure service. Thus the infor- mation returned by it cannot be trusted.

Current practice for REALM to KDC mapping is to use hostnames to indicate KDC hosts (stored in some implementation-dependent location, but generally a local config file). These hostnames are vulnerable to the standard set of DNS attacks (denial of service, spoofed entries, etc). The design of the Kerberos protocol limits attacks of this sort to denial of service. However, the use of SRV records does not change this attack in any way. They have the same vulnerabilities that already exist in the common practice of using hostnames for KDC locations.

Implementations SHOULD provide a way of specifying this information locally without the use of DNS. However, to make this feature worthwhile a lack of any configuration information on a client should be interpretted as permission to use DNS.

3.6 Kerberos via TLS

If Shishi is built with support for GNUTLS, the messages exchanged between clients and Shishid can be protected with TLS. TLS is only available over TCP connections. A full discussion of the features TLS have is out of scope here, but in short it means the communication is integrity and privacy protected, and that users can use OpenPGP, X.509 or SRP (i.e., any mechanism supported by TLS) to authenticate themselves to the Kerberos server. For details on the implementation, See Section B.1 [STARTTLS protected KDC exchanges], page 236.

3.6.1 Setting up TLS resume

Resuming earlier TLS session is supported and enabled by default. This improves the speed of the TLS handshake, because results from earlier negotiations can be re-used. Currently the TLS resume database is stored in memory (in constract to storing it on disk), in both the client and in the server. Because the server typically runs for a long time, this is not a problem for that side. The client is typically not a long-running process though; the client usually is invoked as part of applications like 'telnet' or 'login'. However, because each use of the client library typically result in a ticket, which is stored on disk and re-used by later processes, this is likely not a serious problem because the number of different tickets required by a user is usually quite small. For the client, TLS resume is typically only useful when you perform an initial authentication (using a password) followed by a ticket request for a service, in the same process.

You can configure the server, 'shishid' to never use TLS resume, or to increase or decrease the number of distinct TLS connections that can be resumed before they are garbage collected, see the '--resume-limit' parameter (see Section 4.7 [Parameters for shishid], page 47).

3.6.2 Setting up Anonymous TLS

Anonymous TLS is the simplest to set up and use. In fact, only the client need to be informed that your KDC support TLS. This can be done in the configuration file with the '/tls' parameter for 'kdc-realm' (see [Shishi Configuration], page 43), or by placing the KDC address in DNS using the '_tls' SRV record (see Section 3.5 [Configuring DNS for KDC], page 25).

Let's start Shishid, listening on a TCP socket. TLS require TCP. TCP sockets are automatically upgraded to TLS if the client request it.

```
jas@latte:~$ /usr/local/sbin/shishid -l IPv4:*:4711/tcp
Initializing GNUTLS...done
Listening on IPv4:*:4711/tcp...
Listening on 1 ports...
shishid: Starting (GNUTLS '1.0.4')
shishid: Listening on IPv4:*:4711/tcp socket 4
```

Let's use the client to talk with it, using TLS.

```
jas@latte:~$ shishi -o 'realm-kdc=EXAMPLE.ORG,localhost:4711/tls \
    simon@EXAMPLE.ORG
Enter password for 'simon@EXAMPLE.ORG':
simon@EXAMPLE.ORG:
Authtime:        Tue Dec 16 05:20:47 2003
Endtime:         Tue Dec 16 05:37:27 2003
Server:          krbtgt/EXAMPLE.ORG key aes256-cts-hmac-sha1-96 (18)
Ticket key:      aes256-cts-hmac-sha1-96 (18) protected by aes256-cts-hmac-sha1-96 (18)
Ticket flags:    FORWARDED PROXIABLE (12)
jas@latte:~$
```

On success, the server will print the following debug information.

```
shishid: Accepted socket 6 from socket 4 as IPv4:*:4711/tcp peer 127.0.0.1
shishid: Listening on IPv4:*:4711/tcp socket 4
shishid: Listening on IPv4:*:4711/tcp peer 127.0.0.1 socket 6
shishid: Has 4 bytes from IPv4:*:4711/tcp peer 127.0.0.1 on socket 6
shishid: Trying STARTTLS
shishid: TLS handshake negotiated protocol 'TLS 1.0', key exchange 'Anon DH', certfica
shishid: TLS anonymous authentication with 1024 bit Diffie-Hellman
shishid: Listening on IPv4:*:4711/tcp socket 4
shishid: Listening on IPv4:*:4711/tcp peer 127.0.0.1 socket 6
shishid: Has 131 bytes from IPv4:*:4711/tcp peer 127.0.0.1 on socket 6
```

```
shishid: Processing 131 from IPv4:*:4711/tcp peer 127.0.0.1 on socket 6
shishid: Trying AS-REQ
shishid: AS-REQ from simon@EXAMPLE.ORG for krbtgt/EXAMPLE.ORG@EXAMPLE.ORG
shishid: Matching client etype 18 against user key etype 18
shishid: Have 511 bytes for IPv4:*:4711/tcp peer 127.0.0.1 on socket 6
shishid: Sending 511 bytes to IPv4:*:4711/tcp peer 127.0.0.1 socket 6 via TLS
shishid: Listening on IPv4:*:4711/tcp socket 4
shishid: Listening on IPv4:*:4711/tcp peer 127.0.0.1 socket 6
shishid: Peer IPv4:*:4711/tcp peer 127.0.0.1 disconnected on socket 6
shishid: Closing IPv4:*:4711/tcp peer 127.0.0.1 socket 6
shishid: Listening on IPv4:*:4711/tcp socket 4
```

3.6.3 Setting up X.509 authenticated TLS

Setting up X.509 authentication is slightly more complicated than anonymous authentication. You need a X.509 certificate authority (CA) that can generate certificates for your Kerberos server and Kerberos clients. It is often easiest to setup the CA yourself. Managing a CA can be a daunting task, and we only give the bare essentials to get things up and running. We suggest that you study the relevant literature. As a first step beyond this introduction, you may wish to explore more secure forms of key storage than storing them unencrypted on disk.

The following three sections describe how you create the CA, KDC certificate, and client certificates. You can use any tool you like for this task, as long as they generate X.509 (PKIX) certificates in PEM format and RSA keys in PKCS#1 format. Here we use 'certtool' that come with GNUTLS, which is widely available. We conclude by discussing how you use these certificates in the KDC and in the Shishi client.

3.6.3.1 Create a Kerberos Certificate Authority

First create a CA key.

```
jas@latte:~$ certtool --generate-privkey \
   --outfile /usr/local/etc/shishi/shishi.key
Generating a private key...
Generating a 1024 bit RSA private key...
jas@latte:~$
```

Then create the CA certificate. Use whatever details you prefer.

```
jas@latte:~$ certtool --generate-self-signed \
   --load-privkey /usr/local/etc/shishi/shishi.key \
   --outfile /usr/local/etc/shishi/shishi.cert
Generating a self signed certificate...
Please enter the details of the certificate's distinguished name. \
Just press enter to ignore a field.
Country name (2 chars): SE
Organization name: Shishi Example CA
Organizational unit name:
Locality name:
State or province name:
Common name: CA
```

```
This field should not be used in new certificates.
E-mail:
Enter the certificate's serial number (decimal): 0


Activation/Expiration time.
The generated certificate will expire in (days): 180


Extensions.
Does the certificate belong to an authority? (Y/N): y
Is this a web server certificate? (Y/N): n
Enter the e-mail of the subject of the certificate:


X.509 certificate info:

Version: 3
Serial Number (hex): 00
Validity:
        Not Before: Sun Dec 21 10:59:00 2003
        Not After: Fri Jun 18 11:59:00 2004
Subject: C=SE,O=Shishi Example CA,CN=CA
Subject Public Key Info:
        Public Key Algorithm: RSA

X.509 Extensions:
        Basic Constraints: (critical)
                CA:TRUE

Is the above information ok? (Y/N): y


Signing certificate...
jas@latte:~$
```

3.6.3.2 Create a Kerberos KDC Certificate

First create the key for the KDC.

```
jas@latte:~$ certtool --generate-privkey \
   --outfile /usr/local/etc/shishi/shishid.key
Generating a private key...
Generating a 1024 bit RSA private key...
jas@latte:~$
```

Then create actual KDC certificate, signed by the CA certificate created in the previous step.

```
jas@latte:~$ certtool --generate-certificate \
```

```
    --load-ca-certificate /usr/local/etc/shishi/shishi.cert \
    --load-ca-privkey /usr/local/etc/shishi/shishi.key \
    --load-privkey /usr/local/etc/shishi/shishid.key \
    --outfile /usr/local/etc/shishi/shishid.cert
Generating a signed certificate...
Loading CA's private key...
Loading CA's certificate...
Please enter the details of the certificate's distinguished name. \
Just press enter to ignore a field.
Country name (2 chars): SE
Organization name: Shishi Example KDC
Organizational unit name:
Locality name:
State or province name:
Common name: KDC
This field should not be used in new certificates.
E-mail:
Enter the certificate's serial number (decimal): 0


Activation/Expiration time.
The generated certificate will expire in (days): 180


Extensions.
Does the certificate belong to an authority? (Y/N): n
Is this a web server certificate? (Y/N): n
Enter the e-mail of the subject of the certificate:


X.509 certificate info:

Version: 3
Serial Number (hex): 00
Validity:
        Not Before: Sun Dec 21 11:02:00 2003
        Not After: Fri Jun 18 12:02:00 2004
Subject: C=SE,O=Shishi Example KDC,CN=KDC
Subject Public Key Info:
        Public Key Algorithm: RSA

X.509 Extensions:
        Basic Constraints: (critical)
                CA:FALSE

Is the above information ok? (Y/N): y
```

```
Signing certificate...
jas@latte:~$
```

3.6.3.3 Create a Kerberos Client Certificate

First create the key for the client.

```
jas@latte:~$ certtool --generate-privkey \
   --outfile ~/.shishi/client.key
Generating a private key...
Generating a 1024 bit RSA private key...
jas@latte:~$
```

Then create the client certificate, signed by the CA. An alternative would be to have the KDC sign the client certificates.

```
jas@latte:~$ certtool --generate-certificate \
   --load-ca-certificate /usr/local/etc/shishi/shishi.cert \
   --load-ca-privkey /usr/local/etc/shishi/shishi.key \
   --load-privkey ~/.shishi/client.key \
   --outfile ~/.shishi/client.certs
Generating a signed certificate...
Loading CA's private key...
Loading CA's certificate...
Please enter the details of the certificate's distinguished name. \
Just press enter to ignore a field.
Country name (2 chars): SE
Organization name: Shishi Example Client
Organizational unit name:
Locality name:
State or province name:
Common name: Client
This field should not be used in new certificates.
E-mail:
Enter the certificate's serial number (decimal): 0


Activation/Expiration time.
The generated certificate will expire in (days): 180


Extensions.
Does the certificate belong to an authority? (Y/N): n
Is this a web server certificate? (Y/N): n
Enter the e-mail of the subject of the certificate:


X.509 certificate info:
```

```
Version: 3
Serial Number (hex): 00
Validity:
        Not Before: Sun Dec 21 11:04:00 2003
        Not After: Fri Jun 18 12:04:00 2004
Subject: C=SE,O=Shishi Example Client,CN=Client
Subject Public Key Info:
        Public Key Algorithm: RSA


X.509 Extensions:
        Basic Constraints: (critical)
                CA:FALSE


Is the above information ok? (Y/N): y



Signing certificate...
jas@latte:~$
```

3.6.3.4 Starting KDC with X.509 authentication support

The KDC need the CA certificate (to verify client certificates) and the server certificate and key (to authenticate itself to the clients). See elsewhere (see Section 4.7 [Parameters for shishid], page 47) for the entire description of the parameters.

```
jas@latte:~$ shishid -l *:4711/tcp \
   --x509cafile /usr/local/etc/shishi/shishi.cert \
   --x509certfile /usr/local/etc/shishi/shishid.cert \
   --x509keyfile /usr/local/etc/shishi/shishid.key
Initializing GNUTLS...
Parsed 1 CAs...
Loaded server certificate/key...
Generating Diffie-Hellman parameters...
Initializing GNUTLS...done
Listening on *:4711/tcp...
Listening on 1 ports...
shishid: Starting (GNUTLS '1.0.4')
shishid: Listening on *:4711/tcp socket 4
```

Then acquire tickets as usual. In case you wonder how shishi finds the client certificate and key, the filenames used above when generating the client certificates happen to be the default filenames for these files. So it pick them up automatically.

```
jas@latte:~$ shishi -o 'realm-kdc=EXAMPLE.ORG,localhost:4711/tls' \
   simon@EXAMPLE.ORG
Enter password for 'simon@EXAMPLE.ORG':
simon@EXAMPLE.ORG:
Authtime:       Sun Dec 21 11:15:47 2003
Endtime:        Sun Dec 21 11:32:27 2003
Server:         krbtgt/EXAMPLE.ORG key aes256-cts-hmac-sha1-96 (18)
```

```
    Ticket key:      aes256-cts-hmac-sha1-96 (18) protected by aes256-cts-hmac-sha1-96 (18)
    Ticket flags:    FORWARDED PROXIABLE RENEWABLE HWAUTHENT TRANSITEDPOLICYCHECKED OKASDEI
    jas@latte:~$
```

Here is what the server would print.

```
    shishid: Accepted socket 6 from socket 4 as *:4711/tcp peer 127.0.0.1
    shishid: Listening on *:4711/tcp socket 4
    shishid: Listening on *:4711/tcp peer 127.0.0.1 socket 6
    shishid: Has 4 bytes from *:4711/tcp peer 127.0.0.1 on socket 6
    shishid: Trying STARTTLS
    shishid: TLS handshake negotiated protocol 'TLS 1.0', key exchange 'RSA', certficate t
    shishid: TLS client certificate 'C=SE,O=Shishi Example Client,CN=Client', issued by 'C
    shishid: Listening on *:4711/tcp socket 4
    shishid: Listening on *:4711/tcp peer 127.0.0.1 socket 6
    shishid: Has 131 bytes from *:4711/tcp peer 127.0.0.1 on socket 6
    shishid: Processing 131 from *:4711/tcp peer 127.0.0.1 on socket 6
    shishid: Trying AS-REQ
    shishid: AS-REQ from simon@EXAMPLE.ORG for krbtgt/EXAMPLE.ORG@EXAMPLE.ORG
    shishid: Matching client etype 18 against user key etype 18
    shishid: Have 511 bytes for *:4711/tcp peer 127.0.0.1 on socket 6
    shishid: Sending 511 bytes to *:4711/tcp peer 127.0.0.1 socket 6 via TLS
    shishid: Listening on *:4711/tcp socket 4
    shishid: Listening on *:4711/tcp peer 127.0.0.1 socket 6
    shishid: Peer *:4711/tcp peer 127.0.0.1 disconnected on socket 6
    shishid: Closing *:4711/tcp peer 127.0.0.1 socket 6
    shishid: Listening on *:4711/tcp socket 4
```

3.7 Multiple servers

Setting up multiple servers is as easy as replicating the user database. Since the default 'file' user database is stored in the normal file system, you can use any common tools to replicate a file system. Network file system like NFS (properly secured by, e.g., a point-to-point symmetrically encrypted IPSEC connection) and file synchronizing tools like 'rsync' are typical choices.

The secondary server should be configured just like the master server. If you use the 'file' database over NFS you do not have to make any modifications. If you use, e.g., a cron job to 'rsync' the directory every hour or so, you may want to add a '--read-only' flag to the Shisa 'db' definition (see Section 4.5 [Shisa Configuration], page 45). That way, nobody will be lured into creating or changing information in the database on the secondary server, which only would be overwritten during the next synchronization.

```
    db --read-only file /usr/local/var/backup-shishi
```

The 'file' database is designed so it doesn't require file locking in the file system, which may be unreliable in some network file systems or implementations. It is also designed so that multiple concurrent readers and writers may access the database without causing corruption.

Warning: The last paragraph is currently not completely accurate. There may be race conditions with concurrent writers. None should cause infinite loops or data loss. However, unexpected results might occur if two writers try to update information about a principal simultaneous.

If you use a remote LDAP server or SQL database to store the user database, and access it via a Shisa backend, you have make sure your Shisa backend handle concurrent writers properly. If you use a modern SQL database, this probably is not a concern. If it is a problem, you may be able to work around it by implementing some kind of synchronization or semaphore mechanism. If all else sounds too complicated, you can set up the secondary servers as '--read-only' servers, although you will lose some functionality (like changing passwords via the secondary server, or updating timestamps when the last ticket request occurred).

One function that is of particular use for users with remote databases (be it LDAP or SQL) is the "database override" feature. Using this you can have the security critical principals (such as the ticket granting ticket) stored on local file system storage, but use the remote database for user principals. Of course, you must keep the local file system storage synchronized between all servers, as before. Here is an example configuration.

```
db --read-only file /var/local/master
db ldap kdc.example.org ca=/etc/shisa/kdc-ca.pem
```

This instruct the Shisa library to access the two databases sequentially, for each query using the first database that know about the requested principal. If you put the 'krbtgt/REALM' principal in the local 'file' database, this will override the LDAP interface. Naturally, you can have as many 'db' definition lines as you wish.

Users with remote databases can also investigate a so called *High Availability* mode. This is useful if you wish to have your Kerberos servers be able to continue to operate even when the remote database is offline. This is achieved via the '--ignore-errors' flag in the database definition. Here is a sample configuration.

```
db --ignore-errors ldap kdc.example.org ca=/etc/shisa/kdc-ca.pem
db --read-only file /var/cache/ldap-copy
```

This instruct the Shisa library to try the LDAP backend first, but if it fails, instead of returning an error, continue to try the operation on a read only local 'file' based database. Of course, write requests will still fail, but it may be better than halting the server completely. To make this work, you first need to set up a cron job on a, say, hourly basis, to make a copy of the remote database and store it in the local file database. That way, when the remote server goes away, fairly current information will still be available locally.

If you also wish to experiment with read-write fail over, here is an idea for the configuration.

```
db --ignore-errors ldap kdc.example.org ca=/etc/shisa/kdc-ca.pem
db --ignore-errors --read-only file /var/cache/ldap-copy
db file /var/cache/local-updates
```

This is similar to the previous, but it will ignore errors reading and writing from the first two databases, ultimately causing write attempts to end up in the final 'file' based database. Of course, you would need to create tools to feed back any local updates made while the remote server was down. It may also be necessary to create a special backend for this purpose, which can auto create principals that are used.

We finish with an example that demonstrate all the ideas presented.

```
db --read-only file /var/local/master
db --ignore-errors ldap kdc.example.org ca=/etc/shisa/kdc-ca.pem
db --ignore-errors --read-only file /var/cache/ldap-copy
db file /var/cache/local-updates
```

3.8 Developer information

The Programming API for Shisa is described below (see Section 5.19 [Kerberos Database Functions], page 226); this section is about extending Shisa, and consequently Shishi, to use your own user database system. You may want to store your Kerberos user information on an LDAP database server, for example.

Adding a new backend is straight forward. You need to implement the backend API function set, add the list of API functions to 'db/db.c' and possibly also add any library dependencies to the Makefile.

The simplest way to write a new backend is to start from the existing 'file' based database, in 'db/file.c', and modify the entry points as needed.

Note that the current backend API will likely change before it is frozen. We may describe it in detail here when it has matured. However, currently it is similar to the external Shisa API (see Section 5.19 [Kerberos Database Functions], page 226).

There should be no need to modify anything else in the Shisa library, and certainly not in the Shishi library or the 'shishid' server.

Naturally, we would appreciate if you would send us your new backend, if you believe it is generally useful (see Section 1.9 [Bug Reports], page 11).

4 Reference Manual

This chapter discuss the underlying assumptions of Kerberos, contain a glossary to Kerberos concepts, give you background information on choosing realm and principal names, and describe all parameters and configuration file syntaxes for the Shishi tools.

4.1 Environmental Assumptions

Kerberos imposes a few assumptions on the environment in which it can properly function:

- "Denial of service" attacks are not solved with Kerberos. There are places in the protocols where an intruder can prevent an application from participating in the proper authentication steps. Detection and solution of such attacks (some of which can appear to be not-uncommon "normal" failure modes for the system) is usually best left to the human administrators and users.

- Principals MUST keep their secret keys secret. If an intruder somehow steals a principal's key, it will be able to masquerade as that principal or impersonate any server to the legitimate principal.

- "Password guessing" attacks are not solved by Kerberos. If a user chooses a poor password, it is possible for an attacker to successfully mount an offline dictionary attack by repeatedly attempting to decrypt, with successive entries from a dictionary, messages obtained which are encrypted under a key derived from the user's password.

- Each host on the network MUST have a clock which is "loosely synchronized" to the time of the other hosts; this synchronization is used to reduce the bookkeeping needs of application servers when they do replay detection. The degree of "looseness" can be configured on a per-server basis, but is typically on the order of 5 minutes. If the clocks are synchronized over the network, the clock synchronization protocol MUST itself be secured from network attackers.

- Principal identifiers are not recycled on a short-term basis. A typical mode of access control will use access control lists (ACLs) to grant permissions to particular principals. If a stale ACL entry remains for a deleted principal and the principal identifier is reused, the new principal will inherit rights specified in the stale ACL entry. By not re-using principal identifiers, the danger of inadvertent access is removed.

4.2 Glossary of terms

Authentication
> Verifying the claimed identity of a principal.

Authentication header
> A record containing a Ticket and an Authenticator to be presented to a server as part of the authentication process.

Authentication path
> A sequence of intermediate realms transited in the authentication process when communicating from one realm to another.

Authenticator
> A record containing information that can be shown to have been recently generated using the session key known only by the client and server.

Authorization
>   The process of determining whether a client may use a service, which objects the client is allowed to access, and the type of access allowed for each.

Capability A token that grants the bearer permission to access an object or service. In Kerberos, this might be a ticket whose use is restricted by the contents of the authorization data field, but which lists no network addresses, together with the session key necessary to use the ticket.

Ciphertext
>   The output of an encryption function. Encryption transforms plaintext into ciphertext.

Client   A process that makes use of a network service on behalf of a user. Note that in some cases a Server may itself be a client of some other server (e.g. a print server may be a client of a file server).

Credentials
>   A ticket plus the secret session key necessary to successfully use that ticket in an authentication exchange.

Encryption Type (etype)
>   When associated with encrypted data, an encryption type identifies the algorithm used to encrypt the data and is used to select the appropriate algorithm for decrypting the data. Encryption type tags are communicated in other messages to enumerate algorithms that are desired, supported, preferred, or allowed to be used for encryption of data between parties. This preference is combined with local information and policy to select an algorithm to be used.

KDC   Key Distribution Center, a network service that supplies tickets and temporary session keys; or an instance of that service or the host on which it runs. The KDC services both initial ticket and ticket-granting ticket requests. The initial ticket portion is sometimes referred to as the Authentication Server (or service). The ticket-granting ticket portion is sometimes referred to as the ticket-granting server (or service).

Kerberos   The name given to the Project Athena's authentication service, the protocol used by that service, or the code used to implement the authentication service. The name is adopted from the three-headed dog which guards Hades.

Key Version Number (kvno)
>   A tag associated with encrypted data identifies which key was used for encryption when a long lived key associated with a principal changes over time. It is used during the transition to a new key so that the party decrypting a message can tell whether the data was encrypted using the old or the new key.

Plaintext   The input to an encryption function or the output of a decryption function. Decryption transforms ciphertext into plaintext.

Principal   A named client or server entity that participates in a network communication, with one name that is considered canonical.

Principal identifier
>   The canonical name used to uniquely identify each different principal.

Seal
: To encipher a record containing several fields in such a way that the fields cannot be individually replaced without either knowledge of the encryption key or leaving evidence of tampering.

Secret key
: An encryption key shared by a principal and the KDC, distributed outside the bounds of the system, with a long lifetime. In the case of a human user's principal, the secret key MAY be derived from a password.

Server
: A particular Principal which provides a resource to network clients. The server is sometimes referred to as the Application Server.

Service
: A resource provided to network clients; often provided by more than one server (for example, remote file service).

Session key
: A temporary encryption key used between two principals, with a lifetime limited to the duration of a single login "session". In the Kerberos system, a session key is generated by the KDC. The session key is distinct from the sub-session key, described next..

Sub-session key
: A temporary encryption key used between two principals, selected and exchanged by the principals using the session key, and with a lifetime limited to the duration of a single association. The sub- session key is also referred to as the subkey.

Ticket
: A record that helps a client authenticate itself to a server; it contains the client's identity, a session key, a timestamp, and other information, all sealed using the server's secret key. It only serves to authenticate a client when presented along with a fresh Authenticator.

4.3 Realm and Principal Naming

This section contains the discussion on naming realms and principals from the Kerberos specification.

4.3.1 Realm Names

Although realm names are encoded as GeneralStrings and although a realm can technically select any name it chooses, interoperability across realm boundaries requires agreement on how realm names are to be assigned, and what information they imply.

To enforce these conventions, each realm MUST conform to the conventions itself, and it MUST require that any realms with which inter-realm keys are shared also conform to the conventions and require the same from its neighbors.

Kerberos realm names are case sensitive. Realm names that differ only in the case of the characters are not equivalent. There are presently three styles of realm names: domain, X500, and other. Examples of each style follow:

```
domain:  ATHENA.MIT.EDU
  X500:  C=US/O=OSF
 other:  NAMETYPE:rest/of.name=without-restrictions
```

Domain syle realm names MUST look like domain names: they consist of components separated by periods (.) and they contain neither colons (:) nor slashes (/). Though domain names themselves are case insensitive, in order for realms to match, the case must match as well. When establishing a new realm name based on an internet domain name it is recommended by convention that the characters be converted to upper case.

X.500 names contain an equal (=) and cannot contain a colon (:) before the equal. The realm names for X.500 names will be string representations of the names with components separated by slashes. Leading and trailing slashes will not be included. Note that the slash separator is consistent with Kerberos implementations based on RFC1510, but it is different from the separator recommended in RFC2253.

Names that fall into the other category MUST begin with a prefix that contains no equal (=) or period (.) and the prefix MUST be followed by a colon (:) and the rest of the name. All prefixes must be assigned before they may be used. Presently none are assigned.

The reserved category includes strings which do not fall into the first three categories. All names in this category are reserved. It is unlikely that names will be assigned to this category unless there is a very strong argument for not using the 'other' category.

These rules guarantee that there will be no conflicts between the various name styles. The following additional constraints apply to the assignment of realm names in the domain and X.500 categories: the name of a realm for the domain or X.500 formats must either be used by the organization owning (to whom it was assigned) an Internet domain name or X.500 name, or in the case that no such names are registered, authority to use a realm name MAY be derived from the authority of the parent realm. For example, if there is no domain name for E40.MIT.EDU, then the administrator of the MIT.EDU realm can authorize the creation of a realm with that name.

This is acceptable because the organization to which the parent is assigned is presumably the organization authorized to assign names to its children in the X.500 and domain name systems as well. If the parent assigns a realm name without also registering it in the domain name or X.500 hierarchy, it is the parent's responsibility to make sure that there will not in the future exist a name identical to the realm name of the child unless it is assigned to the same entity as the realm name.

4.3.2 Principal Names

As was the case for realm names, conventions are needed to ensure that all agree on what information is implied by a principal name. The name-type field that is part of the principal name indicates the kind of information implied by the name. The name-type SHOULD be treated only as a hint to interpreting the meaning of a name. It is not significant when checking for equivalence. Principal names that differ only in the name-type identify the same principal. The name type does not partition the name space. Ignoring the name type, no two names can be the same (i.e. at least one of the components, or the realm, MUST be different). The following name types are defined:

```
name-type       value   meaning

NT-UNKNOWN        0   Name type not known
NT-PRINCIPAL      1   Just the name of the principal as in DCE, or for users
NT-SRV-INST       2   Service and other unique instance (krbtgt)
```

```
NT-SRV-HST          3   Service with host name as instance (telnet, rcommands)
NT-SRV-XHST         4   Service with host as remaining components
NT-UID              5   Unique ID
NT-X500-PRINCIPAL 6   Encoded X.509 Distingished name [RFC 2253]
NT-SMTP-NAME        7   Name in form of SMTP email name (e.g. user@foo.com)
NT-ENTERPRISE      10   Enterprise name - may be mapped to principal name
```

When a name implies no information other than its uniqueness at a particular time the name type PRINCIPAL SHOULD be used. The principal name type SHOULD be used for users, and it might also be used for a unique server. If the name is a unique machine generated ID that is guaranteed never to be reassigned then the name type of UID SHOULD be used (note that it is generally a bad idea to reassign names of any type since stale entries might remain in access control lists).

If the first component of a name identifies a service and the remaining components identify an instance of the service in a server specified manner, then the name type of SRV-INST SHOULD be used. An example of this name type is the Kerberos ticket-granting service whose name has a first component of krbtgt and a second component identifying the realm for which the ticket is valid.

If the first component of a name identifies a service and there is a single component following the service name identifying the instance as the host on which the server is running, then the name type SRV- HST SHOULD be used. This type is typically used for Internet services such as telnet and the Berkeley R commands. If the separate components of the host name appear as successive components following the name of the service, then the name type SRV-XHST SHOULD be used. This type might be used to identify servers on hosts with X.500 names where the slash (/) might otherwise be ambiguous.

A name type of NT-X500-PRINCIPAL SHOULD be used when a name from an X.509 certificate is translated into a Kerberos name. The encoding of the X.509 name as a Kerberos principal shall conform to the encoding rules specified in RFC 2253.

A name type of SMTP allows a name to be of a form that resembles a SMTP email name. This name, including an "@" and a domain name, is used as the one component of the principal name.

A name type of UNKNOWN SHOULD be used when the form of the name is not known. When comparing names, a name of type UNKNOWN will match principals authenticated with names of any type. A principal authenticated with a name of type UNKNOWN, however, will only match other names of type UNKNOWN.

Names of any type with an initial component of 'krbtgt' are reserved for the Kerberos ticket granting service. See [Name of the TGS], page 41, for the form of such names.

4.3.2.1 Name of server principals

The principal identifier for a server on a host will generally be composed of two parts: (1) the realm of the KDC with which the server is registered, and (2) a two-component name of type NT-SRV-HST if the host name is an Internet domain name or a multi-component name of type NT-SRV-XHST if the name of the host is of a form such as X.500 that allows slash (/) separators. The first component of the two- or multi-component name will identify the service and the latter components will identify the host. Where the name of the host is not case sensitive (for example, with Internet domain names) the name of the host MUST be lower case. If specified by the application protocol for services such as telnet and the Berkeley R commands which run with system privileges, the first component MAY be the string 'host' instead of a service specific identifier.

4.3.2.2 Name of the TGS

The principal identifier of the ticket-granting service shall be composed of three parts: (1) the realm of the KDC issuing the TGS ticket (2) a two-part name of type NT-SRV-INST, with the first part "krbtgt" and the second part the name of the realm which will accept the ticket-granting ticket. For example, a ticket-granting ticket issued by the ATHENA.MIT.EDU realm to be used to get tickets from the ATHENA.MIT.EDU KDC has a principal identifier of "ATHENA.MIT.EDU" (realm), ("krbtgt", "ATHENA.MIT.EDU") (name). A ticket-granting ticket issued by the ATHENA.MIT.EDU realm to be used to get tickets from the MIT.EDU realm has a principal identifier of "ATHENA.MIT.EDU" (realm), ("krbtgt", "MIT.EDU") (name).

4.3.3 Choosing a principal with which to communicate

The Kerberos protocol provides the means for verifying (subject to the assumptions in Section 4.1 [Environmental Assumptions], page 36) that the entity with which one communicates is the same entity that was registered with the KDC using the claimed identity (principal name). It is still necessary to determine whether that identity corresponds to the entity with which one intends to communicate.

When appropriate data has been exchanged in advance, this determination may be performed syntactically by the application based on the application protocol specification, information provided by the user, and configuration files. For example, the server principal name (including realm) for a telnet server might be derived from the user specified host name (from the telnet command line), the "host/" prefix specified in the application protocol specification, and a mapping to a Kerberos realm derived syntactically from the domain part of the specified hostname and information from the local Kerberos realms database.

One can also rely on trusted third parties to make this determination, but only when the data obtained from the third party is suitably integrity protected while resident on the third party server and when transmitted. Thus, for example, one should not rely on an unprotected domain name system record to map a host alias to the primary name of a server, accepting the primary name as the party one intends to contact, since an attacker can modify the mapping and impersonate the party with which one intended to communicate.

Implementations of Kerberos and protocols based on Kerberos MUST NOT use insecure DNS queries to canonicalize the hostname components of the service principal names. In an environment without secure name service, application authors MAY append a statically configured domain name to unqualified hostnames before passing the name to the security mechanisms, but should do no more than that. Secure name service facilities, if available, might be trusted for hostname canonicalization, but such canonicalization by the client SHOULD NOT be required by KDC implementations.

Implementation note: Many current implementations do some degree of canonicalization of the provided service name, often using DNS even though it creates security problems. However there is no consistency among implementations about whether the service name is case folded to lower case or whether reverse resolution is used. To maximize interoperability and security, applications SHOULD provide security mechanisms with names which result from folding the user-entered name to lower case, without performing any other modifications or canonicalization.

4.3.4 Principal Name Form

Principal names consist of a sequence of strings, which is often tedious to parse. Therefor, Shishi often uses a "printed" form of principal which embed the entire principal name string sequence, and optionally also the realm, into one string. The format is taken from the Kerberos 5 GSS-API mechanism (RFC 1964).

The elements included within this name representation are as follows, proceeding from the beginning of the string:

1. One or more principal name components; if more than one principal name component is included, the components are separated by '/'. Arbitrary octets may be included within principal name components, with the following constraints and special considerations:

    a. Any occurrence of the characters '@' or '/' within a name component must be immediately preceded by the '\' quoting character, to prevent interpretation as a component or realm separator.

    b. The ASCII newline, tab, backspace, and null characters may occur directly within the component or may be represented, respectively, by '\n', '\t', '\b', or '\0'.

    c. If the '\' quoting character occurs outside the contexts described in (1a) and (1b) above, the following character is interpreted literally. As a special case, this allows the doubled representation '\\' to represent a single occurrence of the quoting character.

    d. An occurrence of the '\' quoting character as the last character of a component is illegal.

2. Optionally, a '@' character, signifying that a realm name immediately follows. If no realm name element is included, the local realm name is assumed. The '/', ':', and null characters may not occur within a realm name; the '@', newline, tab, and backspace characters may be included using the quoting conventions described in (1a), (1b), and (1c) above.

4.4 Shishi Configuration

The valid configuration file tokens are described here. The user configuration file is typically located in '`~/.shishi/shishi.conf`' (compare '`shishi --configuration-file`') and the system configuration is typically located in '`/usr/local/etc/shishi/shishi.conf`' (compare '`shishi --system-configuration-file`'). If the first non white space character of a line is a '#', the line is ignored. Empty lines are also ignored.

All tokens are valid in both the system and the user configuration files, and have the same meaning. However, as the system file is supposed to apply to all users on a system, it would not make sense to use some tokens in that file. For example, the '`default-principal`' is rarely useful in a system configuration file.

4.4.1 '`default-realm`'

Specify the default realm, by default the hostname of the host is used. E.g.,

```
default-realm JOSEFSSON.ORG
```

4.4.2 'default-principal'

Specify the default principal, by default the login username is used. E.g.,

```
default-principal jas
```

4.4.3 'client-kdc-etypes'

Specify which encryption types client asks server to respond in during AS/TGS exchanges. List valid encryption types, in preference order. Supported algorithms include aes256-cts-hmac-sha1-96, aes128-cts-hmac-sha1-96, des3-cbc-sha1-kd, des-cbc-md5, des-cbc-md4, des-cbc-crc and null. This option also indicates which encryption types are accepted by the client when receiving the response. Note that the preference order is not cryptographically protected, so a man in the middle can modify the order without being detected. Thus, only specify encryption types you trust completely here. The default only includes aes256-cts-hmac-sha1-96, as suggested by RFC1510bis. E.g.,

```
client-kdc-etypes=aes256-cts-hmac-sha1-96 des3-cbc-sha1-kd des-cbc-md5
```

4.4.4 'verbose', 'verbose-asn1', 'verbose-noise', 'verbose-crypto', 'verbose-crypto-noise'

Enable verbose library messages. E.g.,

```
verbose
verbose-noise
```

4.4.5 'realm-kdc'

Specify KDC addresses for realms. Value is 'REALM,KDCADDRESS[/TRANSPORT][,KDCADDRESS[/TRANSPORT]...

KDCADDRESS is the hostname or IP address of KDC.

Optional TRANSPORT is "udp" for UDP, "tcp" for TCP, and "tls" for TLS connections. By default UDP is tried first, and TCP used as a fallback if the KRB_ERR_RESPONSE_TOO_BIG error is received.

If not specified, Shishi tries to locate the KDC using SRV RRs, which is recommended. This option should normally only be used during experiments, or to access badly maintained realms.

```
realm-kdc=JOSEFSSON.ORG,ristretto.josefsson.org
```

4.4.6 'server-realm'

Specify realm for servers. Value is 'REALM,SERVERREGEXP[,SERVERREGEXP...]'.

SERVERREGEXP is a regular expression matching servers in the realm. The first match is used. E.g.,

```
server-realm=JOSEFSSON.ORG,.josefsson.org
```

Note: currently not used.

4.4.7 'kdc-timeout', 'kdc-retries'

How long shishi waits for a response from a KDC before continuing to next KDC for realm. The default is 5 seconds. E.g.,

```
kdc-timeout=10
```

How many times shishi sends a request to a KDC before giving up. The default is 3 times. E.g.,

```
kdc-retries=5
```

4.4.8 'stringprocess'

How username and passwords entered from the terminal, or taken from the command line, are processed.

"none": no processing is used.

"stringprep": convert from locale charset to UTF-8 and process using experimental RFC 1510 stringprep profile.

It can also be a string indicating a character set supported by iconv via libstringprep, in which case data is converted from locale charset into the indicated character set. E.g., UTF-8, ISO-8859-1, KOI-8, EBCDIC-IS-FRISS are supported on GNU systems. On some systems you can use "locale -m" to list available character sets. By default, the "none" setting is used which is consistent with RFC 1510 that is silent on the issue. In practice, however, converting to UTF-8 improves interoperability.

E.g.,

```
stringprocess=UTF-8
```

4.4.9 'ticket-life'

Specify default ticket life time.

The string can be in almost any common format. It can contain month names, time zones, 'am' and 'pm', 'yesterday', 'ago', 'next', etc. See Section 4.10 [Date input formats], page 50, for the long story.

As an extra feature, if the time specified by your string correspond to a time during the last 24 hours, an extra day is added to it. This allows you to specify relative times such as "17:00" to always mean the next 17:00, even if your system clock happens to be 17:30.

The default is 8 hours.

E.g.,

```
#ticket-life=8 hours
#ticket-life=1 day
ticket-life=17:00
```

4.4.10 'renew-life'

Specify how long a renewable ticket should remain renewable.

See ticket-life for the syntax. The extra feature that handles negative values within the last 2 hours is not active here.

The default is 7 days.

E.g.,

```
#renew-life=1 week
#renew-life=friday 17:00
renew-life=sunday
```

4.5 Shisa Configuration

The configuration file for Shisa is typically stored in '/usr/local/etc/shishi/shisa.conf'. If the first non white space character of a line is a '#', the line is ignored. Empty lines are also ignored.

4.5.1 'db'

Currently the only configuration options available is the db token that define the databases to use. The syntax is:

```
db [OPTIONS] <TYPE> [LOCATION] [PARAMETERS ...]
```

Specify the data sources for Kerberos 5 data. Multiple entries, even of the same data source type, are allowed. The data sources are accessed in the same sequence as they are defined here. If an entry is found in one data source, it will be used for the operations, without searching the remaining data sources. Valid OPTIONS include:

```
--read-only      No data is written to this data source.
--ignore-errors  Ignore failures in this backend.
```

The default (when the configuration file is empty) uses one "file" data source (see below), but for a larger installation you may want to combine several data sources. Here is an example.

```
db --read-only file /var/local/master
db --ignore-errors ldap kdc.example.org ca=/etc/shisa/kdc-ca.pem
db --read-only file /var/cache/ldap-copy
```

This demonstrate how you can store critical principals on local disk (the first entry, /var/local/master) that will always be found without looking in the LDAP directory. The critical principals could be, e.g., krbtgt/EXAMPLE.ORG. The second entry denote a LDAP server that could hold user principals. As you can see, Shisa will not let the caller know about errors with the LDAP source (they will be logged, however). Instead, if for instance the LDAP server has crashed, Shisa would continue and read from the /var/cache/ldap-copy file source. That file source may have been set up to contain a copy of the data in the LDAP server, perhaps made on an hourly basis, so that your server will be able to serve recent data even in case of a crash. Any updates or passwords change requests will however not be possible while the LDAP server is inaccessible, to reduce the problem of synchronizing data back into the LDAP server once it is online again.

Currently only the "file" data source is supported, and denote a data source that use the standard file system for storage.

Valid syntaxes for the "file" database:

```
db file PATH
```

Examples:

```
db file /var/shishi
db file /usr/share/shishi read-only
```

If no 'db' tokens are present, the default will be:

```
db file /usr/local/var/shishi
```

4.6 Parameters for shishi

If no command is given, Shishi try to make sure you have a ticket granting ticket for the default realm, and then display it.

Mandatory arguments to long options are mandatory for short options too.

Usage: `shishi [OPTIONS]... [CLIENT [SERVER]]...`

-h, --help	Print help and exit
-V, --version	Print version and exit

Commands:

-d, --destroy	Destroy tickets in local cache, limited by any --client-name or --server-name. (default=off)
-l, --list	List tickets in local cache, limited by any --client-name and --server-name. (default=off)
-r, --renew	Renew ticket. Use --server-name to specify ticket, default is the most recent renewable ticket granting ticket for the default realm. (default=off)

Flags:

--forwardable	Get a forwardable ticket, i.e., one that can be used to get forwarded tickets. (default=off)
--forwarded	Get a forwarded ticket. (default=off)
--proxiable	Get a proxiable ticket, i.e., one that can be used to get proxy tickets. (default=off)
--proxy	Get a proxy ticket. (default=off)
--renewable	Get a renewable ticket. (default=off)

Options:

--client-name=NAME	Client name. Default is login username.
-E, --encryption-type=ETYPE,[ETYPE...]	Encryption types to use. ETYPE is either registered name or integer. Valid values include 'aes128', 'aes256', 'aes' (same as 'aes256'), '3des', 'des-md5', 'des-md4', 'des-crc', 'des' (same as 'des-md5'), and 'arcfour'.
-e, --endtime=STRING	Specify when ticket validity should

	expire. The time syntax may be relative (to the start time), such as '20 hours', or absolute, such as '2001-02-03 04:05:06 CET'. The default is 8 hours after the start time.
--realm=STRING	Set default realm.
--renew-till=STRING	Specify renewable life of ticket. Implies --renewable. Accepts same time syntax as --endtime. If --renewable is specified, the default is 1 week after the start time.
--server-name=NAME	Server name. Default is 'krbtgt/REALM' where REALM is client realm.
-s, --starttime=STRING	Specify when ticket should start to be valid. Accepts same time syntax as --endtime. The default is to become valid immediately.
--ticket-granter=NAME	Service name in ticket to use for authenticating request. Only for TGS. Defaults to 'krbtgt/REALM@REALM' where REALM is client realm.

Other options:

--configuration-file=FILE	Read user configuration from FILE.
-c, --ticket-file=FILE	Read tickets from FILE.
-o, --library-options=STRING	Parse STRING as a configuration file statement.
-q, --quiet	Don't produce any diagnostic output. (default=off)
--system-configuration-file=FILE	Read system configuration from FILE.
--ticket-write-file=FILE	Write tickets from FILE. Default is to write them back to where they were read from.
-v, --verbose	Produce verbose output. (default=off)

4.7 Parameters for shishid

If no parameters are specified, 'shishid' listens on the defaults interfaces and answers incoming requests using the keys in the default key file.

Mandatory arguments to long options are mandatory for short options too.

    Usage: shishid [OPTIONS]...

```
    -h, --help                          Print help and exit
    -V, --version                       Print version and exit

Commands:
  -l, --listen=[FAMILY:]ADDR:PORT/TYPE
                                        Sockets to listen for queries on.  Family is
                                          'IPv4' or 'IPv6', if absent the family is
                                          decided by gethostbyname(ADDR). An address of
                                          '*' indicates all addresses on the local
                                          host. The default is '*:kerberos/udp,
                                          *:kerberos/tcp'.
    -u, --setuid=NAME                   After binding socket, set user identity.

TLS settings:
      --no-tls                          Disable TLS support  (default=off)
      --x509cafile=FILE                 X.509 certificate authorities used to verify
                                          client certificates, in PEM format.
      --x509certfile=FILE               X.509 server certificate, in PEM format.
      --x509crlfile=FILE                X.509 certificate revocation list to check for
                                          revoked client certificates, in PEM format.
      --x509keyfile=FILE                X.509 server certificate key, in PEM format.
      --resume-limit=SHORT              Keep track of up to this many TLS sessions for
                                          resume purposes (0 to disable TLS resume).
                                          (default='50')

Other options:
   -c, --configuration-file=FILE Use specified configuration file.
    -v, --verbose                       Produce verbose output.
                                          Use multiple times to increase amount of
                                          information.
    -q, --quiet                         Don't produce any diagnostic output.
                                          (default=off)
```

4.8 Parameters for shisa

The purpose of 'shisa' is to manipulate information stored in the Kerberos 5 database used by Shishi.

Mandatory arguments to long options are mandatory for short options too.

```
    Usage: shisa [OPTIONS]... [REALM [PRINCIPAL]]...

    -h, --help                          Print help and exit
    -V, --version                       Print version and exit


Operations:
    -a, --add                           Add realm or principal to database.
    -d, --dump                          Dump entries in database.
    -n, --key-add                       Add new key to a principal in database.
```

```
    --key-remove              Remove a key from a principal in
                                database.
-l, --list                    List entries in database.
-m, --modify                  Modify principal entry in database.
-r, --remove                  Remove realm or principal from database.

Parameters:
-f, --force                   Allow removal of non-empty realms.
                                (default=off)

    --enabled                 Only dump or list enabled principals.
                                (default=off)

    --disabled                Only dump or list disabled principals.
                                (default=off)

    --keys                    Print cryptographic key and password in
                                hostkey format.  (default=off)

Values:
-E, --encryption-type=STRING  Override default key encryption type.
                                Valid values include 'aes128',
                                'aes256', 'aes' (same as 'aes256'),
                                '3des', 'des-md5', 'des-md4',
                                'des-crc', 'des' (same as 'des-md5'),
                                and 'arcfour'.

    --key-version=NUMBER      Version of key.
    --password[=STRING]       Derive key from this password.
    --random                  Use a random key.  (default)
    --salt=STRING             Use specified salt for deriving key.
                                Defaults to concatenation of realm and
                                (unwrapped) principal name.

    --string-to-key-parameter=HEX   Encryption algorithm specific parameter
                                for password derivation.  Currently
                                only the AES algorithm can utilize
                                this, where it is interpreted as the
                                iteration count of the PKCS#5 PBKDF2
                                key deriver.

Other options:
-c, --configuration-file=FILE Use specified configuration file.
-o, --library-options=STRING  Parse string as configuration file
                                statement.

-v, --verbose                 Produce verbose output.
                                (default=off)

-q, --quiet                   Don't produce any diagnostic output.
                                (default=off)
```

4.9 Environment variables

A few of the compile-time defaults may be overridden at run-time by using environment variables. The following variables are supported.

- `SHISHI_CONFIG` Specify the location of the default system configuration file. Used by the Shishi library. If not specified, the default is specified at compile-time and is usually '`$prefix/etc/shishi.conf`'.

- `SHISHI_HOME` Specify the user specific directory for configuration files, ticket cache, etc. Used by the Shishi library. If not specified, it is computed as `$HOME/.shishi`.

- `SHISHI_USER` Specify the default principal user name. Used by the Shishi library. If not specified, it is taken from the environment variable `USER`.

- `SHISHI_TICKETS` Specify the file name of the ticket cache. Used by the Shishi library. If not specified, it will be `$SHISHI_HOME/tickets`, or `$HOME/.shishi/tickets` if `$SHISHI_HOME` is not specified.

4.10 Date input formats

First, a quote:

> Our units of temporal measurement, from seconds on up to months, are so complicated, asymmetrical and disjunctive so as to make coherent mental reckoning in time all but impossible. Indeed, had some tyrannical god contrived to enslave our minds to time, to make it all but impossible for us to escape subjection to sodden routines and unpleasant surprises, he could hardly have done better than handing down our present system. It is like a set of trapezoidal building blocks, with no vertical or horizontal surfaces, like a language in which the simplest thought demands ornate constructions, useless particles and lengthy circumlocutions. Unlike the more successful patterns of language and science, which enable us to face experience boldly or at least level-headedly, our system of temporal calculation silently and persistently encourages our terror of time.
>
> ... It is as though architects had to measure length in feet, width in meters and height in ells; as though basic instruction manuals demanded a knowledge of five different languages. It is no wonder then that we often look into our own immediate past or future, last Tuesday or a week from Sunday, with feelings of helpless confusion. ...
>
> —Robert Grudin, *Time and the Art of Living*.

This section describes the textual date representations that GNU programs accept. These are the strings you, as a user, can supply as arguments to the various programs. The C interface (via the `parse_datetime` function) is not described here.

4.10.1 General date syntax

A *date* is a string, possibly empty, containing many items separated by whitespace. The whitespace may be omitted when no ambiguity arises. The empty string means the beginning of today (i.e., midnight). Order of the items is immaterial. A date string may contain many flavors of items:

- calendar date items

- time of day items

- time zone items

- combined date and time of day items

- day of the week items

- relative items

- pure numbers.

We describe each of these item types in turn, below.

A few ordinal numbers may be written out in words in some contexts. This is most useful for specifying day of the week items or relative items (see below). Among the most commonly used ordinal numbers, the word 'last' stands for −1, 'this' stands for 0, and 'first' and 'next' both stand for 1. Because the word 'second' stands for the unit of time there is no way to write the ordinal number 2, but for convenience 'third' stands for 3, 'fourth' for 4, 'fifth' for 5, 'sixth' for 6, 'seventh' for 7, 'eighth' for 8, 'ninth' for 9, 'tenth' for 10, 'eleventh' for 11 and 'twelfth' for 12.

When a month is written this way, it is still considered to be written numerically, instead of being "spelled in full"; this changes the allowed strings.

In the current implementation, only English is supported for words and abbreviations like 'AM', 'DST', 'EST', 'first', 'January', 'Sunday', 'tomorrow', and 'year'.

The output of the date command is not always acceptable as a date string, not only because of the language problem, but also because there is no standard meaning for time zone items like 'IST'. When using date to generate a date string intended to be parsed later, specify a date format that is independent of language and that does not use time zone items other than 'UTC' and 'Z'. Here are some ways to do this:

```
$ LC_ALL=C TZ=UTC0 date
Mon Mar  1 00:21:42 UTC 2004
$ TZ=UTC0 date +'%Y-%m-%d %H:%M:%SZ'
2004-03-01 00:21:42Z
$ date --rfc-3339=ns  # --rfc-3339 is a GNU extension.
2004-02-29 16:21:42.692722128-08:00
$ date --rfc-2822  # a GNU extension
Sun, 29 Feb 2004 16:21:42 -0800
$ date +'%Y-%m-%d %H:%M:%S %z'  # %z is a GNU extension.
2004-02-29 16:21:42 -0800
$ date +'@%s.%N'  # %s and %N are GNU extensions.
@1078100502.692722128
```

Alphabetic case is completely ignored in dates. Comments may be introduced between round parentheses, as long as included parentheses are properly nested. Hyphens not followed by a digit are currently ignored. Leading zeros on numbers are ignored.

Invalid dates like '2005-02-29' or times like '24:00' are rejected. In the typical case of a host that does not support leap seconds, a time like '23:59:60' is rejected even if it corresponds to a valid leap second.

4.10.2 Calendar date items

A *calendar date item* specifies a day of the year. It is specified differently, depending on whether the month is specified numerically or literally. All these strings specify the same calendar date:

```
1972-09-24       # ISO 8601.
72-9-24          # Assume 19xx for 69 through 99,
                 # 20xx for 00 through 68.
72-09-24         # Leading zeros are ignored.
9/24/72          # Common U.S. writing.
24 September 1972
24 Sept 72       # September has a special abbreviation.
24 Sep 72        # Three-letter abbreviations always allowed.
Sep 24, 1972
24-sep-72
24sep72
```

The year can also be omitted. In this case, the last specified year is used, or the current year if none. For example:

```
9/24
sep 24
```

Here are the rules.

For numeric months, the ISO 8601 format '`year-month-day`' is allowed, where *year* is any positive number, *month* is a number between 01 and 12, and *day* is a number between 01 and 31. A leading zero must be present if a number is less than ten. If *year* is 68 or smaller, then 2000 is added to it; otherwise, if *year* is less than 100, then 1900 is added to it. The construct '`month/day/year`', popular in the United States, is accepted. Also '`month/day`', omitting the year.

Literal months may be spelled out in full: '`January`', '`February`', '`March`', '`April`', '`May`', '`June`', '`July`', '`August`', '`September`', '`October`', '`November`' or '`December`'. Literal months may be abbreviated to their first three letters, possibly followed by an abbreviating dot. It is also permitted to write '`Sept`' instead of '`September`'.

When months are written literally, the calendar date may be given as any of the following:

```
day month year
day month
month day year
day-month-year
```

Or, omitting the year:

```
month day
```

4.10.3 Time of day items

A *time of day item* in date strings specifies the time on a given day. Here are some examples, all of which represent the same time:

```
20:02:00.000000
20:02
8:02pm
```

```
20:02-0500      # In EST (U.S. Eastern Standard Time).
```

More generally, the time of day may be given as '*hour*:*minute*:*second*', where *hour* is a number between 0 and 23, *minute* is a number between 0 and 59, and *second* is a number between 0 and 59 possibly followed by '.' or ',' and a fraction containing one or more digits. Alternatively, ':*second*' can be omitted, in which case it is taken to be zero. On the rare hosts that support leap seconds, *second* may be 60.

If the time is followed by 'am' or 'pm' (or 'a.m.' or 'p.m.'), *hour* is restricted to run from 1 to 12, and ':*minute*' may be omitted (taken to be zero). 'am' indicates the first half of the day, 'pm' indicates the second half of the day. In this notation, 12 is the predecessor of 1: midnight is '12am' while noon is '12pm'. (This is the zero-oriented interpretation of '12am' and '12pm', as opposed to the old tradition derived from Latin which uses '12m' for noon and '12pm' for midnight.)

The time may alternatively be followed by a time zone correction, expressed as '*s hh mm*', where *s* is '+' or '-', *hh* is a number of zone hours and *mm* is a number of zone minutes. The zone minutes term, *mm*, may be omitted, in which case the one- or two-digit correction is interpreted as a number of hours. You can also separate *hh* from *mm* with a colon. When a time zone correction is given this way, it forces interpretation of the time relative to Coordinated Universal Time (UTC), overriding any previous specification for the time zone or the local time zone. For example, '+0530' and '+05:30' both stand for the time zone 5.5 hours ahead of UTC (e.g., India). This is the best way to specify a time zone correction by fractional parts of an hour. The maximum zone correction is 24 hours.

Either 'am'/'pm' or a time zone correction may be specified, but not both.

4.10.4 Time zone items

A *time zone item* specifies an international time zone, indicated by a small set of letters, e.g., 'UTC' or 'Z' for Coordinated Universal Time. Any included periods are ignored. By following a non-daylight-saving time zone by the string 'DST' in a separate word (that is, separated by some white space), the corresponding daylight saving time zone may be specified. Alternatively, a non-daylight-saving time zone can be followed by a time zone correction, to add the two values. This is normally done only for 'UTC'; for example, 'UTC+05:30' is equivalent to '+05:30'.

Time zone items other than 'UTC' and 'Z' are obsolescent and are not recommended, because they are ambiguous; for example, 'EST' has a different meaning in Australia than in the United States. Instead, it's better to use unambiguous numeric time zone corrections like '-0500', as described in the previous section.

If neither a time zone item nor a time zone correction is supplied, time stamps are interpreted using the rules of the default time zone (see Section 4.10.10 [Specifying time zone rules], page 56).

4.10.5 Combined date and time of day items

The ISO 8601 date and time of day extended format consists of an ISO 8601 date, a 'T' character separator, and an ISO 8601 time of day. This format is also recognized if the 'T' is replaced by a space.

In this format, the time of day should use 24-hour notation. Fractional seconds are allowed, with either comma or period preceding the fraction. ISO 8601 fractional minutes and hours are not supported. Typically, hosts support nanosecond timestamp resolution; excess precision is silently discarded.

Here are some examples:

```
2012-09-24T20:02:00.052-0500
2012-12-31T23:59:59,999999999+1100
1970-01-01 00:00Z
```

4.10.6 Day of week items

The explicit mention of a day of the week will forward the date (only if necessary) to reach that day of the week in the future.

Days of the week may be spelled out in full: 'Sunday', 'Monday', 'Tuesday', 'Wednesday', 'Thursday', 'Friday' or 'Saturday'. Days may be abbreviated to their first three letters, optionally followed by a period. The special abbreviations 'Tues' for 'Tuesday', 'Wednes' for 'Wednesday' and 'Thur' or 'Thurs' for 'Thursday' are also allowed.

A number may precede a day of the week item to move forward supplementary weeks. It is best used in expression like 'third monday'. In this context, 'last *day*' or 'next *day*' is also acceptable; they move one week before or after the day that *day* by itself would represent.

A comma following a day of the week item is ignored.

4.10.7 Relative items in date strings

Relative items adjust a date (or the current date if none) forward or backward. The effects of relative items accumulate. Here are some examples:

```
1 year
1 year ago
3 years
2 days
```

The unit of time displacement may be selected by the string 'year' or 'month' for moving by whole years or months. These are fuzzy units, as years and months are not all of equal duration. More precise units are 'fortnight' which is worth 14 days, 'week' worth 7 days, 'day' worth 24 hours, 'hour' worth 60 minutes, 'minute' or 'min' worth 60 seconds, and 'second' or 'sec' worth one second. An 's' suffix on these units is accepted and ignored.

The unit of time may be preceded by a multiplier, given as an optionally signed number. Unsigned numbers are taken as positively signed. No number at all implies 1 for a multiplier. Following a relative item by the string 'ago' is equivalent to preceding the unit by a multiplier with value −1.

The string 'tomorrow' is worth one day in the future (equivalent to 'day'), the string 'yesterday' is worth one day in the past (equivalent to 'day ago').

The strings 'now' or 'today' are relative items corresponding to zero-valued time displacement, these strings come from the fact a zero-valued time displacement represents the current time when not otherwise changed by previous items. They may be used to stress other items, like in '12:00 today'. The string 'this' also has the meaning of a zero-valued time displacement, but is preferred in date strings like 'this thursday'.

When a relative item causes the resulting date to cross a boundary where the clocks were adjusted, typically for daylight saving time, the resulting date and time are adjusted accordingly.

The fuzz in units can cause problems with relative items. For example, '2003-07-31 -1 month' might evaluate to 2003-07-01, because 2003-06-31 is an invalid date. To determine the previous month more reliably, you can ask for the month before the 15th of the current month. For example:

```
$ date -R
Thu, 31 Jul 2003 13:02:39 -0700
$ date --date='-1 month' +'Last month was %B?'
Last month was July?
$ date --date="$(date +%Y-%m-15) -1 month" +'Last month was %B!'
Last month was June!
```

Also, take care when manipulating dates around clock changes such as daylight saving leaps. In a few cases these have added or subtracted as much as 24 hours from the clock, so it is often wise to adopt universal time by setting the TZ environment variable to 'UTC0' before embarking on calendrical calculations.

4.10.8 Pure numbers in date strings

The precise interpretation of a pure decimal number depends on the context in the date string.

If the decimal number is of the form *yyyymmdd* and no other calendar date item (see Section 4.10.2 [Calendar date items], page 52) appears before it in the date string, then *yyyy* is read as the year, *mm* as the month number and *dd* as the day of the month, for the specified calendar date.

If the decimal number is of the form *hhmm* and no other time of day item appears before it in the date string, then *hh* is read as the hour of the day and *mm* as the minute of the hour, for the specified time of day. *mm* can also be omitted.

If both a calendar date and a time of day appear to the left of a number in the date string, but no relative item, then the number overrides the year.

4.10.9 Seconds since the Epoch

If you precede a number with '@', it represents an internal time stamp as a count of seconds. The number can contain an internal decimal point (either '.' or ','); any excess precision not supported by the internal representation is truncated toward minus infinity. Such a number cannot be combined with any other date item, as it specifies a complete time stamp.

Internally, computer times are represented as a count of seconds since an epoch—a well-defined point of time. On GNU and POSIX systems, the epoch is 1970-01-01 00:00:00 UTC, so '@0' represents this time, '@1' represents 1970-01-01 00:00:01 UTC, and so forth. GNU and most other POSIX-compliant systems support such times as an extension to POSIX, using negative counts, so that '@-1' represents 1969-12-31 23:59:59 UTC.

Traditional Unix systems count seconds with 32-bit two's-complement integers and can represent times from 1901-12-13 20:45:52 through 2038-01-19 03:14:07 UTC. More modern systems use 64-bit counts of seconds with nanosecond subcounts, and can represent all the times in the known lifetime of the universe to a resolution of 1 nanosecond.

On most hosts, these counts ignore the presence of leap seconds. For example, on most hosts '@915148799' represents 1998-12-31 23:59:59 UTC, '@915148800' represents 1999-01-01 00:00:00 UTC, and there is no way to represent the intervening leap second 1998-12-31 23:59:60 UTC.

4.10.10 Specifying time zone rules

Normally, dates are interpreted using the rules of the current time zone, which in turn are specified by the TZ environment variable, or by a system default if TZ is not set. To specify a different set of default time zone rules that apply just to one date, start the date with a string of the form 'TZ="*rule*"'. The two quote characters ('"') must be present in the date, and any quotes or backslashes within *rule* must be escaped by a backslash.

For example, with the GNU date command you can answer the question "What time is it in New York when a Paris clock shows 6:30am on October 31, 2004?" by using a date beginning with 'TZ="Europe/Paris"' as shown in the following shell transcript:

```
$ export TZ="America/New_York"
$ date --date='TZ="Europe/Paris" 2004-10-31 06:30'
Sun Oct 31 01:30:00 EDT 2004
```

In this example, the '--date' operand begins with its own TZ setting, so the rest of that operand is processed according to 'Europe/Paris' rules, treating the string '2004-10-31 06:30' as if it were in Paris. However, since the output of the date command is processed according to the overall time zone rules, it uses New York time. (Paris was normally six hours ahead of New York in 2004, but this example refers to a brief Halloween period when the gap was five hours.)

A TZ value is a rule that typically names a location in the 'tz' database. A recent catalog of location names appears in the TWiki Date and Time Gateway. A few non-GNU hosts require a colon before a location name in a TZ setting, e.g., 'TZ=":America/New_York"'.

The 'tz' database includes a wide variety of locations ranging from 'Arctic/Longyearbyen' to 'Antarctica/South_Pole', but if you are at sea and have your own private time zone, or if you are using a non-GNU host that does not support the 'tz' database, you may need to use a POSIX rule instead. Simple POSIX rules like 'UTC0' specify a time zone without daylight saving time; other rules can specify simple daylight saving regimes. See Section "Specifying the Time Zone with TZ" in The GNU C Library.

4.10.11 Authors of parse_datetime

parse_datetime started life as getdate, as originally implemented by Steven M. Bellovin (smb@research.att.com) while at the University of North Carolina at Chapel Hill. The code was later tweaked by a couple of people on Usenet, then completely overhauled by Rich $alz (rsalz@bbn.com) and Jim Berets (jberets@bbn.com) in August, 1990. Various revisions for the GNU system were made by David MacKenzie, Jim Meyering, Paul Eggert and others, including renaming it to get_date to avoid a conflict with the alternative Posix function getdate, and a later rename to parse_datetime. The Posix function getdate can parse more locale-specific dates using strptime, but relies on an environment variable and external file, and lacks the thread-safety of parse_datetime.

This chapter was originally produced by François Pinard (pinard@iro.umontreal.ca) from the 'parse_datetime.y' source code, and then edited by K. Berry (kb@cs.umb.edu).

5 Programming Manual

This chapter describes all the publicly available functions in the library.

5.1 Preparation

To use 'Libshishi', you have to perform some changes to your sources and the build system. The necessary changes are small and explained in the following sections. At the end of this chapter, it is described how the library is initialized, and how the requirements of the library are verified.

A faster way to find out how to adapt your application for use with 'Libshishi' may be to look at the examples at the end of this manual (see Section 5.18 [Examples], page 225).

5.1.1 Header

All interfaces (data types and functions) of the library are defined in the header file 'shishi.h'. You must include this in all programs using the library, either directly or through some other header file, like this:

```
#include <shishi.h>
```

The name space of 'Libshishi' is `shishi_*` for function names, `Shishi*` for data types and `SHISHI_*` for other symbols. In addition the same name prefixes with one prepended underscore are reserved for internal use and should never be used by an application.

5.1.2 Initialization

'Libshishi' must be initialized before it can be used. The library is initialized by calling `shishi_init` (see Section 5.2 [Initialization Functions], page 60). The resources allocated by the initialization process can be released if the application no longer has a need to call 'Libshishi' functions, this is done by calling `shishi_done`.

In order to take advantage of the internationalisation features in 'Libshishi', such as translated error messages, the application must set the current locale using `setlocale` before initializing 'Libshishi'.

5.1.3 Version Check

It is often desirable to check that the version of 'Libshishi' used is indeed one which fits all requirements. Even with binary compatibility new features may have been introduced but due to problem with the dynamic linker an old version is actually used. So you may want to check that the version is okay right after program startup.

shishi_check_version

const char * shishi_check_version (*const char * req_version*)   [Function]
> *req_version*: version string to compare with, or NULL
>
> Check that the version of the library is at minimum the one given as a string in `req_version`.
>
> **Return value:** the actual version string of the library; NULL if the condition is not met. If `NULL` is passed to this function no check is done and only the version string is returned.

The normal way to use the function is to put something similar to the following early in your `main`:

```
if (!shishi_check_version (SHISHI_VERSION))
  {
    printf ("shishi_check_version failed:\n"
            "Header file incompatible with shared library.\n");
    exit (EXIT_FAILURE);
  }
```

5.1.4 Building the source

If you want to compile a source file including the 'shishi.h' header file, you must make sure that the compiler can find it in the directory hierarchy. This is accomplished by adding the path to the directory in which the header file is located to the compilers include file search path (via the '-I' option).

However, the path to the include file is determined at the time the source is configured. To solve this problem, 'Libshishi' uses the external package `pkg-config` that knows the path to the include file and other configuration options. The options that need to be added to the compiler invocation at compile time are output by the '--cflags' option to `pkg-config shishi`. The following example shows how it can be used at the command line:

```
gcc -c foo.c `pkg-config shishi --cflags`
```

Adding the output of '`pkg-config shishi --cflags`' to the compilers command line will ensure that the compiler can find the 'Libshishi' header file.

A similar problem occurs when linking the program with the library. Again, the compiler has to find the library files. For this to work, the path to the library files has to be added to the library search path (via the '-L' option). For this, the option '--libs' to `pkg-config shishi` can be used. For convenience, this option also outputs all other options that are required to link the program with the 'Libshishi' libararies (in particular, the '-lshishi' option). The example shows how to link 'foo.o' with the 'Libshishi' library to a program `foo`.

```
gcc -o foo foo.o `pkg-config shishi --libs`
```

Of course you can also combine both examples to a single command by specifying both options to `pkg-config`:

```
gcc -o foo foo.c `pkg-config shishi --cflags --libs`
```

5.1.5 Autoconf tests

If you work on a project that uses Autoconf (see ⟨undefined⟩ [top], page ⟨undefined⟩) to help find installed libraries, the suggestions in the previous section are not the entire story. There are a few methods to detect and incorporate Shishi into your Autoconf based package. The preferred approach, is to use Libtool in your project, and use the normal Autoconf header file and library tests.

5.1.5.1 Autoconf test via 'pkg-config'

If your audience is a typical GNU/Linux desktop, you can often assume they have the 'pkg-config' tool installed, in which you can use its Autoconf M4 macro to find and set up your package for use with Shishi. The following illustrate this scenario.

```
AC_ARG_ENABLE(kerberos_v5,
AC_HELP_STRING([--disable-kerberos_v5],
                       [don't use the KERBEROS_V5 mechanism]),
kerberos_v5=$enableval)
if test "$kerberos_v5" != "no" ; then
PKG_CHECK_MODULES(SHISHI, shishi >= 0.0.0,
[kerberos_v5=yes],
                       [kerberos_v5=no])
if test "$kerberos_v5" != "yes" ; then
kerberos_v5=no
AC_MSG_WARN([shishi not found, disabling Kerberos 5])
else
kerberos_v5=yes
AC_DEFINE(USE_KERBEROS_V5, 1,
                       [Define to 1 if you want Kerberos 5.])
fi
fi
AC_MSG_CHECKING([if Kerberos 5 should be used])
AC_MSG_RESULT($kerberos_v5)
```

5.1.5.2 Standalone Autoconf test using Libtool

If your package uses Libtool(see ⟨undefined⟩ [top], page ⟨undefined⟩), you can use the normal Autoconf tests to find the Shishi library and rely on the Libtool dependency tracking to include the proper dependency libraries (e.g., Libidn). The following illustrate this scenario.

```
AC_CHECK_HEADER(shishi.h,
AC_CHECK_LIB(shishi, shishi_check_version,
[kerberos5=yes AC_SUBST(SHISHI_LIBS, -lshishi)],
kerberos5=no),
kerberos5=no)
AC_ARG_ENABLE(kerberos5,
AC_HELP_STRING([--disable-kerberos5],
                       [disable Kerberos 5 unconditionally]),
kerberos5=$enableval)
if test "$kerberos5" != "no" ; then
AC_DEFINE(USE_KERBEROS_V5, 1,
  [Define to 1 if you want Kerberos 5.])
else
AC_MSG_WARN([Shishi not found, disabling Kerberos 5])
fi
AC_MSG_CHECKING([if Kerberos 5 should be used])
AC_MSG_RESULT($kerberos5)
```

5.1.5.3 Standalone Autoconf test

If your package does not use Libtool, as well as detecting the Shishi library as in the previous case, you must also detect whatever dependencies Shishi requires to work (e.g., libidn). Since the dependencies are in a state of flux, we do not provide an example and we do not recommend this approach, unless you are experienced developer.

5.2 Initialization Functions

shishi

Shishi * shishi (*void*)   [Function]
> Initializes the Shishi library, and set up, using `shishi_error_set_outputtype()`, the library so that future warnings and informational messages are printed to stderr. If this function fails, it may print diagnostic errors to stderr.
>
> **Return value:** Returns Shishi library handle, or NULL on error.

shishi_server

Shishi * shishi_server (*void*)   [Function]
> Initializes the Shishi library, and set up, using `shishi_error_set_outputtype()`, the library so that future warnings and informational messages are printed to the syslog. If this function fails, it may print diagnostic errors to the syslog.
>
> **Return value:** Returns Shishi library handle, or NULL on error.

shishi_done

void shishi_done (*Shishi * handle*)   [Function]
> *handle*: shishi handle as allocated by `shishi_init()`.
>
> Deallocates the shishi library handle. The handle must not be used in any calls to shishi functions after this.
>
> If there is a default tkts, it is written to the default tkts file (call `shishi_tkts_default_file_set()` to change the default tkts file). If you do not wish to write the default tkts file, close the default tkts with shishi_tkts_done(handle, NULL) before calling this function.

shishi_init

int shishi_init (*Shishi ** handle*)   [Function]
> *handle*: pointer to handle to be created.
>
> Create a Shishi library handle, using `shishi()`, and read the system configuration file, user configuration file and user tickets from their default locations. The paths to the system configuration file is decided at compile time, and is $sysconfdir/shishi.conf. The user configuration file is $HOME/.shishi/config, and the user ticket file is $HOME/.shishi/ticket.
>
> The handle is allocated regardless of return values, except for SHISHI_HANDLE_ERROR which indicates a problem allocating the handle. (The other error conditions comes from reading the files.)
>
> **Return value:** Returns SHISHI_OK iff successful.

shishi_init_with_paths

int shishi_init_with_paths (*Shishi* ** *handle*, *const char* *   [Function]
    tktsfile, *const char* * *systemcfgfile*, *const char* * *usercfgfile*)

handle: pointer to handle to be created.

tktsfile: Filename of ticket file, or NULL.

systemcfgfile: Filename of system configuration, or NULL.

usercfgfile: Filename of user configuration, or NULL.

Create a Shishi library handle, using `shishi()`, and read the system configuration file, user configuration file, and user tickets from the specified locations. If any of `usercfgfile` or `systemcfgfile` is NULL, the file is read from its default location, which for the system configuration file is decided at compile time, and is $sysconfdir/shishi.conf, and for the user configuration file is $HOME/.shishi/config. If the ticket file is NULL, a ticket file is not read at all.

The handle is allocated regardless of return values, except for SHISHI_HANDLE_ERROR which indicates a problem allocating the handle. (The other error conditions comes from reading the files.)

Return value: Returns SHISHI_OK iff successful.

shishi_init_server

int shishi_init_server (*Shishi* ** *handle*)   [Function]

handle: pointer to handle to be created.

Create a Shishi library handle, using `shishi_server()`, and read the system configuration file. The paths to the system configuration file is decided at compile time, and is $sysconfdir/shishi.conf.

The handle is allocated regardless of return values, except for SHISHI_HANDLE_ERROR which indicates a problem allocating the handle. (The other error conditions comes from reading the file.)

Return value: Returns SHISHI_OK iff successful.

shishi_init_server_with_paths

int shishi_init_server_with_paths (*Shishi* ** *handle*, *const char* *   [Function]
    systemcfgfile)

handle: pointer to handle to be created.

systemcfgfile: Filename of system configuration, or NULL.

Create a Shishi library handle, using `shishi_server()`, and read the system configuration file from specified location. The paths to the system configuration file is decided at compile time, and is $sysconfdir/shishi.conf. The handle is allocated regardless of return values, except for SHISHI_HANDLE_ERROR which indicates a problem allocating the handle. (The other error conditions comes from reading the file.)

Return value: Returns SHISHI_OK iff successful.

shishi_cfg

int shishi_cfg (*Shishi* * **handle**, *const char* * **option**)   [Function]
handle: Shishi library handle create by `shishi_init()`.

option: string with shishi library option.

Configure shishi library with given option.

Return Value: Returns SHISHI_OK if option was valid.

shishi_cfg_from_file

int shishi_cfg_from_file (*Shishi* * **handle**, *const char* * **cfg**)   [Function]
handle: Shishi library handle create by `shishi_init()`.

cfg: filename to read configuration from.

Configure shishi library using configuration file.

Return Value: Returns `SHISHI_OK` iff successful.

shishi_cfg_print

int shishi_cfg_print (*Shishi* * **handle**, *FILE* * **fh**)   [Function]
handle: Shishi library handle create by `shishi_init()`.

fh: file descriptor opened for writing.

Print library configuration status, mostly for debugging purposes.

Return Value: Returns SHISHI_OK.

shishi_cfg_default_systemfile

const char * shishi_cfg_default_systemfile (*Shishi* * **handle**)   [Function]
handle: Shishi library handle create by `shishi_init()`.

The system configuration file name is decided at compile-time, but may be overridden
by the environment variable SHISHI_CONFIG.

Return value: Return system configuration file name.

shishi_cfg_default_userdirectory

const char * shishi_cfg_default_userdirectory (*Shishi* *   [Function]
        handle)
handle: Shishi library handle create by `shishi_init()`.

The default user directory (used for, e.g. Shishi ticket cache) is normally computed
by appending BASE_DIR ("/.shishi") to the content of the environment variable
$HOME, but can be overridden by specifying the complete path in the environment
variable SHISHI_HOME.

Return value: Return directory with configuration files etc.

shishi_cfg_userdirectory_file

char * shishi_cfg_userdirectory_file (*Shishi* * *handle*, *const*   [Function]
    char * *file*)
> *handle*: Shishi library handle create by `shishi_init()`.
>
> *file*: basename of file to find in user directory.
>
> Get the full path to specified `file` in the users' configuration directory.
>
> **Return value:** Return full path to given relative filename, relative to the user specific Shishi configuration directory as returned by `shishi_cfg_default_userdirectory()` (typically $HOME/.shishi).

shishi_cfg_default_userfile

const char * shishi_cfg_default_userfile (*Shishi* * *handle*)   [Function]
> *handle*: Shishi library handle create by `shishi_init()`.
>
> Get filename of default user configuration file, typically $HOME/shishi.conf.
>
> **Return value:** Return user configuration filename.

shishi_cfg_clientkdcetype

int shishi_cfg_clientkdcetype (*Shishi* * *handle*, *int32_t* **   [Function]
    etypes)
> *handle*: Shishi library handle create by `shishi_init()`.
>
> *etypes*: output array with encryption types.
>
> Set the etypes variable to the array of preferred client etypes.
>
> **Return value:** Return the number of encryption types in the array, 0 means none.

shishi_cfg_clientkdcetype_fast

int32_t shishi_cfg_clientkdcetype_fast (*Shishi* * *handle*)   [Function]
> *handle*: Shishi library handle create by `shishi_init()`.
>
> Extract the default etype from the list of preferred client etypes.
>
> **Return value:** Return the default encryption types.

shishi_cfg_clientkdcetype_set

int shishi_cfg_clientkdcetype_set (*Shishi* * *handle*, *char* *   [Function]
    value)
> *handle*: Shishi library handle created by `shishi_init()`.
>
> *value*: string with encryption types.
>
> Set the "client-kdc-etypes" configuration option from given string. The string contains encryption types (integer or names) separated by comma or whitespace, e.g. "aes256-cts-hmac-sha1-96 des3-cbc-sha1-kd des-cbc-md5".
>
> **Return value:** Returns SHISHI_OK if successful.

shishi_cfg_authorizationtype_set

int shishi_cfg_authorizationtype_set (*Shishi * handle*, *char **   [Function]
    value)

handle: Shishi library handle created by shishi_init().

value: string with authorization types.

Set the "authorization-types" configuration option from given string. The string
contains authorization types (integer or names) separated by comma or whitespace,
e.g. "basic k5login".

Return value: Returns SHISHI_OK if successful.

5.3 Ticket Set Functions

A "ticket set" is, as the name implies, a collection of tickets. Functions are provided to read
tickets from file into a ticket set, to query number of tickets in the set, to extract a given
ticket from the set, to search the ticket set for tickets matching certain criterium, to write
the ticket set to a file, etc. High level functions for performing a initial authentication (see
Section 5.7 [AS Functions], page 113) or subsequent authentication (see Section 5.8 [TGS
Functions], page 118) and storing the new ticket in the ticket set are also provided.

See Section 5.6 [Ticket Functions], page 102, to manipulate each individual ticket. See
Section 5.9 [Ticket (ASN.1) Functions], page 124, for low-level ASN.1 manipulation.

shishi_tkts_default_file_guess

char * shishi_tkts_default_file_guess (*Shishi * handle*)   [Function]

handle: Shishi library handle create by shishi_init().

Guesses the default ticket filename; it is $SHISHI_TICKETS, $SHISHI_HOME/tickets,
or $HOME/.shishi/tickets.

Return value: Returns default tkts filename as a string that has to be deallocated
with free() by the caller.

shishi_tkts_default_file

const char * shishi_tkts_default_file (*Shishi * handle*)   [Function]

handle: Shishi library handle create by shishi_init().

Get filename of default ticket set.

Return value: Returns the default ticket set filename used in the library. The string
is not a copy, so don't modify or deallocate it.

shishi_tkts_default_file_set

void shishi_tkts_default_file_set (*Shishi * handle*, *const char **   [Function]
    tktsfile)

handle: Shishi library handle create by shishi_init().

tktsfile: string with new default tkts file name, or NULL to reset to default.

Set the default ticket set filename used in the library. The string is copied into the
library, so you can dispose of the variable immediately after calling this function.

shishi_tkts_default

Shishi_tkts * shishi_tkts_default (*Shishi* * `handle`)   [Function]
> *handle*: Shishi library handle create by `shishi_init()`.
>
> Get the default ticket set for library handle.
>
> **Return value:** Return the handle global ticket set.

shishi_tkts

int shishi_tkts (*Shishi* * `handle`, *Shishi_tkts* ** `tkts`)   [Function]
> *handle*: shishi handle as allocated by `shishi_init()`.
>
> *tkts*: output pointer to newly allocated tkts handle.
>
> Get a new ticket set handle.
>
> **Return value:** Returns `SHISHI_OK` iff successful.

shishi_tkts_done

void shishi_tkts_done (*Shishi_tkts* ** `tkts`)   [Function]
> *tkts*: ticket set handle as allocated by `shishi_tkts()`.
>
> Deallocates all resources associated with ticket set. The ticket set handle must not be used in calls to other shishi_tkts_*() functions after this.

shishi_tkts_size

int shishi_tkts_size (*Shishi_tkts* * `tkts`)   [Function]
> *tkts*: ticket set handle as allocated by `shishi_tkts()`.
>
> Get size of ticket set.
>
> **Return value:** Returns number of tickets stored in ticket set.

shishi_tkts_nth

Shishi_tkt * shishi_tkts_nth (*Shishi_tkts* * `tkts`, *int* `ticketno`)   [Function]
> *tkts*: ticket set handle as allocated by `shishi_tkts()`.
>
> *ticketno*: integer indicating requested ticket in ticket set.
>
> **Get the n:** th ticket in ticket set.
>
> **Return value:** Returns a ticket handle to the ticketno:th ticket in the ticket set, or NULL if ticket set is invalid or ticketno is out of bounds. The first ticket is ticketno 0, the second ticketno 1, and so on.

shishi_tkts_remove

int shishi_tkts_remove (*Shishi_tkts* * `tkts`, *int* `ticketno`)   [Function]
> *tkts*: ticket set handle as allocated by `shishi_tkts()`.
>
> *ticketno*: ticket number of ticket in the set to remove. The first ticket is ticket number 0.
>
> Remove a ticket, indexed by `ticketno`, in ticket set.
>
> **Return value:** `SHISHI_OK` if successful or if `ticketno` larger than size of ticket set.

shishi_tkts_add

int shishi_tkts_add (*Shishi_tkts* * *tkts*, *Shishi_tkt* * *tkt*)   [Function]

> *tkts*: ticket set handle as allocated by `shishi_tkts()`.
>
> *tkt*: ticket to be added to ticket set.
>
> Add a ticket to the ticket set. Only the pointer is stored, so if you modify `tkt`, the ticket in the ticket set will also be modified.
>
> **Return value:** Returns SHISHI_OK iff successful.

shishi_tkts_new

int shishi_tkts_new (*Shishi_tkts* * *tkts*, *Shishi_asn1* `ticket`,   [Function]
    Shishi_asn1 `enckdcreppart`, *Shishi_asn1* `kdcrep`)

> *tkts*: ticket set handle as allocated by `shishi_tkts()`.
>
> *ticket*: input ticket variable.
>
> *enckdcreppart*: input ticket detail variable.
>
> *kdcrep*: input KDC-REP variable.
>
> Allocate a new ticket and add it to the ticket set.
>
> Note that `ticket`, `enckdcreppart` and `kdcrep` are stored by reference, so you must not de-allocate them before the ticket is removed from the ticket set and de-allocated.
>
> **Return value:** Returns SHISHI_OK iff successful.

shishi_tkts_read

int shishi_tkts_read (*Shishi_tkts* * *tkts*, *FILE* * *fh*)   [Function]

> *tkts*: ticket set handle as allocated by `shishi_tkts()`.
>
> *fh*: file descriptor to read from.
>
> Read tickets from file descriptor and add them to the ticket set.
>
> **Return value:** Returns SHISHI_OK iff successful.

shishi_tkts_from_file

int shishi_tkts_from_file (*Shishi_tkts* * *tkts*, const char *   [Function]
    `filename`)

> *tkts*: ticket set handle as allocated by `shishi_tkts()`.
>
> *filename*: filename to read tickets from.
>
> Read tickets from file and add them to the ticket set.
>
> **Return value:** Returns SHISHI_OK iff successful.

shishi_tkts_write

int shishi_tkts_write (*Shishi_tkts* * *tkts*, *FILE* * *fh*)   [Function]

> *tkts*: ticket set handle as allocated by `shishi_tkts()`.
>
> *fh*: file descriptor to write tickets to.
>
> Write tickets in set to file descriptor.
>
> **Return value:** Returns SHISHI_OK iff successful.

shishi_tkts_expire

int shishi_tkts_expire (*Shishi_tkts* * tkts)   [Function]
    tkts: ticket set handle as allocated by shishi_tkts().

Remove expired tickets from ticket set.

Return value: Returns SHISHI_OK iff successful.

shishi_tkts_to_file

int shishi_tkts_to_file (*Shishi_tkts* * tkts, *const char* * filename)   [Function]
    tkts: ticket set handle as allocated by shishi_tkts().

filename: filename to write tickets to.

Write tickets in set to file.

Return value: Returns SHISHI_OK iff successful.

shishi_tkts_print_for_service

int shishi_tkts_print_for_service (*Shishi_tkts* * tkts, *FILE* * fh,   [Function]
        const char * service)
    tkts: ticket set handle as allocated by shishi_tkts().

fh: file descriptor to print to.

service: service to limit tickets printed to, or NULL.

Print description of tickets for specified service to file descriptor. If service is NULL,
all tickets are printed.

Return value: Returns SHISHI_OK iff successful.

shishi_tkts_print

int shishi_tkts_print (*Shishi_tkts* * tkts, *FILE* * fh)   [Function]
    tkts: ticket set handle as allocated by shishi_tkts().

fh: file descriptor to print to.

Print description of all tickets to file descriptor.

Return value: Returns SHISHI_OK iff successful.

shishi_tkt_match_p

int shishi_tkt_match_p (*Shishi_tkt* * tkt, *Shishi_tkts_hint* * hint)   [Function]
    tkt: ticket to test hints on.

hint: structure with characteristics of ticket to be found.

Test if a ticket matches specified hints.

Return value: Returns 0 iff ticket fails to match given criteria.

shishi_tkts_find

`Shishi_tkt * shishi_tkts_find` (*Shishi_tkts * `tkts`, Shishi_tkts_hint*   [Function]
      * `hint`)

> *tkts*: ticket set handle as allocated by `shishi_tkts()`.
>
> *hint*: structure with characteristics of ticket to be found.
>
> Search the ticketset sequentially (from ticket number 0 through all tickets in the set) for a ticket that fits the given characteristics. If a ticket is found, the hint->startpos field is updated to point to the next ticket in the set, so this function can be called repeatedly with the same hint argument in order to find all tickets matching a certain criterium. Note that if tickets are added to, or removed from, the ticketset during a query with the same hint argument, the hint->startpos field must be updated appropriately.
>
> **Here is how you would typically use this function:** Shishi_tkts_hint hint;
>
> Shishi_tkt tkt;
>
> memset(&hint, 0, sizeof(hint));
>
> hint.server = "imap/mail.example.org";
>
> tkt = shishi_tkts_find (shishi_tkts_default(handle), &hint);
>
> if (!tkt)
>
> printf("No ticket found...\n");
>
> else
>
> do_something_with_ticket (tkt);
>
> **Return value:** Returns a ticket if found, or NULL if no further matching tickets could be found.

shishi_tkts_find_for_clientserver

`Shishi_tkt * shishi_tkts_find_for_clientserver` (*Shishi_tkts **   [Function]
      `tkts`, *const char * `client`, const char * `server`*)

> *tkts*: ticket set handle as allocated by `shishi_tkts()`.
>
> *client*: client name to find ticket for.
>
> *server*: server name to find ticket for.
>
> Short-hand function for searching the ticket set for a ticket for the given client and server. See `shishi_tkts_find()`.
>
> **Return value:** Returns a ticket if found, or NULL.

shishi_tkts_find_for_server

`Shishi_tkt * shishi_tkts_find_for_server` (*Shishi_tkts * `tkts`,*   [Function]
      const char * `server`)

> *tkts*: ticket set handle as allocated by `shishi_tkts()`.
>
> *server*: server name to find ticket for.
>
> Short-hand function for searching the ticket set for a ticket for the given server using the default client principal. See `shishi_tkts_find_for_clientserver()` and `shishi_tkts_find()`.

Return value: Returns a ticket if found, or NULL.

shishi_tkts_get_tgt

Shishi_tkt * shishi_tkts_get_tgt (*Shishi_tkts* * **tkts**,   [Function]
    Shishi_tkts_hint * **hint**)

    tkts: ticket set handle as allocated by `shishi_tkts()`.

    hint: structure with characteristics of ticket to begot.

    Get a ticket granting ticket (TGT) suitable for acquiring ticket matching the hint. I.e., get a TGT for the server realm in the hint structure (hint->serverrealm), or the default realm if the serverrealm field is NULL. Can result in AS exchange.

    Currently this function do not implement cross realm logic.

    This function is used by `shishi_tkts_get()`, which is probably what you really want to use unless you have special needs.

    Return value: Returns a ticket granting ticket if successful, or NULL if this function is unable to acquire on.

shishi_tkts_get_tgs

Shishi_tkt * shishi_tkts_get_tgs (*Shishi_tkts* * **tkts**,   [Function]
    Shishi_tkts_hint * **hint**, *Shishi_tkt* * **tgt**)

    tkts: ticket set handle as allocated by `shishi_tkts()`.

    hint: structure with characteristics of ticket to begot.

    tgt: ticket granting ticket to use.

    Get a ticket via TGS exchange using specified ticket granting ticket.

    This function is used by `shishi_tkts_get()`, which is probably what you really want to use unless you have special needs.

    Return value: Returns a ticket if successful, or NULL if this function is unable to acquire on.

shishi_tkts_get

Shishi_tkt * shishi_tkts_get (*Shishi_tkts* * **tkts**, *Shishi_tkts_hint* *   [Function]
    hint)

    tkts: ticket set handle as allocated by `shishi_tkts()`.

    hint: structure with characteristics of ticket to be found.

    Get a ticket matching given characteristics. This function first looks in the ticket set for a ticket, then tries to find a suitable TGT, possibly via an AS exchange, using `shishi_tkts_get_tgt()`, and then uses that TGT in a TGS exchange to get the ticket.

    Currently this function does not implement cross realm logic.

    Return value: Returns a ticket if found, or NULL if this function is unable to get the ticket.

shishi_tkts_get_for_clientserver

Shishi_tkt * shishi_tkts_get_for_clientserver (*Shishi_tkts **   [Function]
      tkts, *const char *** `client`, *const char *** `server`)

> *tkts*: ticket set handle as allocated by `shishi_tkts()`.
>
> *client*: client name to get ticket for.
>
> *server*: server name to get ticket for.
>
> Short-hand function for getting a ticket for the given client and server. See `shishi_tkts_get()`.
>
> **Return value:** Returns a ticket if found, or NULL.

shishi_tkts_get_for_server

Shishi_tkt * shishi_tkts_get_for_server (*Shishi_tkts ** `tkts`,   [Function]
      *const char *** `server`)

> *tkts*: ticket set handle as allocated by `shishi_tkts()`.
>
> *server*: server name to get ticket for.
>
> Short-hand function for getting a ticket to the given server and for the default principal client. See `shishi_tkts_get()`.
>
> **Return value:** Returns a ticket if found, or NULL.

shishi_tkts_get_for_localservicepasswd

Shishi_tkt * shishi_tkts_get_for_localservicepasswd   [Function]
      (*Shishi_tkts *** `tkts`, *const char *** `service`, *const char *** `passwd`)

> *tkts*: ticket set handle as allocated by `shishi_tkts()`.
>
> *service*: service name to get ticket for.
>
> *passwd*: password for the default client principal.
>
> Short-hand function for getting a ticket to the given local service, and for the default principal client. The latter's password is given as argument. See `shishi_tkts_get()`.
>
> **Return value:** Returns a ticket if found, or NULL otherwise.

5.4 AP-REQ and AP-REP Functions

The "AP-REQ" and "AP-REP" are ASN.1 structures used by application client and servers to prove to each other who they are. The structures contain auxilliary information, together with an authenticator (see Section 5.11 [Authenticator Functions], page 152) which is the real cryptographic proof. The following illustrates the AP-REQ and AP-REP ASN.1 structures.

```
AP-REQ          ::= [APPLICATION 14] SEQUENCE {
      pvno            [0] INTEGER (5),
      msg-type        [1] INTEGER (14),
      ap-options      [2] APOptions,
      ticket          [3] Ticket,
      authenticator   [4] EncryptedData {Authenticator,
                          { keyuse-pa-TGSReq-authenticator
```

```
                            | keyuse-APReq-authenticator }}
}

AP-REP           ::= [APPLICATION 15] SEQUENCE {
      pvno             [0] INTEGER (5),
      msg-type         [1] INTEGER (15),
      enc-part         [2] EncryptedData {EncAPRepPart,
                             { keyuse-EncAPRepPart }}
}

EncAPRepPart     ::= [APPLICATION 27] SEQUENCE {
      ctime            [0] KerberosTime,
      cusec            [1] Microseconds,
      subkey           [2] EncryptionKey OPTIONAL,
      seq-number       [3] UInt32 OPTIONAL
}
```

shishi_ap

int shishi_ap (*Shishi* * *handle*, *Shishi_ap* ** *ap*)   [Function]
> *handle*: shishi handle as allocated by `shishi_init()`.

> *ap*: pointer to new structure that holds information about AP exchange

> Create a new AP exchange with a random subkey of the default encryption type from configuration. Note that there is no guarantee that the receiver will understand that key type, you should probably use `shishi_ap_etype()` or `shishi_ap_nosubkey()` instead. In the future, this function will likely behave as `shishi_ap_nosubkey()` and `shishi_ap_nosubkey()` will be removed.

> **Return value:** Returns SHISHI_OK iff successful.

shishi_ap_etype

int shishi_ap_etype (*Shishi* * *handle*, *Shishi_ap* ** *ap*, *int* *etype*)   [Function]
> *handle*: shishi handle as allocated by `shishi_init()`.

> *ap*: pointer to new structure that holds information about AP exchange

> *etype*: encryption type of newly generated random subkey.

> Create a new AP exchange with a random subkey of indicated encryption type.

> **Return value:** Returns SHISHI_OK iff successful.

shishi_ap_nosubkey

int shishi_ap_nosubkey (*Shishi* * *handle*, *Shishi_ap* ** *ap*)   [Function]
> *handle*: shishi handle as allocated by `shishi_init()`.

> *ap*: pointer to new structure that holds information about AP exchange

> Create a new AP exchange without subkey in authenticator.

> **Return value:** Returns SHISHI_OK iff successful.

shishi_ap_done

void **shishi_ap_done** (*Shishi_ap* * **ap**)   [Function]
> *ap*: structure that holds information about AP exchange

> Deallocate resources associated with AP exchange. This should be called by the application when it no longer need to utilize the AP exchange handle.

shishi_ap_set_tktoptions

int **shishi_ap_set_tktoptions** (*Shishi_ap* * **ap**, *Shishi_tkt* * **tkt**, *int*   [Function]
> **options**)

> *ap*: structure that holds information about AP exchange

> *tkt*: ticket to set in AP.

> *options*: AP-REQ options to set in AP.

> Set the ticket (see **shishi_ap_tkt_set()**) and set the AP-REQ apoptions (see **shishi_apreq_options_set()**).

> **Return value:** Returns SHISHI_OK iff successful.

shishi_ap_set_tktoptionsdata

int **shishi_ap_set_tktoptionsdata** (*Shishi_ap* * **ap**, *Shishi_tkt* *   [Function]
> **tkt**, *int* **options**, *const char* * **data**, *size_t* **len**)

> *ap*: structure that holds information about AP exchange

> *tkt*: ticket to set in AP.

> *options*: AP-REQ options to set in AP.

> *data*: input array with data to checksum in Authenticator.

> *len*: length of input array with data to checksum in Authenticator.

> Set the ticket (see **shishi_ap_tkt_set()**) and set the AP-REQ apoptions (see **shishi_apreq_options_set()**) and set the Authenticator checksum data.

> **Return value:** Returns SHISHI_OK iff successful.

shishi_ap_set_tktoptionsraw

int **shishi_ap_set_tktoptionsraw** (*Shishi_ap* * **ap**, *Shishi_tkt* * **tkt**,   [Function]
> *int* **options**, *int32_t* **cksumtype**, *const char* * **data**, *size_t* **len**)

> *ap*: structure that holds information about AP exchange

> *tkt*: ticket to set in AP.

> *options*: AP-REQ options to set in AP.

> *cksumtype*: authenticator checksum type to set in AP.

> *data*: input array with data to store in checksum field in Authenticator.

> *len*: length of input array with data to store in checksum field in Authenticator.

> Set the ticket (see **shishi_ap_tkt_set()**) and set the AP-REQ apoptions (see **shishi_apreq_options_set()**) and set the raw Authenticator checksum data.

> **Return value:** Returns SHISHI_OK iff successful.

shishi_ap_set_tktoptionsasn1usage

int shishi_ap_set_tktoptionsasn1usage (*Shishi_ap* * ap, *Shishi_tkt*   [Function]
        * `tkt`, *int* `options`, *Shishi_asn1* `node`, *const char* * `field`, *int*
        `authenticatorcksumkeyusage`, *int* `authenticatorkeyusage`)

> *ap*: structure that holds information about AP exchange
>
> *tkt*: ticket to set in AP.
>
> *options*: AP-REQ options to set in AP.
>
> *node*: input ASN.1 structure to store as authenticator checksum data.
>
> *field*: field in ASN.1 structure to use.
>
> *authenticatorcksumkeyusage*: key usage for checksum in authenticator.
>
> *authenticatorkeyusage*: key usage for authenticator.
>
> Set ticket, options and authenticator checksum data using `shishi_ap_set_tktoptionsdata()`. The authenticator checksum data is the DER encoding of the ASN.1 field provided.
>
> **Return value:** Returns SHISHI_OK iff successful.

shishi_ap_tktoptions

int shishi_ap_tktoptions (*Shishi* * `handle`, *Shishi_ap* ** `ap`,   [Function]
        Shishi_tkt * `tkt`, *int* `options`)

> *handle*: shishi handle as allocated by `shishi_init()`.
>
> *ap*: pointer to new structure that holds information about AP exchange
>
> *tkt*: ticket to set in newly created AP.
>
> *options*: AP-REQ options to set in newly created AP.
>
> Create a new AP exchange using `shishi_ap()`, and set the ticket and AP-REQ apoptions using `shishi_ap_set_tktoptions()`. A random session key is added to the authenticator, using the same keytype as the ticket.
>
> **Return value:** Returns SHISHI_OK iff successful.

shishi_ap_tktoptionsdata

int shishi_ap_tktoptionsdata (*Shishi* * `handle`, *Shishi_ap* ** `ap`,   [Function]
        Shishi_tkt * `tkt`, *int* `options`, *const char* * `data`, *size_t* `len`)

> *handle*: shishi handle as allocated by `shishi_init()`.
>
> *ap*: pointer to new structure that holds information about AP exchange
>
> *tkt*: ticket to set in newly created AP.
>
> *options*: AP-REQ options to set in newly created AP.
>
> *data*: input array with data to checksum in Authenticator.
>
> *len*: length of input array with data to checksum in Authenticator.
>
> Create a new AP exchange using `shishi_ap()`, and set the ticket, AP-REQ apoptions and the Authenticator checksum data using `shishi_ap_set_tktoptionsdata()`. A random session key is added to the authenticator, using the same keytype as the ticket.
>
> **Return value:** Returns SHISHI_OK iff successful.

shishi_ap_tktoptionsraw

int shishi_ap_tktoptionsraw (*Shishi * handle, Shishi_ap ** `ap`,   [Function]
     *Shishi_tkt * `tkt`, int `options`, int32_t `cksumtype`, const char * `data`, size_t
     `len`*)

handle: shishi handle as allocated by `shishi_init()`.

ap: pointer to new structure that holds information about AP exchange

tkt: ticket to set in newly created AP.

options: AP-REQ options to set in newly created AP.

cksumtype: authenticator checksum type to set in AP.

data: input array with data to store in checksum field in Authenticator.

len: length of input array with data to store in checksum field in Authenticator.

Create a new AP exchange using `shishi_ap()`, and set the ticket, AP-REQ apoptions and the raw Authenticator checksum data field using `shishi_ap_set_tktoptionsraw()`. A random session key is added to the authenticator, using the same keytype as the ticket.

Return value: Returns SHISHI_OK iff successful.

shishi_ap_etype_tktoptionsdata

int shishi_ap_etype_tktoptionsdata (*Shishi * handle, Shishi_ap*   [Function]
     ** `ap`, int32_t `etype`, Shishi_tkt * `tkt`, int `options`, const char * `data`, size_t
     `len`*)

handle: shishi handle as allocated by `shishi_init()`.

ap: pointer to new structure that holds information about AP exchange

etype: encryption type of newly generated random subkey.

tkt: ticket to set in newly created AP.

options: AP-REQ options to set in newly created AP.

data: input array with data to checksum in Authenticator.

len: length of input array with data to checksum in Authenticator.

Create a new AP exchange using `shishi_ap()`, and set the ticket, AP-REQ apoptions and the Authenticator checksum data using `shishi_ap_set_tktoptionsdata()`. A random session key is added to the authenticator, using the same keytype as the ticket.

Return value: Returns SHISHI_OK iff successful.

shishi_ap_tktoptionsasn1usage

int shishi_ap_tktoptionsasn1usage (*Shishi * handle, Shishi_ap **   [Function]
     `ap`, Shishi_tkt * `tkt`, int `options`, Shishi_asn1 `node`, const char * `field`, int
     `authenticatorcksumkeyusage`, int `authenticatorkeyusage`*)

handle: shishi handle as allocated by `shishi_init()`.

ap: pointer to new structure that holds information about AP exchange

tkt: ticket to set in newly created AP.

options: AP-REQ options to set in newly created AP.

node: input ASN.1 structure to store as authenticator checksum data.

field: field in ASN.1 structure to use.

authenticatorcksumkeyusage: key usage for checksum in authenticator.

authenticatorkeyusage: key usage for authenticator.

Create a new AP exchange using `shishi_ap()`, and set ticket, options and authenticator checksum data from the DER encoding of the ASN.1 field using `shishi_ap_set_tktoptionsasn1usage()`. A random session key is added to the authenticator, using the same keytype as the ticket.

Return value: Returns SHISHI_OK iff successful.

shishi_ap_tkt

Shishi_tkt * shishi_ap_tkt (*Shishi_ap* * ap)   [Function]
    ap: structure that holds information about AP exchange

Get Ticket from AP exchange.

Return value: Returns the ticket from the AP exchange, or NULL if not yet set or an error occured.

shishi_ap_tkt_set

void shishi_ap_tkt_set (*Shishi_ap* * ap, *Shishi_tkt* * tkt)   [Function]
    ap: structure that holds information about AP exchange

    tkt: ticket to store in AP.

Set the Ticket in the AP exchange.

shishi_ap_authenticator_cksumdata

int shishi_ap_authenticator_cksumdata (*Shishi_ap* * ap, *char* *   [Function]
    out, *size_t* * len)
    ap: structure that holds information about AP exchange

    out: output array that holds authenticator checksum data.

    len: on input, maximum length of output array that holds authenticator checksum data, on output actual length of output array that holds authenticator checksum data.

Get checksum data from Authenticator.

Return value: Returns `SHISHI_OK` if successful, or `SHISHI_TOO_SMALL_BUFFER` if buffer provided was too small (then `len` will hold necessary buffer size).

shishi_ap_authenticator_cksumdata_set

void shishi_ap_authenticator_cksumdata_set (*Shishi_ap* * ap,   [Function]
    const char * `authenticatorcksumdata`, *size_t*
    `authenticatorcksumdatalen`)
    ap: structure that holds information about AP exchange

    authenticatorcksumdata: input array with data to compute checksum on and store in Authenticator in AP-REQ.

authenticatorcksumdatalen: length of input array with data to compute checksum on and store in Authenticator in AP-REQ.

Set the Authenticator Checksum Data in the AP exchange. This is the data that will be checksumed, and the checksum placed in the checksum field. It is not the actual checksum field. See also shishi_ap_authenticator_cksumraw_set.

shishi_ap_authenticator_cksumraw_set

void **shishi_ap_authenticator_cksumraw_set** (*Shishi_ap* * **ap**,   [Function]
    int32_t **authenticatorcksumtype**, *const char* * **authenticatorcksumraw**,
    size_t **authenticatorcksumrawlen**)

ap: structure that holds information about AP exchange

authenticatorcksumtype: authenticator checksum type to set in AP.

authenticatorcksumraw: input array with authenticator checksum field value to set in Authenticator in AP-REQ.

authenticatorcksumrawlen: length of input array with authenticator checksum field value to set in Authenticator in AP-REQ.

Set the Authenticator Checksum Data in the AP exchange. This is the actual checksum field, not data to compute checksum on and then store in the checksum field. See also shishi_ap_authenticator_cksumdata_set.

shishi_ap_authenticator_cksumtype

int32_t **shishi_ap_authenticator_cksumtype** (*Shishi_ap* * **ap**)   [Function]
    ap: structure that holds information about AP exchange

Get the Authenticator Checksum Type in the AP exchange.

Return value: Return the authenticator checksum type.

shishi_ap_authenticator_cksumtype_set

void **shishi_ap_authenticator_cksumtype_set** (*Shishi_ap* * **ap**,   [Function]
    int32_t **cksumtype**)

ap: structure that holds information about AP exchange

cksumtype: authenticator checksum type to set in AP.

Set the Authenticator Checksum Type in the AP exchange.

shishi_ap_authenticator

Shishi_asn1 **shishi_ap_authenticator** (*Shishi_ap* * **ap**)   [Function]
    ap: structure that holds information about AP exchange

Get ASN.1 Authenticator structure from AP exchange.

Return value: Returns the Authenticator from the AP exchange, or NULL if not yet set or an error occured.

shishi_ap_authenticator_set

void **shishi_ap_authenticator_set** (*Shishi_ap* * **ap**, *Shishi_asn1*   [Function]
    authenticator)

> *ap*: structure that holds information about AP exchange
>
> *authenticator*: authenticator to store in AP.
>
> Set the Authenticator in the AP exchange.

shishi_ap_req

Shishi_asn1 **shishi_ap_req** (*Shishi_ap* * **ap**)   [Function]

> *ap*: structure that holds information about AP exchange
>
> Get ASN.1 AP-REQ structure from AP exchange.
>
> **Return value:** Returns the AP-REQ from the AP exchange, or NULL if not yet set or an error occured.

shishi_ap_req_set

void **shishi_ap_req_set** (*Shishi_ap* * **ap**, *Shishi_asn1* **apreq**)   [Function]

> *ap*: structure that holds information about AP exchange
>
> *apreq*: apreq to store in AP.
>
> Set the AP-REQ in the AP exchange.

shishi_ap_req_der

int **shishi_ap_req_der** (*Shishi_ap* * **ap**, *char* ** **out**, *size_t* * **outlen**)   [Function]

> *ap*: structure that holds information about AP exchange
>
> *out*: pointer to output array with der encoding of AP-REQ.
>
> *outlen*: pointer to length of output array with der encoding of AP-REQ.
>
> Build AP-REQ using **shishi_ap_req_build()** and DER encode it. **out** is allocated by this function, and it is the responsibility of caller to deallocate it.
>
> **Return value:** Returns SHISHI_OK iff successful.

shishi_ap_req_der_set

int **shishi_ap_req_der_set** (*Shishi_ap* * **ap**, *char* * **der**, *size_t*   [Function]
    derlen)

> *ap*: structure that holds information about AP exchange
>
> *der*: input array with DER encoded AP-REQ.
>
> *derlen*: length of input array with DER encoded AP-REQ.
>
> DER decode AP-REQ and set it AP exchange. If decoding fails, the AP-REQ in the AP exchange is lost.
>
> **Return value:** Returns SHISHI_OK.

shishi_ap_req_build

int shishi_ap_req_build (*Shishi_ap* * **ap**) [Function]

> *ap*: structure that holds information about AP exchange
>
> Checksum data in authenticator and add ticket and authenticator to AP-REQ.
>
> **Return value:** Returns SHISHI_OK iff successful.

shishi ap_req_decode

int shishi_ap_req_decode (*Shishi_ap* * **ap**) [Function]

> *ap*: structure that holds information about AP exchange
>
> Decode ticket in AP-REQ and set the Ticket fields in the AP exchange.
>
> **Return value:** Returns SHISHI_OK iff successful.

shishi_ap_req_process_keyusage

int shishi_ap_req_process_keyusage (*Shishi_ap* * **ap**, *Shishi_key* * [Function]
> **key**, *int32_t* **keyusage**)
>
> *ap*: structure that holds information about AP exchange
>
> *key*: cryptographic key used to decrypt ticket in AP-REQ.
>
> *keyusage*: key usage to use during decryption, for normal AP-REQ's this is normally SHISHI_KEYUSAGE_APREQ_AUTHENTICATOR, for AP-REQ's part of TGS-REQ's, this is normally SHISHI_KEYUSAGE_TGSREQ_APREQ_AUTHENTICATOR.
>
> Decrypt ticket in AP-REQ using supplied key and decrypt Authenticator in AP-REQ using key in decrypted ticket, and on success set the Ticket and Authenticator fields in the AP exchange.
>
> **Return value:** Returns SHISHI_OK iff successful.

shishi_ap_req_process

int shishi_ap_req_process (*Shishi_ap* * **ap**, *Shishi_key* * **key**) [Function]

> *ap*: structure that holds information about AP exchange
>
> *key*: cryptographic key used to decrypt ticket in AP-REQ.
>
> Decrypt ticket in AP-REQ using supplied key and decrypt Authenticator in AP-REQ using key in decrypted ticket, and on success set the Ticket and Authenticator fields in the AP exchange.
>
> **Return value:** Returns SHISHI_OK iff successful.

shishi_ap_req_asn1

int shishi_ap_req_asn1 (*Shishi_ap* * **ap**, *Shishi_asn1* * **apreq**) [Function]

> *ap*: structure that holds information about AP exchange
>
> *apreq*: output AP-REQ variable.
>
> Build AP-REQ using `shishi_ap_req_build()` and return it.
>
> **Return value:** Returns SHISHI_OK iff successful.

shishi_ap_key

Shishi_key * shishi_ap_key (*Shishi_ap* * `ap`)   [Function]
> *ap*: structure that holds information about AP exchange

> Extract the application key from AP. If subkeys are used, it is taken from the Authenticator, otherwise the session key is used.

> **Return value:** Return application key from AP.

shishi_ap_rep

Shishi_asn1 shishi_ap_rep (*Shishi_ap* * `ap`)   [Function]
> *ap*: structure that holds information about AP exchange

> Get ASN.1 AP-REP structure from AP exchange.

> **Return value:** Returns the AP-REP from the AP exchange, or NULL if not yet set or an error occured.

shishi_ap_rep_set

void shishi_ap_rep_set (*Shishi_ap* * `ap`, *Shishi_asn1* `aprep`)   [Function]
> *ap*: structure that holds information about AP exchange

> *aprep*: aprep to store in AP.

> Set the AP-REP in the AP exchange.

shishi_ap_rep_der

int shishi_ap_rep_der (*Shishi_ap* * `ap`, *char* ** `out`, *size_t* * `outlen`)   [Function]
> *ap*: structure that holds information about AP exchange

> *out*: output array with newly allocated DER encoding of AP-REP.

> *outlen*: length of output array with DER encoding of AP-REP.

> Build AP-REP using `shishi_ap_rep_build()` and DER encode it. `out` is allocated by this function, and it is the responsibility of caller to deallocate it.

> **Return value:** Returns SHISHI_OK iff successful.

shishi_ap_rep_der_set

int shishi_ap_rep_der_set (*Shishi_ap* * `ap`, *char* * `der`, *size_t*   [Function]
> `derlen`)

> *ap*: structure that holds information about AP exchange

> *der*: input array with DER encoded AP-REP.

> *derlen*: length of input array with DER encoded AP-REP.

> DER decode AP-REP and set it AP exchange. If decoding fails, the AP-REP in the AP exchange remains.

> **Return value:** Returns SHISHI_OK.

shishi_ap_rep_build

int shishi_ap_rep_build (*Shishi_ap* * ap)   [Function]
> *ap*: structure that holds information about AP exchange

> Checksum data in authenticator and add ticket and authenticator to AP-REP.

> **Return value:** Returns SHISHI_OK iff successful.

shishi_ap_rep_asn1

int shishi_ap_rep_asn1 (*Shishi_ap* * ap, *Shishi_asn1* * aprep)   [Function]
> *ap*: structure that holds information about AP exchange

> *aprep*: output AP-REP variable.

> Build AP-REP using shishi_ap_rep_build() and return it.

> **Return value:** Returns SHISHI_OK iff successful.

shishi_ap_rep_verify

int shishi_ap_rep_verify (*Shishi_ap* * ap)   [Function]
> *ap*: structure that holds information about AP exchange

> Verify AP-REP compared to Authenticator.

> **Return value:** Returns SHISHI_OK, SHISHI_APREP_VERIFY_FAILED or an error.

shishi_ap_rep_verify_der

int shishi_ap_rep_verify_der (*Shishi_ap* * ap, *char* * der, *size_t*   [Function]
> der1en)

> *ap*: structure that holds information about AP exchange

> *der*: input array with DER encoded AP-REP.

> *der1en*: length of input array with DER encoded AP-REP.

> DER decode AP-REP and set it in AP exchange using shishi_ap_rep_der_set()
> and verify it using shishi_ap_rep_verify().

> **Return value:** Returns SHISHI_OK, SHISHI_APREP_VERIFY_FAILED or an error.

shishi_ap_rep_verify_asn1

int shishi_ap_rep_verify_asn1 (*Shishi_ap* * ap, *Shishi_asn1* aprep)   [Function]
> *ap*: structure that holds information about AP exchange

> *aprep*: input AP-REP.

> Set the AP-REP in the AP exchange using shishi_ap_rep_set() and verify it using
> shishi_ap_rep_verify().

> **Return value:** Returns SHISHI_OK, SHISHI_APREP_VERIFY_FAILED or an error.

shishi_ap_encapreppart

`Shishi_asn1 shishi_ap_encapreppart (Shishi_ap * ap)` [Function]

> *ap*: structure that holds information about AP exchange

> Get ASN.1 EncAPRepPart structure from AP exchange.

> **Return value:** Returns the EncAPREPPart from the AP exchange, or NULL if not yet set or an error occured.

shishi_ap_encapreppart_set

`void shishi_ap_encapreppart_set (Shishi_ap * ap, Shishi_asn1 encapreppart)` [Function]

> *ap*: structure that holds information about AP exchange

> *encapreppart*: EncAPRepPart to store in AP.

> Set the EncAPRepPart in the AP exchange.

shishi_ap_option2string

`const char * shishi_ap_option2string (Shishi_apoptions option)` [Function]

> *option*: enumerated AP-Option type, see Shishi_apoptions.

> Convert AP-Option type to AP-Option name string. Note that `option` must be just one of the AP-Option types, it cannot be an binary ORed indicating several AP-Options.

> **Return value:** Returns static string with name of AP-Option that must not be deallocated, or "unknown" if AP-Option was not understood.

shishi_ap_string2option

`Shishi_apoptions shishi_ap_string2option (const char * str)` [Function]

> *str*: zero terminated character array with name of AP-Option, e.g. "use-session-key".

> Convert AP-Option name to AP-Option type.

> **Return value:** Returns enumerated type member corresponding to AP-Option, or 0 if string was not understood.

shishi_apreq

`Shishi_asn1 shishi_apreq (Shishi * handle)` [Function]

> *handle*: shishi handle as allocated by `shishi_init()`.

> This function creates a new AP-REQ, populated with some default values.

> **Return value:** Returns the AP-REQ or NULL on failure.

shishi_apreq_print

`int shishi_apreq_print (Shishi * handle, FILE * fh, Shishi_asn1 apreq)` [Function]

> *handle*: shishi handle as allocated by `shishi_init()`.

> *fh*: file handle open for writing.

apreq: AP-REQ to print.

Print ASCII armored DER encoding of AP-REQ to file.

Return value: Returns SHISHI_OK iff successful.

shishi_apreq_save

int shishi_apreq_save (*Shishi * handle, FILE * fh, Shishi_asn1*   [Function]
      apreq)

handle: shishi handle as allocated by shishi_init().

fh: file handle open for writing.

apreq: AP-REQ to save.

Save DER encoding of AP-REQ to file.

Return value: Returns SHISHI_OK iff successful.

shishi_apreq_to_file

int shishi_apreq_to_file (*Shishi * handle, Shishi_asn1 apreq, int*   [Function]
      filetype, const char * filename)

handle: shishi handle as allocated by shishi_init().

apreq: AP-REQ to save.

filetype: input variable specifying type of file to be written, see Shishi_filetype.

filename: input variable with filename to write to.

Write AP-REQ to file in specified TYPE. The file will be truncated if it exists.

Return value: Returns SHISHI_OK iff successful.

shishi_apreq_parse

int shishi_apreq_parse (*Shishi * handle, FILE * fh, Shishi_asn1 **   [Function]
      apreq)

handle: shishi handle as allocated by shishi_init().

fh: file handle open for reading.

apreq: output variable with newly allocated AP-REQ.

Read ASCII armored DER encoded AP-REQ from file and populate given variable.

Return value: Returns SHISHI_OK iff successful.

shishi_apreq_read

int shishi_apreq_read (*Shishi * handle, FILE * fh, Shishi_asn1 **   [Function]
      apreq)

handle: shishi handle as allocated by shishi_init().

fh: file handle open for reading.

apreq: output variable with newly allocated AP-REQ.

Read DER encoded AP-REQ from file and populate given variable.

Return value: Returns SHISHI_OK iff successful.

shishi_apreq_from_file

int shishi_apreq_from_file (*Shishi * handle*, *Shishi_asn1 * apreq*,   [Function]
    int filetype, *const char * filename*)

handle: shishi handle as allocated by shishi_init().

apreq: output variable with newly allocated AP-REQ.

filetype: input variable specifying type of file to be read, see Shishi_filetype.

filename: input variable with filename to read from.

Read AP-REQ from file in specified TYPE.

Return value: Returns SHISHI_OK iff successful.

shishi_apreq_set_authenticator

int shishi_apreq_set_authenticator (*Shishi * handle*, *Shishi_asn1*   [Function]
    apreq, *int32_t etype*, *uint32_t kvno*, *const char * buf*, *size_t buflen*)

handle: shishi handle as allocated by shishi_init().

apreq: AP-REQ to add authenticator field to.

etype: encryption type used to encrypt authenticator.

kvno: version of the key used to encrypt authenticator.

buf: input array with encrypted authenticator.

buflen: size of input array with encrypted authenticator.

Set the encrypted authenticator field in the AP-REP. The encrypted data is usually created by calling shishi_encrypt() on the DER encoded authenticator. To save time, you may want to use shishi_apreq_add_authenticator() instead, which calculates the encrypted data and calls this function in one step.

Return value: Returns SHISHI_OK on success.

shishi_apreq_add_authenticator

int shishi_apreq_add_authenticator (*Shishi * handle*, *Shishi_asn1*   [Function]
    apreq, *Shishi_key * key*, *int keyusage*, *Shishi_asn1 authenticator*)

handle: shishi handle as allocated by shishi_init().

apreq: AP-REQ to add authenticator field to.

key: key to to use for encryption.

keyusage: cryptographic key usage value to use in encryption.

authenticator: authenticator as allocated by shishi_authenticator().

Encrypts DER encoded authenticator using key and store it in the AP-REQ.

Return value: Returns SHISHI_OK iff successful.

shishi_apreq_set_ticket

int shishi_apreq_set_ticket (*Shishi* * **handle**, *Shishi_asn1* **apreq**,   [Function]
        Shishi_asn1 **ticket**)

> *handle*: shishi handle as allocated by shishi_init().
>
> *apreq*: AP-REQ to add ticket field to.
>
> *ticket*: input ticket to copy into AP-REQ ticket field.
>
> Copy ticket into AP-REQ.
>
> **Return value:** Returns SHISHI_OK iff successful.

shishi_apreq_options

int shishi_apreq_options (*Shishi* * **handle**, *Shishi_asn1* **apreq**,   [Function]
        uint32_t * **flags**)

> *handle*: shishi handle as allocated by shishi_init().
>
> *apreq*: AP-REQ to get options from.
>
> *flags*: Output integer containing options from AP-REQ.
>
> Extract the AP-Options from AP-REQ into output integer.
>
> **Return value:** Returns SHISHI_OK iff successful.

shishi_apreq_use_session_key_p

int shishi_apreq_use_session_key_p (*Shishi* * **handle**, *Shishi_asn1*   [Function]
        apreq)

> *handle*: shishi handle as allocated by shishi_init().
>
> *apreq*: AP-REQ as allocated by shishi_apreq().
>
> Return non-0 iff the "Use session key" option is set in the AP-REQ.
>
> **Return value:** Returns SHISHI_OK iff successful.

shishi_apreq_mutual_required_p

int shishi_apreq_mutual_required_p (*Shishi* * **handle**, *Shishi_asn1*   [Function]
        apreq)

> *handle*: shishi handle as allocated by shishi_init().
>
> *apreq*: AP-REQ as allocated by shishi_apreq().
>
> Return non-0 iff the "Mutual required" option is set in the AP-REQ.
>
> **Return value:** Returns SHISHI_OK iff successful.

shishi_apreq_options_set

int shishi_apreq_options_set (*Shishi* * **handle**, *Shishi_asn1* **apreq**,   [Function]
        uint32_t **options**)

> *handle*: shishi handle as allocated by shishi_init().
>
> *apreq*: AP-REQ as allocated by shishi_apreq().
>
> *options*: Options to set in AP-REQ.
>
> Set the AP-Options in AP-REQ to indicate integer.
>
> **Return value:** Returns SHISHI_OK iff successful.

shishi_apreq_options_add

int shishi_apreq_options_add (*Shishi * handle*, *Shishi_asn1* apreq,   [Function]
    uint32_t option)

handle: shishi handle as allocated by shishi_init().

apreq: AP-REQ as allocated by shishi_apreq().

option: Options to add in AP-REQ.

Add the AP-Options in AP-REQ. Options not set in input parameter option are preserved in the AP-REQ.

Return value: Returns SHISHI_OK iff successful.

shishi_apreq_options_remove

int shishi_apreq_options_remove (*Shishi * handle*, *Shishi_asn1*   [Function]
    apreq, *uint32_t* option)

handle: shishi handle as allocated by shishi_init().

apreq: AP-REQ as allocated by shishi_apreq().

option: Options to remove from AP-REQ.

Remove the AP-Options from AP-REQ. Options not set in input parameter option are preserved in the AP-REQ.

Return value: Returns SHISHI_OK iff successful.

shishi_apreq_get_authenticator_etype

int shishi_apreq_get_authenticator_etype (*Shishi * handle*,   [Function]
    Shishi_asn1 apreq, *int32_t ** etype)

handle: shishi handle as allocated by shishi_init().

apreq: AP-REQ variable to get value from.

etype: output variable that holds the value.

Extract AP-REQ.authenticator.etype.

Return value: Returns SHISHI_OK iff successful.

shishi_apreq_get_ticket

int shishi_apreq_get_ticket (*Shishi * handle*, *Shishi_asn1* apreq,   [Function]
    Shishi_asn1 * ticket)

handle: shishi handle as allocated by shishi_init().

apreq: AP-REQ variable to get ticket from.

ticket: output variable to hold extracted ticket.

Extract ticket from AP-REQ.

Return value: Returns SHISHI_OK iff successful.

shishi_aprep

Shishi_asn1 shishi_aprep (*Shishi* * `handle`)   [Function]

> *handle*: shishi handle as allocated by `shishi_init()`.
>
> This function creates a new AP-REP, populated with some default values.
>
> **Return value:** Returns the authenticator or NULL on failure.

shishi_aprep_print

int shishi_aprep_print (*Shishi* * `handle`, *FILE* * `fh`, *Shishi_asn1*   [Function]
> `aprep`)
>
> *handle*: shishi handle as allocated by `shishi_init()`.
>
> *fh*: file handle open for writing.
>
> *aprep*: AP-REP to print.
>
> Print ASCII armored DER encoding of AP-REP to file.
>
> **Return value:** Returns SHISHI_OK iff successful.

shishi_aprep_save

int shishi_aprep_save (*Shishi* * `handle`, *FILE* * `fh`, *Shishi_asn1*   [Function]
> `aprep`)
>
> *handle*: shishi handle as allocated by `shishi_init()`.
>
> *fh*: file handle open for writing.
>
> *aprep*: AP-REP to save.
>
> Save DER encoding of AP-REP to file.
>
> **Return value:** Returns SHISHI_OK iff successful.

shishi_aprep_to_file

int shishi_aprep_to_file (*Shishi* * `handle`, *Shishi_asn1* `aprep`, *int*   [Function]
> `filetype`, *const char* * `filename`)
>
> *handle*: shishi handle as allocated by `shishi_init()`.
>
> *aprep*: AP-REP to save.
>
> *filetype*: input variable specifying type of file to be written, see Shishi_filetype.
>
> *filename*: input variable with filename to write to.
>
> Write AP-REP to file in specified TYPE. The file will be truncated if it exists.
>
> **Return value:** Returns SHISHI_OK iff successful.

shishi_aprep_parse

int shishi_aprep_parse (*Shishi* * `handle`, *FILE* * `fh`, *Shishi_asn1* *   [Function]
> `aprep`)
>
> *handle*: shishi handle as allocated by `shishi_init()`.
>
> *fh*: file handle open for reading.
>
> *aprep*: output variable with newly allocated AP-REP.
>
> Read ASCII armored DER encoded AP-REP from file and populate given variable.
>
> **Return value:** Returns SHISHI_OK iff successful.

shishi_aprep_read

int shishi_aprep_read (*Shishi* * `handle`, *FILE* * `fh`, *Shishi_asn1* *   [Function]
    `aprep`)

> *handle*: shishi handle as allocated by `shishi_init()`.
>
> *fh*: file handle open for reading.
>
> *aprep*: output variable with newly allocated AP-REP.
>
> Read DER encoded AP-REP from file and populate given variable.
>
> **Return value:** Returns SHISHI_OK iff successful.

shishi_aprep_from_file

int shishi_aprep_from_file (*Shishi* * `handle`, *Shishi_asn1* * `aprep`,   [Function]
    int `filetype`, *const char* * `filename`)

> *handle*: shishi handle as allocated by `shishi_init()`.
>
> *aprep*: output variable with newly allocated AP-REP.
>
> *filetype*: input variable specifying type of file to be read, see Shishi_filetype.
>
> *filename*: input variable with filename to read from.
>
> Read AP-REP from file in specified TYPE.
>
> **Return value:** Returns SHISHI_OK iff successful.

shishi_aprep_get_enc_part_etype

int shishi_aprep_get_enc_part_etype (*Shishi* * `handle`,   [Function]
    Shishi_asn1 `aprep`, *int32_t* * `etype`)

> *handle*: shishi handle as allocated by `shishi_init()`.
>
> *aprep*: AP-REP variable to get value from.
>
> *etype*: output variable that holds the value.
>
> Extract AP-REP.enc-part.etype.
>
> **Return value:** Returns SHISHI_OK iff successful.

shishi_encappreppart

Shishi_asn1 shishi_encappreppart (*Shishi* * `handle`)   [Function]

> *handle*: shishi handle as allocated by `shishi_init()`.
>
> This function creates a new EncAPRepPart, populated with some default values. It
> uses the current time as returned by the system for the ctime and cusec fields.
>
> **Return value:** Returns the encappreppart or NULL on failure.

shishi_encappreppart_print

int shishi_encappreppart_print (*Shishi* * `handle`, *FILE* * `fh`,   [Function]
    Shishi_asn1 `encappreppart`)

> *handle*: shishi handle as allocated by `shishi_init()`.
>
> *fh*: file handle open for writing.

encapreppart: EncAPRepPart to print.

Print ASCII armored DER encoding of EncAPRepPart to file.

Return value: Returns SHISHI_OK iff successful.

shishi_encapreppart_save

`int shishi_encapreppart_save` (*Shishi* `* handle`, *FILE* `* fh`,   [Function]
    Shishi_asn1 `encapreppart`)

handle: shishi handle as allocated by `shishi_init()`.

fh: file handle open for writing.

encapreppart: EncAPRepPart to save.

Save DER encoding of EncAPRepPart to file.

Return value: Returns SHISHI_OK iff successful.

shishi_encapreppart_to_file

`int shishi_encapreppart_to_file` (*Shishi* `* handle`, *Shishi_asn1*   [Function]
    `encapreppart`, *int* `filetype`, *const char* `* filename`)

handle: shishi handle as allocated by `shishi_init()`.

encapreppart: EncAPRepPart to save.

filetype: input variable specifying type of file to be written, see Shishi_filetype.

filename: input variable with filename to write to.

Write EncAPRepPart to file in specified TYPE. The file will be truncated if it exists.

Return value: Returns SHISHI_OK iff successful.

shishi_encapreppart_parse

`int shishi_encapreppart_parse` (*Shishi* `* handle`, *FILE* `* fh`,   [Function]
    Shishi_asn1 `* encapreppart`)

handle: shishi handle as allocated by `shishi_init()`.

fh: file handle open for reading.

encapreppart: output variable with newly allocated EncAPRepPart.

Read ASCII armored DER encoded EncAPRepPart from file and populate given variable.

Return value: Returns SHISHI_OK iff successful.

shishi_encapreppart_read

`int shishi_encapreppart_read` (*Shishi* `* handle`, *FILE* `* fh`,   [Function]
    Shishi_asn1 `* encapreppart`)

handle: shishi handle as allocated by `shishi_init()`.

fh: file handle open for reading.

encapreppart: output variable with newly allocated EncAPRepPart.

Read DER encoded EncAPRepPart from file and populate given variable.

Return value: Returns SHISHI_OK iff successful.

shishi_encapreppart_from_file

int shishi_encapreppart_from_file (*Shishi* * handle, *Shishi_asn1* *   [Function]
    encapreppart, *int* filetype, *const char* * filename)
handle: shishi handle as allocated by shishi_init().

encapreppart: output variable with newly allocated EncAPRepPart.

filetype: input variable specifying type of file to be read, see Shishi_filetype.

filename: input variable with filename to read from.

Read EncAPRepPart from file in specified TYPE.

Return value: Returns SHISHI_OK iff successful.

shishi_encapreppart_get_key

int shishi_encapreppart_get_key (*Shishi* * handle, *Shishi_asn1*   [Function]
    encapreppart, *Shishi_key* ** key)
handle: shishi handle as allocated by shishi_init().

encapreppart: input EncAPRepPart variable.

key: newly allocated key.

Extract the subkey from the encrypted AP-REP part.

Return value: Returns SHISHI_OK iff successful.

shishi_encapreppart_ctime

int shishi_encapreppart_ctime (*Shishi* * handle, *Shishi_asn1*   [Function]
    encapreppart, *char* ** t)
handle: shishi handle as allocated by shishi_init().

encapreppart: EncAPRepPart as allocated by shishi_encapreppart().

t: newly allocated zero-terminated character array with client time.

Extract client time from EncAPRepPart.

Return value: Returns SHISHI_OK iff successful.

shishi_encapreppart_ctime_set

int shishi_encapreppart_ctime_set (*Shishi* * handle, *Shishi_asn1*   [Function]
    encapreppart, *const char* * t)
handle: shishi handle as allocated by shishi_init().

encapreppart: EncAPRepPart as allocated by shishi_encapreppart().

t: string with generalized time value to store in EncAPRepPart.

Store client time in EncAPRepPart.

Return value: Returns SHISHI_OK iff successful.

shishi_encapreppart_cusec_get

int shishi_encapreppart_cusec_get (*Shishi* * *handle*, *Shishi_asn1*   [Function]
       encapreppart, *uint32_t* * *cusec*)

handle: shishi handle as allocated by shishi_init().

encapreppart: EncAPRepPart as allocated by shishi_encapreppart().

cusec: output integer with client microseconds field.

Extract client microseconds field from EncAPRepPart.

Return value: Returns SHISHI_OK iff successful.

shishi_encapreppart_cusec_set

int shishi_encapreppart_cusec_set (*Shishi* * *handle*, *Shishi_asn1*   [Function]
       encapreppart, *uint32_t* *cusec*)

handle: shishi handle as allocated by shishi_init().

encapreppart: EncAPRepPart as allocated by shishi_encapreppart().

cusec: client microseconds to set in authenticator, 0-999999.

Set the cusec field in the Authenticator.

Return value: Returns SHISHI_OK iff successful.

shishi_encapreppart_seqnumber_get

int shishi_encapreppart_seqnumber_get (*Shishi* * *handle*,   [Function]
       Shishi_asn1 *encapreppart*, *uint32_t* * *seqnumber*)

handle: shishi handle as allocated by shishi_init().

encapreppart: EncAPRepPart as allocated by shishi_encapreppart().

seqnumber: output integer with sequence number field.

Extract sequence number field from EncAPRepPart.

Return value: Returns SHISHI_OK iff successful.

shishi_encapreppart_seqnumber_remove

int shishi_encapreppart_seqnumber_remove (*Shishi* * *handle*,   [Function]
       Shishi_asn1 *encapreppart*)

handle: shishi handle as allocated by shishi_init().

encapreppart: encapreppart as allocated by shishi_encapreppart().

Remove sequence number field in EncAPRepPart.

Return value: Returns SHISHI_OK iff successful.

shishi_encapreppart_seqnumber_set

int shishi_encapreppart_seqnumber_set (*Shishi* * *handle*,   [Function]
       Shishi_asn1 *encapreppart*, *uint32_t* *seqnumber*)

handle: shishi handle as allocated by shishi_init().

encapreppart: encapreppart as allocated by shishi_encapreppart().

seqnumber: integer with sequence number field to store in encapreppart.

Store sequence number field in EncAPRepPart.

Return value: Returns `SHISHI_OK` iff successful.

shishi_encapreppart_time_copy

int shishi_encapreppart_time_copy (*Shishi * handle*, *Shishi_asn1*   [Function]
        encapreppart, *Shishi_asn1 authenticator*)
    handle: shishi handle as allocated by `shishi_init()`.

    encapreppart: EncAPRepPart as allocated by `shishi_encapreppart()`.

    authenticator: Authenticator to copy time fields from.

    Copy time fields from Authenticator into EncAPRepPart.

    Return value: Returns SHISHI_OK iff successful.

5.5 SAFE and PRIV Functions

The "KRB-SAFE" is an ASN.1 structure used by application client and servers to exchange integrity protected data. The integrity protection is keyed, usually with a key agreed on via the AP exchange (see Section 5.4 [AP-REQ and AP-REP Functions], page 70). The following illustrates the KRB-SAFE ASN.1 structure.

```
KRB-SAFE        ::= [APPLICATION 20] SEQUENCE {
        pvno            [0] INTEGER (5),
        msg-type        [1] INTEGER (20),
        safe-body       [2] KRB-SAFE-BODY,
        cksum           [3] Checksum
}

KRB-SAFE-BODY   ::= SEQUENCE {
        user-data       [0] OCTET STRING,
        timestamp       [1] KerberosTime OPTIONAL,
        usec            [2] Microseconds OPTIONAL,
        seq-number      [3] UInt32 OPTIONAL,
        s-address       [4] HostAddress,
        r-address       [5] HostAddress OPTIONAL
}
```

shishi_safe

int shishi_safe (*Shishi * handle*, *Shishi_safe ** safe*)   [Function]
    handle: shishi handle as allocated by `shishi_init()`.

    safe: pointer to new structure that holds information about SAFE exchange

    Create a new SAFE exchange.

    Return value: Returns SHISHI_OK iff successful.

shishi_safe_done

void shishi_safe_done (*Shishi_safe* * `safe`)   [Function]
> *safe*: structure that holds information about SAFE exchange
>
> Deallocate resources associated with SAFE exchange. This should be called by the application when it no longer need to utilize the SAFE exchange handle.

shishi_safe_key

Shishi_key * shishi_safe_key (*Shishi_safe* * `safe`)   [Function]
> *safe*: structure that holds information about SAFE exchange
>
> Get key structured from SAFE exchange.
>
> **Return value:** Returns the key used in the SAFE exchange, or NULL if not yet set or an error occured.

shishi_safe_key_set

void shishi_safe_key_set (*Shishi_safe* * `safe`, *Shishi_key* * `key`)   [Function]
> *safe*: structure that holds information about SAFE exchange
>
> *key*: key to store in SAFE.
>
> Set the Key in the SAFE exchange.

shishi_safe_safe

Shishi_asn1 shishi_safe_safe (*Shishi_safe* * `safe`)   [Function]
> *safe*: structure that holds information about SAFE exchange
>
> Get ASN.1 SAFE structured from SAFE exchange.
>
> **Return value:** Returns the ASN.1 safe in the SAFE exchange, or NULL if not yet set or an error occured.

shishi_safe_safe_set

void shishi_safe_safe_set (*Shishi_safe* * `safe`, *Shishi_asn1*   [Function]
`asn1safe`)
> *safe*: structure that holds information about SAFE exchange
>
> *asn1safe*: KRB-SAFE to store in SAFE exchange.
>
> Set the KRB-SAFE in the SAFE exchange.

shishi_safe_safe_der

int shishi_safe_safe_der (*Shishi_safe* * `safe`, char ** `out`, *size_t* *   [Function]
`outlen`)
> *safe*: safe as allocated by `shishi_safe()`.
>
> *out*: output array with newly allocated DER encoding of SAFE.
>
> *outlen*: length of output array with DER encoding of SAFE.

DER encode SAFE structure. Typically `shishi_safe_build()` is used to build the SAFE structure first. `out` is allocated by this function, and it is the responsibility of caller to deallocate it.

Return value: Returns SHISHI_OK iff successful.

shishi_safe_safe_der_set

`int shishi_safe_safe_der_set` (*Shishi_safe* * `safe`, *char* * `der`, *size_t*   [Function]
     `derlen`)

safe: safe as allocated by `shishi_safe()`.

der: input array with DER encoded KRB-SAFE.

derlen: length of input array with DER encoded KRB-SAFE.

DER decode KRB-SAFE and set it SAFE exchange. If decoding fails, the KRB-SAFE in the SAFE exchange remains.

Return value: Returns SHISHI_OK.

shishi_safe_print

`int shishi_safe_print` (*Shishi* * `handle`, *FILE* * `fh`, *Shishi_asn1*   [Function]
     `safe`)

handle: shishi handle as allocated by `shishi_init()`.

fh: file handle open for writing.

safe: SAFE to print.

Print ASCII armored DER encoding of SAFE to file.

Return value: Returns SHISHI_OK iff successful.

shishi_safe_save

`int shishi_safe_save` (*Shishi* * `handle`, *FILE* * `fh`, *Shishi_asn1* `safe`)   [Function]

handle: shishi handle as allocated by `shishi_init()`.

fh: file handle open for writing.

safe: SAFE to save.

Save DER encoding of SAFE to file.

Return value: Returns SHISHI_OK iff successful.

shishi_safe_to_file

`int shishi_safe_to_file` (*Shishi* * `handle`, *Shishi_asn1* `safe`, *int*   [Function]
     `filetype`, *const char* * `filename`)

handle: shishi handle as allocated by `shishi_init()`.

safe: SAFE to save.

filetype: input variable specifying type of file to be written, see Shishi_filetype.

filename: input variable with filename to write to.

Write SAFE to file in specified TYPE. The file will be truncated if it exists.

Return value: Returns SHISHI_OK iff successful.

shishi_safe_parse

int shishi_safe_parse (*Shishi * handle*, *FILE * fh*, *Shishi_asn1 **   [Function]
        safe)

handle: shishi handle as allocated by shishi_init().

fh: file handle open for reading.

safe: output variable with newly allocated SAFE.

Read ASCII armored DER encoded SAFE from file and populate given variable.

Return value: Returns SHISHI_OK iff successful.

shishi_safe_read

int shishi_safe_read (*Shishi * handle*, *FILE * fh*, *Shishi_asn1 **   [Function]
        safe)

handle: shishi handle as allocated by shishi_init().

fh: file handle open for reading.

safe: output variable with newly allocated SAFE.

Read DER encoded SAFE from file and populate given variable.

Return value: Returns SHISHI_OK iff successful.

shishi_safe_from_file

int shishi_safe_from_file (*Shishi * handle*, *Shishi_asn1 * safe*, *int*   [Function]
        filetype, *const char * filename*)

handle: shishi handle as allocated by shishi_init().

safe: output variable with newly allocated SAFE.

filetype: input variable specifying type of file to be read, see Shishi_filetype.

filename: input variable with filename to read from.

Read SAFE from file in specified TYPE.

Return value: Returns SHISHI_OK iff successful.

shishi_safe_cksum

int shishi_safe_cksum (*Shishi * handle*, *Shishi_asn1 safe*, *int32_t **   [Function]
        cksumtype, *char ** cksum*, *size_t * cksumlen*)

handle: shishi handle as allocated by shishi_init().

safe: safe as allocated by shishi_safe().

cksumtype: output checksum type.

cksum: output array with newly allocated checksum data from SAFE.

cksumlen: output size of output checksum data buffer.

Read checksum value from KRB-SAFE. cksum is allocated by this function, and it is the responsibility of caller to deallocate it.

Return value: Returns SHISHI_OK iff successful.

shishi_safe_set_cksum

int shishi_safe_set_cksum (*Shishi* * `handle`, *Shishi_asn1* `safe`,   [Function]
     int32_t `cksumtype`, *const char* * `cksum`, *size_t* `cksumlen`)

handle: shishi handle as allocated by `shishi_init()`.

safe: safe as allocated by `shishi_safe()`.

cksumtype: input checksum type to store in SAFE.

cksum: input checksum data to store in SAFE.

cksumlen: size of input checksum data to store in SAFE.

Store checksum value in SAFE. A checksum is usually created by calling `shishi_checksum()` on some application specific data using the key from the ticket that is being used. To save time, you may want to use `shishi_safe_build()` instead, which calculates the checksum and calls this function in one step.

Return value: Returns SHISHI_OK iff successful.

shishi_safe_user_data

int shishi_safe_user_data (*Shishi* * `handle`, *Shishi_asn1* `safe`, *char*   [Function]
     ** `userdata`, *size_t* * `userdatalen`)

handle: shishi handle as allocated by `shishi_init()`.

safe: safe as allocated by `shishi_safe()`.

userdata: output array with newly allocated user data from KRB-SAFE.

userdatalen: output size of output user data buffer.

Read user data value from KRB-SAFE. `userdata` is allocated by this function, and it is the responsibility of caller to deallocate it.

Return value: Returns SHISHI_OK iff successful.

shishi_safe_set_user_data

int shishi_safe_set_user_data (*Shishi* * `handle`, *Shishi_asn1* `safe`,   [Function]
     const char * `userdata`, *size_t* `userdatalen`)

handle: shishi handle as allocated by `shishi_init()`.

safe: safe as allocated by `shishi_safe()`.

userdata: input user application to store in SAFE.

userdatalen: size of input user application to store in SAFE.

Set the application data in SAFE.

Return value: Returns SHISHI_OK iff successful.

shishi_safe_build

int shishi_safe_build (*Shishi_safe* * `safe`, *Shishi_key* * `key`)   [Function]

safe: safe as allocated by `shishi_safe()`.

key: key for session, used to compute checksum.

Build checksum and set it in KRB-SAFE. Note that this follows RFC 1510bis and is incompatible with RFC 1510, although presumably few implementations use the RFC1510 algorithm.

Return value: Returns SHISHI_OK iff successful.

shishi_safe_verify

int **shishi_safe_verify** (*Shishi_safe* * `safe`, *Shishi_key* * `key`)   [Function]
safe: safe as allocated by `shishi_safe()`.

key: key for session, used to verify checksum.

Verify checksum in KRB-SAFE. Note that this follows RFC 1510bis and is incompatible with RFC 1510, although presumably few implementations use the RFC1510 algorithm.

Return value: Returns SHISHI_OK iff successful, SHISHI_SAFE_BAD_KEYTYPE if an incompatible key type is used, or SHISHI_SAFE_VERIFY_FAILED if the actual verification failed.

The "KRB-PRIV" is an ASN.1 structure used by application client and servers to exchange confidential data. The confidentiality is keyed, usually with a key agreed on via the AP exchange (see Section 5.4 [AP-REQ and AP-REP Functions], page 70). The following illustrates the KRB-PRIV ASN.1 structure.

```
KRB-PRIV        ::= [APPLICATION 21] SEQUENCE {
        pvno            [0] INTEGER (5),
        msg-type        [1] INTEGER (21),
                        -- NOTE: there is no [2] tag
        enc-part        [3] EncryptedData -- EncKrbPrivPart
}


EncKrbPrivPart  ::= [APPLICATION 28] SEQUENCE {
        user-data       [0] OCTET STRING,
        timestamp       [1] KerberosTime OPTIONAL,
        usec            [2] Microseconds OPTIONAL,
        seq-number      [3] UInt32 OPTIONAL,
        s-address       [4] HostAddress -- sender's addr --,
        r-address       [5] HostAddress OPTIONAL -- recip's addr
}
```

shishi_priv

int **shishi_priv** (*Shishi* * `handle`, *Shishi_priv* ** `priv`)   [Function]
handle: shishi handle as allocated by `shishi_init()`.

priv: pointer to new structure that holds information about PRIV exchange

Create a new PRIV exchange.

Return value: Returns SHISHI_OK iff successful.

shishi_priv_done

void **shishi_priv_done** (*Shishi_priv* * **priv**) [Function]
> *priv*: structure that holds information about PRIV exchange

> Deallocate resources associated with PRIV exchange. This should be called by the application when it no longer need to utilize the PRIV exchange handle.

shishi_priv_key

Shishi_key * **shishi_priv_key** (*Shishi_priv* * **priv**) [Function]
> *priv*: structure that holds information about PRIV exchange

> Get key from PRIV exchange.

> **Return value:** Returns the key used in the PRIV exchange, or NULL if not yet set or an error occured.

shishi_priv_key_set

void **shishi_priv_key_set** (*Shishi_priv* * **priv**, *Shishi_key* * **key**) [Function]
> *priv*: structure that holds information about PRIV exchange

> *key*: key to store in PRIV.

> Set the Key in the PRIV exchange.

shishi_priv_priv

Shishi_asn1 **shishi_priv_priv** (*Shishi_priv* * **priv**) [Function]
> *priv*: structure that holds information about PRIV exchange

> Get ASN.1 PRIV structure in PRIV exchange.

> **Return value:** Returns the ASN.1 priv in the PRIV exchange, or NULL if not yet set or an error occured.

shishi_priv_priv_set

void **shishi_priv_priv_set** (*Shishi_priv* * **priv**, *Shishi_asn1* **asn1priv**) [Function]
> *priv*: structure that holds information about PRIV exchange

> *asn1priv*: KRB-PRIV to store in PRIV exchange.

> Set the KRB-PRIV in the PRIV exchange.

shishi_priv_priv_der

int **shishi_priv_priv_der** (*Shishi_priv* * **priv**, *char* ** **out**, *size_t* * **outlen**) [Function]
> *priv*: priv as allocated by **shishi_priv**().

> *out*: output array with newly allocated DER encoding of PRIV.

> *outlen*: length of output array with DER encoding of PRIV.

DER encode PRIV structure. Typically `shishi_priv_build()` is used to build the PRIV structure first. `out` is allocated by this function, and it is the responsibility of caller to deallocate it.

Return value: Returns SHISHI_OK iff successful.

shishi_priv_priv_der_set

`int` **`shishi_priv_priv_der_set`** (*Shishi_priv* * **`priv`**, *char* * *der*, *size_t*   [Function]
       `derlen`)
priv: priv as allocated by `shishi_priv()`.

der: input array with DER encoded KRB-PRIV.

derlen: length of input array with DER encoded KRB-PRIV.

DER decode KRB-PRIV and set it PRIV exchange. If decoding fails, the KRB-PRIV in the PRIV exchange remains.

Return value: Returns SHISHI_OK.

shishi_priv_encprivpart

`Shishi_asn1` **`shishi_priv_encprivpart`** (*Shishi_priv* * **`priv`**)   [Function]
       priv: structure that holds information about PRIV exchange

Get ASN.1 EncPrivPart structure from PRIV exchange.

Return value: Returns the ASN.1 encprivpart in the PRIV exchange, or NULL if not yet set or an error occured.

shishi_priv_encprivpart_set

`void` **`shishi_priv_encprivpart_set`** (*Shishi_priv* * **`priv`**, *Shishi_asn1*   [Function]
       `asn1encprivpart`)
priv: structure that holds information about PRIV exchange

asn1encprivpart: ENCPRIVPART to store in PRIV exchange.

Set the ENCPRIVPART in the PRIV exchange.

shishi_priv_encprivpart_der

`int` **`shishi_priv_encprivpart_der`** (*Shishi_priv* * **`priv`**, *char* ** **`out`**,   [Function]
       size_t * **`outlen`**)
priv: priv as allocated by `shishi_priv()`.

out: output array with newly allocated DER encoding of ENCPRIVPART.

outlen: length of output array with DER encoding of ENCPRIVPART.

DER encode ENCPRIVPART structure. `out` is allocated by this function, and it is the responsibility of caller to deallocate it.

Return value: Returns SHISHI_OK iff successful.

shishi_priv_encprivpart_der_set

int shishi_priv_encprivpart_der_set (*Shishi_priv* **priv**, *char* *   [Function]
    der, *size_t* **derlen**)

priv: priv as allocated by `shishi_priv()`.

der: input array with DER encoded ENCPRIVPART.

derlen: length of input array with DER encoded ENCPRIVPART.

DER decode ENCPRIVPART and set it PRIV exchange. If decoding fails, the ENCPRIVPART in the PRIV exchange remains.

Return value: Returns SHISHI_OK.

shishi_priv_print

int shishi_priv_print (*Shishi* * **handle**, *FILE* * **fh**, *Shishi_asn1*   [Function]
    priv)

handle: shishi handle as allocated by `shishi_init()`.

fh: file handle open for writing.

priv: PRIV to print.

Print ASCII armored DER encoding of PRIV to file.

Return value: Returns SHISHI_OK iff successful.

shishi_priv_save

int shishi_priv_save (*Shishi* * **handle**, *FILE* * **fh**, *Shishi_asn1* **priv**)   [Function]

handle: shishi handle as allocated by `shishi_init()`.

fh: file handle open for writing.

priv: PRIV to save.

Save DER encoding of PRIV to file.

Return value: Returns SHISHI_OK iff successful.

shishi_priv_to_file

int shishi_priv_to_file (*Shishi* * **handle**, *Shishi_asn1* **priv**, *int*   [Function]
    filetype, *const char* * **filename**)

handle: shishi handle as allocated by `shishi_init()`.

priv: PRIV to save.

filetype: input variable specifying type of file to be written, see Shishi_filetype.

filename: input variable with filename to write to.

Write PRIV to file in specified TYPE. The file will be truncated if it exists.

Return value: Returns SHISHI_OK iff successful.

shishi_priv_parse

int shishi_priv_parse (*Shishi* * **handle**, *FILE* * **fh**, *Shishi_asn1* *   [Function]
    priv)

handle: shishi handle as allocated by `shishi_init()`.

fh: file handle open for reading.

priv: output variable with newly allocated PRIV.

Read ASCII armored DER encoded PRIV from file and populate given variable.

Return value: Returns SHISHI_OK iff successful.

shishi_priv_read

int shishi_priv_read (*Shishi* * **handle**, *FILE* * **fh**, *Shishi_asn1* *   [Function]
    priv)

handle: shishi handle as allocated by `shishi_init()`.

fh: file handle open for reading.

priv: output variable with newly allocated PRIV.

Read DER encoded PRIV from file and populate given variable.

Return value: Returns SHISHI_OK iff successful.

shishi_priv_from_file

int shishi_priv_from_file (*Shishi* * **handle**, *Shishi_asn1* * **priv**, *int*   [Function]
    filetype, *const char* * **filename**)

handle: shishi handle as allocated by `shishi_init()`.

priv: output variable with newly allocated PRIV.

filetype: input variable specifying type of file to be read, see Shishi_filetype.

filename: input variable with filename to read from.

Read PRIV from file in specified TYPE.

Return value: Returns SHISHI_OK iff successful.

shishi_priv_enc_part_etype

int shishi_priv_enc_part_etype (*Shishi* * **handle**, *Shishi_asn1*   [Function]
    priv, *int32_t* * **etype**)

handle: shishi handle as allocated by `shishi_init()`.

priv: PRIV variable to get value from.

etype: output variable that holds the value.

Extract PRIV.enc-part.etype.

Return value: Returns SHISHI_OK iff successful.

shishi_priv_set_enc_part

int shishi_priv_set_enc_part (*Shishi * handle*, *Shishi_asn1 priv*, [Function]
    int32_t etype, *const char * encpart*, *size_t encpartlen*)

    handle: shishi handle as allocated by shishi_init().

    priv: priv as allocated by shishi_priv().

    etype: input encryption type to store in PRIV.

    encpart: input encrypted data to store in PRIV.

    encpartlen: size of input encrypted data to store in PRIV.

    Store encrypted data in PRIV. The encrypted data is usually created by calling shishi_encrypt() on some application specific data using the key from the ticket that is being used. To save time, you may want to use shishi_priv_build() instead, which encryptes the data and calls this function in one step.

    Return value: Returns SHISHI_OK iff successful.

shishi_encprivpart_user_data

int shishi_encprivpart_user_data (*Shishi * handle*, *Shishi_asn1* [Function]
    encprivpart, *char ** userdata*, *size_t * userdatalen*)

    handle: shishi handle as allocated by shishi_init().

    encprivpart: encprivpart as allocated by shishi_priv().

    userdata: output array with newly allocated user data from KRB-PRIV.

    userdatalen: output size of output user data buffer.

    Read user data value from KRB-PRIV. userdata is allocated by this function, and it is the responsibility of caller to deallocate it.

    Return value: Returns SHISHI_OK iff successful.

shishi_encprivpart_set_user_data

int shishi_encprivpart_set_user_data (*Shishi * handle*, [Function]
    Shishi_asn1 encprivpart, *const char * userdata*, *size_t userdatalen*)

    handle: shishi handle as allocated by shishi_init().

    encprivpart: encprivpart as allocated by shishi_priv().

    userdata: input user application to store in PRIV.

    userdatalen: size of input user application to store in PRIV.

    Set the application data in PRIV.

    Return value: Returns SHISHI_OK iff successful.

shishi_priv_build

int shishi_priv_build (*Shishi_priv * priv*, *Shishi_key * key*) [Function]

    priv: priv as allocated by shishi_priv().

    key: key for session, used to encrypt data.

Build checksum and set it in KRB-PRIV. Note that this follows RFC 1510bis and is incompatible with RFC 1510, although presumably few implementations use the RFC1510 algorithm.

Return value: Returns SHISHI_OK iff successful.

shishi_priv_process

int **shishi_priv_process** (*Shishi_priv* * **priv**, *Shishi_key* * **key**)   [Function]
    priv: priv as allocated by **shishi_priv**().

key: key to use to decrypt EncPrivPart.

Decrypt encrypted data in KRB-PRIV and set the EncPrivPart in the PRIV exchange.

Return value: Returns SHISHI_OK iff successful, SHISHI_PRIV_BAD_KEYTYPE if an incompatible key type is used, or SHISHI_CRYPTO_ERROR if the actual decryption failed.

5.6 Ticket Functions

A Ticket is an ASN.1 structured that can be used to authenticate the holder to services. It contain an encrypted part, which the ticket holder cannot see, but can be encrypted by the service, and various information about the user and service, including an encryption key to use for the connection. See Section 5.9 [Ticket (ASN.1) Functions], page 124, for more details on the ASN.1 structure of a ticket.

shishi_tkt

int **shishi_tkt** (*Shishi* * **handle**, *Shishi_tkt* ** **tkt**)   [Function]
    handle: shishi handle as allocated by **shishi_init**().

tkt: output variable with newly allocated ticket.

Create a new ticket handle.

Return value: Returns SHISHI_OK iff successful.

shishi_tkt2

Shishi_tkt * **shishi_tkt2** (*Shishi* * **handle**, *Shishi_asn1* **ticket**,   [Function]
        Shishi_asn1 **enckdcreppart**, *Shishi_asn1* **kdcrep**)
    handle: shishi handle as allocated by **shishi_init**().

ticket: input variable with ticket.

enckdcreppart: input variable with auxiliary ticket information.

kdcrep: input variable with KDC-REP ticket information.

Create a new ticket handle.

Return value: Returns new ticket handle, or **NULL** on error.

shishi_tkt_done

void shishi_tkt_done (*Shishi_tkt* * `tkt`)   [Function]

> *tkt*: input variable with ticket info.
>
> Deallocate resources associated with ticket. The ticket must not be used again after this call.

shishi_tkt_ticket

Shishi_asn1 shishi_tkt_ticket (*Shishi_tkt* * `tkt`)   [Function]

> *tkt*: input variable with ticket info.
>
> Get ASN.1 Ticket structure from ticket.
>
> **Return value:** Returns actual ticket.

shishi_tkt_ticket_set

void shishi_tkt_ticket_set (*Shishi_tkt* * `tkt`, *Shishi_asn1* `ticket`)   [Function]

> *tkt*: input variable with ticket info.
>
> *ticket*: ASN.1 Ticket to store in ticket.
>
> Set the ASN.1 Ticket in the Ticket.

shishi_tkt_enckdcreppart

Shishi_asn1 shishi_tkt_enckdcreppart (*Shishi_tkt* * `tkt`)   [Function]

> *tkt*: input variable with ticket info.
>
> Get ASN.1 EncKDCRepPart structure from ticket.
>
> **Return value:** Returns auxiliary ticket information.

shishi_tkt_enckdcreppart_set

void shishi_tkt_enckdcreppart_set (*Shishi_tkt* * `tkt`, *Shishi_asn1* [Function]
`enckdcreppart`)

> *tkt*: structure that holds information about Ticket exchange
>
> *enckdcreppart*: EncKDCRepPart to store in Ticket.
>
> Set the EncKDCRepPart in the Ticket.

shishi_tkt_kdcrep

Shishi_asn1 shishi_tkt_kdcrep (*Shishi_tkt* * `tkt`)   [Function]

> *tkt*: input variable with ticket info.
>
> Get ASN.1 KDCRep structure from ticket.
>
> **Return value:** Returns KDC-REP information.

shishi_tkt_encticketpart

Shishi_asn1 shishi_tkt_encticketpart (*Shishi_tkt* * `tkt`)   [Function]

> *tkt*: input variable with ticket info.
>
> Get ASN.1 EncTicketPart structure from ticket.
>
> **Return value:** Returns EncTicketPart information.

shishi_tkt_encticketpart_set

void **shishi_tkt_encticketpart_set** (*Shishi_tkt* * **tkt**, *Shishi_asn1*   [Function]
    encticketpart)

tkt: input variable with ticket info.

encticketpart: encticketpart to store in ticket.

Set the EncTicketPart in the Ticket.

shishi_tkt_key

Shishi_key * **shishi_tkt_key** (*Shishi_tkt* * **tkt**)   [Function]
    tkt: input variable with ticket info.

Get key used in ticket, by looking first in EncKDCRepPart and then in EncTicketPart. If key is already populated, it is not extracted again.

Return value: Returns key extracted from EncKDCRepPart or EncTicketPart.

shishi_tkt_key_set

int **shishi_tkt_key_set** (*Shishi_tkt* * **tkt**, *Shishi_key* * **key**)   [Function]
    tkt: input variable with ticket info.

key: key to store in ticket.

Set the key in the EncTicketPart.

Return value: Returns SHISHI_OK iff successful.

shishi_tkt_client

int **shishi_tkt_client** (*Shishi_tkt* * **tkt**, *char* ** **client**, *size_t* *   [Function]
    clientlen)

tkt: input variable with ticket info.

client: pointer to newly allocated zero terminated string containing principal name. May be NULL (to only populate clientlen).

clientlen: pointer to length of client on output, excluding terminating zero. May be NULL (to only populate client).

Represent client principal name in Ticket KDC-REP as zero-terminated string. The string is allocate by this function, and it is the responsibility of the caller to deallocate it. Note that the output length clientlen does not include the terminating zero.

Return value: Returns SHISHI_OK iff successful.

shishi_tkt_client_p

int **shishi_tkt_client_p** (*Shishi_tkt* * **tkt**, *const char* * **client**)   [Function]
    tkt: input variable with ticket info.

client: client name of ticket.

Determine if ticket is for specified client.

Return value: Returns non-0 iff ticket is for specified client.

shishi_tkt_clientrealm

int **shishi_tkt_clientrealm** (*Shishi_tkt * **tkt**, char ** **client**,   [Function]
    *size_t * **clientlen**)

tkt: input variable with ticket info.

client: pointer to newly allocated zero terminated string containing principal name and realm. May be NULL (to only populate clientlen).

clientlen: pointer to length of client on output, excluding terminating zero. May be NULL (to only populate client).

Convert cname and realm fields from AS-REQ to printable principal name format. The string is allocate by this function, and it is the responsibility of the caller to deallocate it. Note that the output length clientlen does not include the terminating zero.

Return value: Returns SHISHI_OK iff successful.

shishi_tkt_clientrealm_p

int **shishi_tkt_clientrealm_p** (*Shishi_tkt * **tkt**, const char *   [Function]
    client)

tkt: input variable with ticket info.

client: principal name (client name and realm) of ticket.

Determine if ticket is for specified client principal.

Return value: Returns non-0 iff ticket is for specified client principal.

shishi_tkt_realm

int **shishi_tkt_realm** (*Shishi_tkt * **tkt**, char ** **realm**, size_t *   [Function]
    realmlen)

tkt: input variable with ticket info.

realm: pointer to newly allocated character array with realm name.

realmlen: length of newly allocated character array with realm name.

Extract realm of server in ticket.

Return value: Returns SHISHI_OK iff successful.

shishi_tkt_server

int **shishi_tkt_server** (*Shishi_tkt * **tkt**, char ** **server**, size_t *   [Function]
    serverlen)

tkt: input variable with ticket info.

server: pointer to newly allocated zero terminated string containing principal name. May be NULL (to only populate serverlen).

serverlen: pointer to length of server on output, excluding terminating zero. May be NULL (to only populate server).

Represent server principal name in Ticket as zero-terminated string. The string is allocate by this function, and it is the responsibility of the caller to deallocate it. Note that the output length serverlen does not include the terminating zero.

Return value: Returns SHISHI_OK iff successful.

shishi_tkt_server_p

int shishi_tkt_server_p (*Shishi_tkt* * **tkt**, *const char* * **server**)   [Function]
> *tkt*: input variable with ticket info.

> *server*: server name of ticket.

> Determine if ticket is for specified server.

> **Return value:** Returns non-0 iff ticket is for specified server.

shishi_tkt_flags

int shishi_tkt_flags (*Shishi_tkt* * **tkt**, *uint32_t* * **flags**)   [Function]
> *tkt*: input variable with ticket info.

> *flags*: pointer to output integer with flags.

> Extract flags in ticket (i.e., EncKDCRepPart).

> **Return value:** Returns SHISHI_OK iff successful.

shishi_tkt_flags_set

int shishi_tkt_flags_set (*Shishi_tkt* * **tkt**, *uint32_t* **flags**)   [Function]
> *tkt*: input variable with ticket info.

> *flags*: integer with flags to store in ticket.

> Set flags in ticket, i.e., both EncTicketPart and EncKDCRepPart. Note that this reset any already existing flags.

> **Return value:** Returns SHISHI_OK iff successful.

shishi_tkt_flags_add

int shishi_tkt_flags_add (*Shishi_tkt* * **tkt**, *uint32_t* **flag**)   [Function]
> *tkt*: input variable with ticket info.

> *flag*: integer with flags to store in ticket.

> Add ticket flags to Ticket and EncKDCRepPart. This preserves all existing options.

> **Return value:** Returns SHISHI_OK iff successful.

shishi_tkt_forwardable_p

int shishi_tkt_forwardable_p (*Shishi_tkt* * **tkt**)   [Function]
> *tkt*: input variable with ticket info.

> Determine if ticket is forwardable.

> The FORWARDABLE flag in a ticket is normally only interpreted by the ticket-granting service. It can be ignored by application servers. The FORWARDABLE flag has an interpretation similar to that of the PROXIABLE flag, except ticket-granting tickets may also be issued with different network addresses. This flag is reset by default, but users MAY request that it be set by setting the FORWARDABLE option in the AS request when they request their initial ticket-granting ticket.

> **Return value:** Returns non-0 iff forwardable flag is set in ticket.

shishi_tkt_forwarded_p

int shishi_tkt_forwarded_p (*Shishi_tkt* * **tkt**)   [Function]
    tkt: input variable with ticket info.

Determine if ticket is forwarded.

The FORWARDED flag is set by the TGS when a client presents a ticket with the FORWARDABLE flag set and requests a forwarded ticket by specifying the FORWARDED KDC option and supplying a set of addresses for the new ticket. It is also set in all tickets issued based on tickets with the FORWARDED flag set. Application servers may choose to process FORWARDED tickets differently than non-FORWARDED tickets.

Return value: Returns non-0 iff forwarded flag is set in ticket.

shishi_tkt_proxiable_p

int shishi_tkt_proxiable_p (*Shishi_tkt* * **tkt**)   [Function]
    tkt: input variable with ticket info.

Determine if ticket is proxiable.

The PROXIABLE flag in a ticket is normally only interpreted by the ticket-granting service. It can be ignored by application servers. When set, this flag tells the ticket-granting server that it is OK to issue a new ticket (but not a ticket-granting ticket) with a different network address based on this ticket. This flag is set if requested by the client on initial authentication. By default, the client will request that it be set when requesting a ticket-granting ticket, and reset when requesting any other ticket.

Return value: Returns non-0 iff proxiable flag is set in ticket.

shishi_tkt_proxy_p

int shishi_tkt_proxy_p (*Shishi_tkt* * **tkt**)   [Function]
    tkt: input variable with ticket info.

Determine if ticket is proxy ticket.

The PROXY flag is set in a ticket by the TGS when it issues a proxy ticket. Application servers MAY check this flag and at their option they MAY require additional authentication from the agent presenting the proxy in order to provide an audit trail.

Return value: Returns non-0 iff proxy flag is set in ticket.

shishi_tkt_may_postdate_p

int shishi_tkt_may_postdate_p (*Shishi_tkt* * **tkt**)   [Function]
    tkt: input variable with ticket info.

Determine if ticket may be used to grant postdated tickets.

The MAY-POSTDATE flag in a ticket is normally only interpreted by the ticket-granting service. It can be ignored by application servers. This flag MUST be set in a ticket-granting ticket in order to issue a postdated ticket based on the presented ticket. It is reset by default; it MAY be requested by a client by setting the ALLOW-POSTDATE option in the KRB_AS_REQ message. This flag does not allow a client to obtain a postdated ticket-granting ticket; postdated ticket-granting tickets can only by obtained by requesting the postdating in the KRB_AS_REQ message. The life (endtime-starttime) of a postdated ticket will be the remaining life of the ticket-granting ticket at the time of the request, unless the RENEWABLE option is also set, in which case it can be the full life (endtime-starttime) of the ticket-granting ticket. The KDC MAY limit how far in the future a ticket may be postdated.

Return value: Returns non-0 iff may-postdate flag is set in ticket.

shishi_tkt_postdated_p

int **shishi_tkt_postdated_p** (*Shishi_tkt* * **tkt**)   [Function]
    tkt: input variable with ticket info.

Determine if ticket is postdated.

The POSTDATED flag indicates that a ticket has been postdated. The application server can check the authtime field in the ticket to see when the original authentication occurred. Some services MAY choose to reject postdated tickets, or they may only accept them within a certain period after the original authentication. When the KDC issues a POSTDATED ticket, it will also be marked as INVALID, so that the application client MUST present the ticket to the KDC to be validated before use.

Return value: Returns non-0 iff postdated flag is set in ticket.

shishi_tkt_invalid_p

int **shishi_tkt_invalid_p** (*Shishi_tkt* * **tkt**)   [Function]
    tkt: input variable with ticket info.

Determine if ticket is invalid.

The INVALID flag indicates that a ticket is invalid. Application servers MUST reject tickets which have this flag set. A postdated ticket will be issued in this form. Invalid tickets MUST be validated by the KDC before use, by presenting them to the KDC in a TGS request with the VALIDATE option specified. The KDC will only validate tickets after their starttime has passed. The validation is required so that postdated tickets which have been stolen before their starttime can be rendered permanently invalid (through a hot-list mechanism).

Return value: Returns non-0 iff invalid flag is set in ticket.

shishi_tkt_renewable_p

int **shishi_tkt_renewable_p** (*Shishi_tkt* * **tkt**)   [Function]
    tkt: input variable with ticket info.

Determine if ticket is renewable.

The RENEWABLE flag in a ticket is normally only interpreted by the ticket-granting service (discussed below in section 3.3). It can usually be ignored by application servers. However, some particularly careful application servers MAY disallow renewable tickets.

Return value: Returns non-0 iff renewable flag is set in ticket.

shishi_tkt_initial_p

`int shishi_tkt_initial_p` (*Shishi_tkt* * `tkt`)   [Function]
    tkt: input variable with ticket info.

Determine if ticket was issued using AS exchange.

The INITIAL flag indicates that a ticket was issued using the AS protocol, rather than issued based on a ticket-granting ticket. Application servers that want to require the demonstrated knowledge of a client's secret key (e.g. a password-changing program) can insist that this flag be set in any tickets they accept, and thus be assured that the client's key was recently presented to the application client.

Return value: Returns non-0 iff initial flag is set in ticket.

shishi_tkt_pre_authent_p

`int shishi_tkt_pre_authent_p` (*Shishi_tkt* * `tkt`)   [Function]
    tkt: input variable with ticket info.

Determine if ticket was pre-authenticated.

The PRE-AUTHENT and HW-AUTHENT flags provide additional information about the initial authentication, regardless of whether the current ticket was issued directly (in which case INITIAL will also be set) or issued on the basis of a ticket-granting ticket (in which case the INITIAL flag is clear, but the PRE-AUTHENT and HW-AUTHENT flags are carried forward from the ticket-granting ticket).

Return value: Returns non-0 iff pre-authent flag is set in ticket.

shishi_tkt_hw_authent_p

`int shishi_tkt_hw_authent_p` (*Shishi_tkt* * `tkt`)   [Function]
    tkt: input variable with ticket info.

Determine if ticket is authenticated using a hardware token.

The PRE-AUTHENT and HW-AUTHENT flags provide additional information about the initial authentication, regardless of whether the current ticket was issued directly (in which case INITIAL will also be set) or issued on the basis of a ticket-granting ticket (in which case the INITIAL flag is clear, but the PRE-AUTHENT and HW-AUTHENT flags are carried forward from the ticket-granting ticket).

Return value: Returns non-0 iff hw-authent flag is set in ticket.

shishi_tkt_transited_policy_checked_p

`int shishi_tkt_transited_policy_checked_p` (*Shishi_tkt* * `tkt`)   [Function]
    tkt: input variable with ticket info.

Determine if ticket has been policy checked for transit.

The application server is ultimately responsible for accepting or rejecting authentication and SHOULD check that only suitably trusted KDCs are relied upon to authenticate a principal. The transited field in the ticket identifies which realms (and thus which KDCs) were involved in the authentication process and an application server would normally check this field. If any of these are untrusted to authenticate the indicated client principal (probably determined by a realm-based policy), the authentication attempt MUST be rejected. The presence of trusted KDCs in this list does not provide any guarantee; an untrusted KDC may have fabricated the list.

While the end server ultimately decides whether authentication is valid, the KDC for the end server's realm MAY apply a realm specific policy for validating the transited field and accepting credentials for cross realm authentication. When the KDC applies such checks and accepts such cross-realm authentication it will set the TRANSITED-POLICY-CHECKED flag in the service tickets it issues based on the cross-realm TGT. A client MAY request that the KDCs not check the transited field by setting the DISABLE-TRANSITED-CHECK flag. KDCs are encouraged but not required to honor this flag.

Application servers MUST either do the transited-realm checks themselves, or reject cross-realm tickets without TRANSITED-POLICY- CHECKED set.

Return value: Returns non-0 iff transited-policy-checked flag is set in ticket.

shishi_tkt_ok_as_delegate_p

int **shishi_tkt_ok_as_delegate_p** (*Shishi_tkt * tkt*)   [Function]
  tkt: input variable with ticket info.

  Determine if ticket is ok as delegated ticket.

  The copy of the ticket flags in the encrypted part of the KDC reply may have the OK-AS-DELEGATE flag set to indicates to the client that the server specified in the ticket has been determined by policy of the realm to be a suitable recipient of delegation. A client can use the presence of this flag to help it make a decision whether to delegate credentials (either grant a proxy or a forwarded ticket- granting ticket) to this server. It is acceptable to ignore the value of this flag. When setting this flag, an administrator should consider the security and placement of the server on which the service will run, as well as whether the service requires the use of delegated credentials.

  Return value: Returns non-0 iff ok-as-delegate flag is set in ticket.

shishi_tkt_keytype

int **shishi_tkt_keytype** (*Shishi_tkt * tkt*, *int32_t * etype*)   [Function]
  tkt: input variable with ticket info.

  etype: pointer to encryption type that is set, see Shishi_etype.

  Extract encryption type of key in ticket (really EncKDCRepPart).

  Return value: Returns SHISHI_OK iff successful.

shishi_tkt_keytype_fast

int32_t **shishi_tkt_keytype_fast** (*Shishi_tkt * tkt*)   [Function]
  tkt: input variable with ticket info.

  Extract encryption type of key in ticket (really EncKDCRepPart).

Return value: Returns encryption type of session key in ticket (really EncKDCRep-Part), or -1 on error.

shishi_tkt_keytype_p

`int shishi_tkt_keytype_p` (*Shishi_tkt* `* tkt`, *int32_t* `etype`)   [Function]
> *tkt*: input variable with ticket info.
>
> *etype*: encryption type, see Shishi_etype.
>
> Determine if key in ticket (really EncKDCRepPart) is of specified key type (really encryption type).
>
> **Return value:** Returns non-0 iff key in ticket is of specified encryption type.

shishi_tkt_lastreqc

`time_t shishi_tkt_lastreqc` (*Shishi_tkt* `* tkt`, *Shishi_lrtype* `lrtype`)   [Function]
> *tkt*: input variable with ticket info.
>
> *lrtype*: lastreq type to extract, see Shishi_lrtype. E.g., SHISHI_LRTYPE_LAST_REQUEST.
>
> Extract C time corresponding to given lastreq type field in the ticket.
>
> **Return value:** Returns C time interpretation of the specified lastreq field, or (time_t) -1.

shishi_tkt_authctime

`time_t shishi_tkt_authctime` (*Shishi_tkt* `* tkt`)   [Function]
> *tkt*: input variable with ticket info.
>
> Extract C time corresponding to the authtime field. The field holds the time when the original authentication took place that later resulted in this ticket.
>
> **Return value:** Returns C time interpretation of the endtime in ticket.

shishi_tkt_startctime

`time_t shishi_tkt_startctime` (*Shishi_tkt* `* tkt`)   [Function]
> *tkt*: input variable with ticket info.
>
> Extract C time corresponding to the starttime field. The field holds the time where the ticket start to be valid (typically in the past).
>
> **Return value:** Returns C time interpretation of the endtime in ticket.

shishi_tkt_endctime

`time_t shishi_tkt_endctime` (*Shishi_tkt* `* tkt`)   [Function]
> *tkt*: input variable with ticket info.
>
> Extract C time corresponding to the endtime field. The field holds the time where the ticket stop being valid.
>
> **Return value:** Returns C time interpretation of the endtime in ticket.

shishi_tkt_renew_tillc

time_t shishi_tkt_renew_tillc (*Shishi_tkt* * **tkt**)   [Function]
> *tkt*: input variable with ticket info.
>
> Extract C time corresponding to the renew-till field. The field holds the time where the ticket stop being valid for renewal.
>
> **Return value:** Returns C time interpretation of the renew-till in ticket.

shishi_tkt_valid_at_time_p

int shishi_tkt_valid_at_time_p (*Shishi_tkt* * **tkt**, *time_t* **now**)   [Function]
> *tkt*: input variable with ticket info.
>
> *now*: time to check for.
>
> Determine if ticket is valid at a specific point in time.
>
> **Return value:** Returns non-0 iff ticket is valid (not expired and after starttime) at specified time.

shishi_tkt_valid_now_p

int shishi_tkt_valid_now_p (*Shishi_tkt* * **tkt**)   [Function]
> *tkt*: input variable with ticket info.
>
> Determine if ticket is valid now.
>
> **Return value:** Returns 0 iff ticket is invalid (expired or not yet valid).

shishi_tkt_expired_p

int shishi_tkt_expired_p (*Shishi_tkt* * **tkt**)   [Function]
> *tkt*: input variable with ticket info.
>
> Determine if ticket has expired (i.e., endtime is in the past).
>
> **Return value:** Returns 0 iff ticket has expired.

shishi_tkt_lastreq_pretty_print

void shishi_tkt_lastreq_pretty_print (*Shishi_tkt* * **tkt**, *FILE* *   [Function]
     fh)
> *tkt*: input variable with ticket info.
>
> *fh*: file handle open for writing.
>
> Print a human readable representation of the various lastreq fields in the ticket (really EncKDCRepPart).

shishi_tkt_pretty_print

void shishi_tkt_pretty_print (*Shishi_tkt* * **tkt**, *FILE* * **fh**)   [Function]
> *tkt*: input variable with ticket info.
>
> *fh*: file handle open for writing.
>
> Print a human readable representation of a ticket to file handle.

5.7 AS Functions

The Authentication Service (AS) is used to get an initial ticket using e.g. your password.
The following illustrates the AS-REQ and AS-REP ASN.1 structures.

```
-- Request --

AS-REQ            ::= KDC-REQ {10}

KDC-REQ {INTEGER:tagnum}          ::= [APPLICATION tagnum] SEQUENCE {
        pvno            [1] INTEGER (5) -- first tag is [1], not [0] --,
        msg-type        [2] INTEGER (tagnum),
        padata          [3] SEQUENCE OF PA-DATA OPTIONAL,
        req-body        [4] KDC-REQ-BODY
}

KDC-REQ-BODY    ::= SEQUENCE {
        kdc-options             [0] KDCOptions,
        cname                   [1] PrincipalName OPTIONAL
                                    -- Used only in AS-REQ --,
        realm                   [2] Realm
                                    -- Server's realm
                                    -- Also client's in AS-REQ --,
        sname                   [3] PrincipalName OPTIONAL,
        from                    [4] KerberosTime OPTIONAL,
        till                    [5] KerberosTime,
        rtime                   [6] KerberosTime OPTIONAL,
        nonce                   [7] UInt32,
        etype                   [8] SEQUENCE OF Int32 -- EncryptionType
                                    -- in preference order --,
        addresses               [9] HostAddresses OPTIONAL,
        enc-authorization-data  [10] EncryptedData {
                                        AuthorizationData,
                                        { keyuse-TGSReqAuthData-sesskey
                                          | keyuse-TGSReqAuthData-subkey }
                                    } OPTIONAL,
        additional-tickets      [11] SEQUENCE OF Ticket OPTIONAL
}

-- Reply --

AS-REP            ::= KDC-REP {11, EncASRepPart, {keyuse-EncASRepPart}}

KDC-REP {INTEGER:tagnum,
        TypeToEncrypt,
        UInt32:KeyUsages}         ::= [APPLICATION tagnum] SEQUENCE {
        pvno            [0] INTEGER (5),
        msg-type        [1] INTEGER (tagnum),
```

```
        padata          [2] SEQUENCE OF PA-DATA OPTIONAL,
        crealm          [3] Realm,
        cname           [4] PrincipalName,
        ticket          [5] Ticket,
        enc-part        [6] EncryptedData {TypeToEncrypt, KeyUsages}
}

EncASRepPart    ::= [APPLICATION 25] EncKDCRepPart

EncKDCRepPart   ::= SEQUENCE {
        key             [0] EncryptionKey,
        last-req        [1] LastReq,
        nonce           [2] UInt32,
        key-expiration  [3] KerberosTime OPTIONAL,
        flags           [4] TicketFlags,
        authtime        [5] KerberosTime,
        starttime       [6] KerberosTime OPTIONAL,
        endtime         [7] KerberosTime,
        renew-till      [8] KerberosTime OPTIONAL,
        srealm          [9] Realm,
        sname           [10] PrincipalName,
        caddr           [11] HostAddresses OPTIONAL
}
```

shishi_as

int shishi_as (*Shishi * handle*, *Shishi_as ** as*)   [Function]

> *handle*: shishi handle as allocated by **shishi_init()**.
>
> *as*: holds pointer to newly allocate Shishi_as structure.
>
> Allocate a new AS exchange variable.
>
> **Return value:** Returns SHISHI_OK iff successful.

shishi_as_done

void shishi_as_done (*Shishi_as * as*)   [Function]

> *as*: structure that holds information about AS exchange
>
> Deallocate resources associated with AS exchange. This should be called by the application when it no longer need to utilize the AS exchange handle.

shishi_as_req

Shishi_asn1 shishi_as_req (*Shishi_as * as*)   [Function]

> *as*: structure that holds information about AS exchange
>
> Get ASN.1 AS-REQ structure from AS exchange.
>
> **Return value:** Returns the generated AS-REQ packet from the AS exchange, or NULL if not yet set or an error occured.

shishi_as_req_build

int shishi_as_req_build (*Shishi_as* * `as`)   [Function]
> *as*: structure that holds information about AS exchange

> Possibly remove unset fields (e.g., rtime).

> **Return value:** Returns SHISHI_OK iff successful.

shishi_as_req_set

void shishi_as_req_set (*Shishi_as* * `as`, *Shishi_asn1* `asreq`)   [Function]
> *as*: structure that holds information about AS exchange

> *asreq*: asreq to store in AS.

> Set the AS-REQ in the AS exchange.

shishi_as_req_der

int shishi_as_req_der (*Shishi_as* * `as`, *char* ** `out`, *size_t* * `outlen`)   [Function]
> *as*: structure that holds information about AS exchange

> *out*: output array with newly allocated DER encoding of AS-REQ.

> *outlen*: length of output array with DER encoding of AS-REQ.

> DER encode AS-REQ. `out` is allocated by this function, and it is the responsibility of caller to deallocate it.

> **Return value:** Returns SHISHI_OK iff successful.

shishi_as_req_der_set

int shishi_as_req_der_set (*Shishi_as* * `as`, *char* * `der`, *size_t*   [Function]
    `derlen`)
> *as*: structure that holds information about AS exchange

> *der*: input array with DER encoded AP-REQ.

> *derlen*: length of input array with DER encoded AP-REQ.

> DER decode AS-REQ and set it AS exchange. If decoding fails, the AS-REQ in the AS exchange remains.

> **Return value:** Returns SHISHI_OK.

shishi_as_rep

Shishi_asn1 shishi_as_rep (*Shishi_as* * `as`)   [Function]
> *as*: structure that holds information about AS exchange

> Get ASN.1 AS-REP structure from AS exchange.

> **Return value:** Returns the received AS-REP packet from the AS exchange, or NULL if not yet set or an error occured.

shishi_as_rep_process

int shishi_as_rep_process (*Shishi_as* * **as**, *Shishi_key* * **key**, *const*   [Function]
    char * **password**)

as: structure that holds information about AS exchange

key: user's key, used to encrypt the encrypted part of the AS-REP.

password: user's password, used if key is NULL.

Process new AS-REP and set ticket. The key is used to decrypt the AP-REP. If both key and password is NULL, the user is queried for it.

Return value: Returns SHISHI_OK iff successful.

shishi_as_rep_build

int shishi_as_rep_build (*Shishi_as* * **as**, *Shishi_key* * **key**)   [Function]

as: structure that holds information about AS exchange

key: user's key, used to encrypt the encrypted part of the AS-REP.

Build AS-REP.

Return value: Returns SHISHI_OK iff successful.

shishi_as_rep_der

int shishi_as_rep_der (*Shishi_as* * **as**, *char* ** **out**, *size_t* * **outlen**)   [Function]

as: structure that holds information about AS exchange

out: output array with newly allocated DER encoding of AS-REP.

outlen: length of output array with DER encoding of AS-REP.

DER encode AS-REP. out is allocated by this function, and it is the responsibility of caller to deallocate it.

Return value: Returns SHISHI_OK iff successful.

shishi_as_rep_set

void shishi_as_rep_set (*Shishi_as* * **as**, *Shishi_asn1* **asrep**)   [Function]

as: structure that holds information about AS exchange

asrep: asrep to store in AS.

Set the AS-REP in the AS exchange.

shishi_as_rep_der_set

int shishi_as_rep_der_set (*Shishi_as* * **as**, *char* * **der**, *size_t*   [Function]
    derlen)

as: structure that holds information about AS exchange

der: input array with DER encoded AP-REP.

derlen: length of input array with DER encoded AP-REP.

DER decode AS-REP and set it AS exchange. If decoding fails, the AS-REP in the AS exchange remains.

Return value: Returns SHISHI_OK.

shishi_as_krberror

Shishi_asn1 shishi_as_krberror (*Shishi_as* * **as**)   [Function]
> *as*: structure that holds information about AS exchange

> Get ASN.1 KRB-ERROR structure from AS exchange.

> **Return value:** Returns the received KRB-ERROR packet from the AS exchange, or NULL if not yet set or an error occured.

shishi_as_krberror_der

int shishi_as_krberror_der (*Shishi_as* * **as**, *char* ** **out**, *size_t* *   [Function]
> **outlen**)
> *as*: structure that holds information about AS exchange

> *out*: output array with newly allocated DER encoding of KRB-ERROR.

> *outlen*: length of output array with DER encoding of KRB-ERROR.

> DER encode KRB-ERROR. **out** is allocated by this function, and it is the responsibility of caller to deallocate it.

> **Return value:** Returns SHISHI_OK iff successful.

shishi_as_krberror_set

void shishi_as_krberror_set (*Shishi_as* * **as**, *Shishi_asn1*   [Function]
> **krberror**)
> *as*: structure that holds information about AS exchange

> *krberror*: krberror to store in AS.

> Set the KRB-ERROR in the AS exchange.

shishi_as_tkt

Shishi_tkt * shishi_as_tkt (*Shishi_as* * **as**)   [Function]
> *as*: structure that holds information about AS exchange

> Get Ticket in AS exchange.

> **Return value:** Returns the newly acquired tkt from the AS exchange, or NULL if not yet set or an error occured.

shishi_as_tkt_set

void shishi_as_tkt_set (*Shishi_as* * **as**, *Shishi_tkt* * **tkt**)   [Function]
> *as*: structure that holds information about AS exchange

> *tkt*: tkt to store in AS.

> Set the Tkt in the AS exchange.

shishi_as_sendrecv_hint

int shishi_as_sendrecv_hint (*Shishi_as* * **as**, *Shishi_tkts_hint* *   [Function]
      hint)

> *as*: structure that holds information about AS exchange
>
> *hint*: additional parameters that modify connection behaviour, or NULL.
>
> Send AS-REQ and receive AS-REP or KRB-ERROR. This is the initial authentication, usually used to acquire a Ticket Granting Ticket. The hint structure can be used to set, e.g., parameters for TLS authentication.
>
> **Return value:** Returns SHISHI_OK iff successful.

shishi_as_sendrecv

int shishi_as_sendrecv (*Shishi_as* * **as**)   [Function]

> *as*: structure that holds information about AS exchange
>
> Send AS-REQ and receive AS-REP or KRB-ERROR. This is the initial authentication, usually used to acquire a Ticket Granting Ticket.
>
> **Return value:** Returns SHISHI_OK iff successful.

5.8 TGS Functions

The Ticket Granting Service (TGS) is used to get subsequent tickets, authenticated by other tickets (so called ticket granting tickets). The following illustrates the TGS-REQ and TGS-REP ASN.1 structures.

```
-- Request --

TGS-REQ            ::= KDC-REQ {12}

KDC-REQ {INTEGER:tagnum}          ::= [APPLICATION tagnum] SEQUENCE {
        pvno            [1] INTEGER (5) -- first tag is [1], not [0] --,
        msg-type        [2] INTEGER (tagnum),
        padata          [3] SEQUENCE OF PA-DATA OPTIONAL,
        req-body        [4] KDC-REQ-BODY
}

KDC-REQ-BODY    ::= SEQUENCE {
        kdc-options             [0] KDCOptions,
        cname                   [1] PrincipalName OPTIONAL
                                    -- Used only in AS-REQ --,
        realm                   [2] Realm
                                    -- Server's realm
                                    -- Also client's in AS-REQ --,
        sname                   [3] PrincipalName OPTIONAL,
        from                    [4] KerberosTime OPTIONAL,
        till                    [5] KerberosTime,
        rtime                   [6] KerberosTime OPTIONAL,
        nonce                   [7] UInt32,
```

```
        etype                   [8] SEQUENCE OF Int32 -- EncryptionType
                                    -- in preference order --,
        addresses               [9] HostAddresses OPTIONAL,
        enc-authorization-data  [10] EncryptedData {
                                        AuthorizationData,
                                          { keyuse-TGSReqAuthData-sesskey
                                            | keyuse-TGSReqAuthData-subkey }
                                    } OPTIONAL,
        additional-tickets      [11] SEQUENCE OF Ticket OPTIONAL
}


-- Reply --


TGS-REP           ::= KDC-REP {13, EncTGSRepPart,
                    { keyuse-EncTGSRepPart-sesskey
                      | keyuse-EncTGSRepPart-subkey }}


KDC-REP {INTEGER:tagnum,
        TypeToEncrypt,
        UInt32:KeyUsages}        ::= [APPLICATION tagnum] SEQUENCE {
        pvno            [0] INTEGER (5),
        msg-type        [1] INTEGER (tagnum),
        padata          [2] SEQUENCE OF PA-DATA OPTIONAL,
        crealm          [3] Realm,
        cname           [4] PrincipalName,
        ticket          [5] Ticket,
        enc-part        [6] EncryptedData {TypeToEncrypt, KeyUsages}
}


EncTGSRepPart   ::= [APPLICATION 26] EncKDCRepPart


EncKDCRepPart   ::= SEQUENCE {
        key             [0] EncryptionKey,
        last-req        [1] LastReq,
        nonce           [2] UInt32,
        key-expiration  [3] KerberosTime OPTIONAL,
        flags           [4] TicketFlags,
        authtime        [5] KerberosTime,
        starttime       [6] KerberosTime OPTIONAL,
        endtime         [7] KerberosTime,
        renew-till      [8] KerberosTime OPTIONAL,
        srealm          [9] Realm,
        sname           [10] PrincipalName,
        caddr           [11] HostAddresses OPTIONAL
}
```

shishi_tgs

int shishi_tgs (*Shishi* * `handle`, *Shishi_tgs* ** `tgs`)   [Function]
> *handle*: shishi handle as allocated by `shishi_init()`.

> *tgs*: holds pointer to newly allocate Shishi_tgs structure.

> Allocate a new TGS exchange variable.

> **Return value:** Returns SHISHI_OK iff successful.

shishi_tgs_done

void shishi_tgs_done (*Shishi_tgs* * `tgs`)   [Function]
> *tgs*: structure that holds information about AS exchange

> Deallocate resources associated with TGS exchange. This should be called by the application when it no longer need to utilize the TGS exchange handle.

shishi_tgs_tgtkt

Shishi_tkt * shishi_tgs_tgtkt (*Shishi_tgs* * `tgs`)   [Function]
> *tgs*: structure that holds information about TGS exchange

> Get Ticket-granting-ticket from TGS exchange.

> **Return value:** Returns the ticket-granting-ticket used in the TGS exchange, or NULL if not yet set or an error occured.

shishi_tgs_tgtkt_set

void shishi_tgs_tgtkt_set (*Shishi_tgs* * `tgs`, *Shishi_tkt* * `tgtkt`)   [Function]
> *tgs*: structure that holds information about TGS exchange

> *tgtkt*: ticket granting ticket to store in TGS.

> Set the Ticket in the TGS exchange.

shishi_tgs_ap

Shishi_ap * shishi_tgs_ap (*Shishi_tgs* * `tgs`)   [Function]
> *tgs*: structure that holds information about TGS exchange

> Get the AP from TGS exchange.

> **Return value:** Returns the AP exchange (part of TGS-REQ) from the TGS exchange, or NULL if not yet set or an error occured.

shishi_tgs_req

Shishi_asn1 shishi_tgs_req (*Shishi_tgs* * `tgs`)   [Function]
> *tgs*: structure that holds information about TGS exchange

> Get the TGS-REQ from TGS exchange.

> **Return value:** Returns the generated TGS-REQ from the TGS exchange, or NULL if not yet set or an error occured.

shishi_tgs_req_set

void **shishi_tgs_req_set** (*Shishi_tgs* * **tgs**, *Shishi_asn1* **tgsreq**)   [Function]
> *tgs*: structure that holds information about TGS exchange
>
> *tgsreq*: tgsreq to store in TGS.
>
> Set the TGS-REQ in the TGS exchange.

shishi_tgs_req_der

int **shishi_tgs_req_der** (*Shishi_tgs* * **tgs**, *char* ** **out**, *size_t* *   [Function]
> **outlen**)
>
> *tgs*: structure that holds information about TGS exchange
>
> *out*: output array with newly allocated DER encoding of TGS-REQ.
>
> *outlen*: length of output array with DER encoding of TGS-REQ.
>
> DER encode TGS-REQ. out is allocated by this function, and it is the responsibility of caller to deallocate it.
>
> **Return value:** Returns SHISHI_OK iff successful.

shishi_tgs_req_der_set

int **shishi_tgs_req_der_set** (*Shishi_tgs* * **tgs**, *char* * **der**, *size_t*   [Function]
> **derlen**)
>
> *tgs*: structure that holds information about TGS exchange
>
> *der*: input array with DER encoded AP-REQ.
>
> *derlen*: length of input array with DER encoded AP-REQ.
>
> DER decode TGS-REQ and set it TGS exchange. If decoding fails, the TGS-REQ in the TGS exchange remains.
>
> **Return value:** Returns SHISHI_OK.

shishi_tgs_req_process

int **shishi_tgs_req_process** (*Shishi_tgs* * **tgs**)   [Function]
> *tgs*: structure that holds information about TGS exchange
>
> Process new TGS-REQ and set ticket. The key to decrypt the TGS-REQ is taken from the EncKDCReqPart of the TGS tgticket.
>
> **Return value:** Returns SHISHI_OK iff successful.

shishi_tgs_req_build

int **shishi_tgs_req_build** (*Shishi_tgs* * **tgs**)   [Function]
> *tgs*: structure that holds information about TGS exchange
>
> Checksum data in authenticator and add ticket and authenticator to TGS-REQ.
>
> **Return value:** Returns SHISHI_OK iff successful.

shishi_tgs_rep

Shishi_asn1 shishi_tgs_rep (*Shishi_tgs* * **tgs**)   [Function]
> *tgs*: structure that holds information about TGS exchange

> Get TGS-REP from TGS exchange.

> **Return value:** Returns the received TGS-REP from the TGS exchange, or NULL if
> not yet set or an error occured.

shishi_tgs_rep_der

int shishi_tgs_rep_der (*Shishi_tgs* * **tgs**, *char* ** **out**, *size_t* *   [Function]
>   **outlen**)
> *tgs*: structure that holds information about TGS exchange

> *out*: output array with newly allocated DER encoding of TGS-REP.

> *outlen*: length of output array with DER encoding of TGS-REP.

> DER encode TGS-REP. **out** is allocated by this function, and it is the responsibility
> of caller to deallocate it.

> **Return value:** Returns SHISHI_OK iff successful.

shishi_tgs_rep_process

int shishi_tgs_rep_process (*Shishi_tgs* * **tgs**)   [Function]
> *tgs*: structure that holds information about TGS exchange

> Process new TGS-REP and set ticket. The key to decrypt the TGS-REP is taken
> from the EncKDCRepPart of the TGS tgticket.

> **Return value:** Returns SHISHI_OK iff successful.

shishi_tgs_rep_build

int shishi_tgs_rep_build (*Shishi_tgs* * **tgs**, *int* **keyusage**,   [Function]
>   *Shishi_key* * **key**)
> *tgs*: structure that holds information about TGS exchange

> *keyusage*: keyusage integer.

> *key*: user's key, used to encrypt the encrypted part of the TGS-REP.

> Build TGS-REP.

> **Return value:** Returns SHISHI_OK iff successful.

shishi_tgs_krberror

Shishi_asn1 shishi_tgs_krberror (*Shishi_tgs* * **tgs**)   [Function]
> *tgs*: structure that holds information about TGS exchange

> Get KRB-ERROR from TGS exchange.

> **Return value:** Returns the received TGS-REP from the TGS exchange, or NULL if
> not yet set or an error occured.

shishi_tgs_krberror_der

int **shishi_tgs_krberror_der** (*Shishi_tgs* * **tgs**, *char* ** **out**, *size_t* *   [Function]
    `outlen`)

tgs: structure that holds information about TGS exchange

out: output array with newly allocated DER encoding of KRB-ERROR.

outlen: length of output array with DER encoding of KRB-ERROR.

DER encode KRB-ERROR. `out` is allocated by this function, and it is the responsibility of caller to deallocate it.

Return value: Returns SHISHI_OK iff successful.

shishi_tgs_krberror_set

void **shishi_tgs_krberror_set** (*Shishi_tgs* * **tgs**, *Shishi_asn1*   [Function]
    `krberror`)

tgs: structure that holds information about TGS exchange

krberror: krberror to store in TGS.

Set the KRB-ERROR in the TGS exchange.

shishi_tgs_tkt

Shishi_tkt * **shishi_tgs_tkt** (*Shishi_tgs* * **tgs**)   [Function]

tgs: structure that holds information about TGS exchange

Get Ticket from TGS exchange.

Return value: Returns the newly acquired ticket from the TGS exchange, or NULL if not yet set or an error occured.

shishi_tgs_tkt_set

void **shishi_tgs_tkt_set** (*Shishi_tgs* * **tgs**, *Shishi_tkt* * **tkt**)   [Function]

tgs: structure that holds information about TGS exchange

tkt: ticket to store in TGS.

Set the Ticket in the TGS exchange.

shishi_tgs_sendrecv_hint

int **shishi_tgs_sendrecv_hint** (*Shishi_tgs* * **tgs**, *Shishi_tkts_hint* *   [Function]
    `hint`)

tgs: structure that holds information about TGS exchange

hint: additional parameters that modify connection behaviour, or `NULL`.

Send TGS-REQ and receive TGS-REP or KRB-ERROR. This is the subsequent authentication, usually used to acquire server tickets. The `hint` structure can be used to set, e.g., parameters for TLS authentication.

Return value: Returns SHISHI_OK iff successful.

shishi_tgs_sendrecv

int shishi_tgs_sendrecv (*Shishi_tgs* * **tgs**)   [Function]
    tgs: structure that holds information about TGS exchange

    Send TGS-REQ and receive TGS-REP or KRB-ERROR. This is the subsequent authentication, usually used to acquire server tickets.

    Return value: Returns SHISHI_OK iff successful.

shishi_tgs_set_server

int shishi_tgs_set_server (*Shishi_tgs* * **tgs**, *const char* * **server**)   [Function]
    tgs: structure that holds information about TGS exchange

    server: indicates the server to acquire ticket for.

    Set the server in the TGS-REQ.

    Return value: Returns SHISHI_OK iff successful.

shishi_tgs_set_realm

int shishi_tgs_set_realm (*Shishi_tgs* * **tgs**, *const char* * **realm**)   [Function]
    tgs: structure that holds information about TGS exchange

    realm: indicates the realm to acquire ticket for.

    Set the server in the TGS-REQ.

    Return value: Returns SHISHI_OK iff successful.

shishi_tgs_set_realmserver

int shishi_tgs_set_realmserver (*Shishi_tgs* * **tgs**, *const char* *   [Function]
    realm, *const char* * **server**)
    tgs: structure that holds information about TGS exchange

    realm: indicates the realm to acquire ticket for.

    server: indicates the server to acquire ticket for.

    Set the realm and server in the TGS-REQ.

    Return value: Returns SHISHI_OK iff successful.

5.9 Ticket (ASN.1) Functions

See Section 5.6 [Ticket Functions], page 102, for an high-level overview of tickets. The following illustrates the Ticket and EncTicketPart ASN.1 structures.

```
Ticket              ::= [APPLICATION 1] SEQUENCE {
        tkt-vno         [0] INTEGER (5),
        realm           [1] Realm,
        sname           [2] PrincipalName,
        enc-part        [3] EncryptedData -- EncTicketPart
}

-- Encrypted part of ticket
```

```
EncTicketPart    ::= [APPLICATION 3] SEQUENCE {
      flags                     [0] TicketFlags,
      key                       [1] EncryptionKey,
      crealm                    [2] Realm,
      cname                     [3] PrincipalName,
      transited                 [4] TransitedEncoding,
      authtime                  [5] KerberosTime,
      starttime                 [6] KerberosTime OPTIONAL,
      endtime                   [7] KerberosTime,
      renew-till                [8] KerberosTime OPTIONAL,
      caddr                     [9] HostAddresses OPTIONAL,
      authorization-data        [10] AuthorizationData OPTIONAL
}
```

shishi_ticket

Shishi_asn1 shishi_ticket (*Shishi* * *handle*)   [Function]

> *handle*: shishi handle as allocated by `shishi_init()`.
>
> This function creates a new ASN.1 Ticket, populated with some default values.
>
> **Return value:** Returns the ticket or NULL on failure.

shishi_ticket_realm_get

int shishi_ticket_realm_get (*Shishi* * *handle*, *Shishi_asn1* *ticket*,   [Function]
     char ** *realm*, *size_t* * *realmlen*)

> *handle*: shishi handle as allocated by `shishi_init()`.
>
> *ticket*: input variable with ticket info.
>
> *realm*: output array with newly allocated name of realm in ticket.
>
> *realmlen*: size of output array.
>
> Extract realm from ticket.
>
> **Return value:** Returns SHISHI_OK iff successful.

shishi_ticket_realm_set

int shishi_ticket_realm_set (*Shishi* * *handle*, *Shishi_asn1* *ticket*,   [Function]
     const char * *realm*)

> *handle*: shishi handle as allocated by `shishi_init()`.
>
> *ticket*: input variable with ticket info.
>
> *realm*: input array with name of realm.
>
> Set the realm field in the Ticket.
>
> **Return value:** Returns SHISHI_OK iff successful.

shishi_ticket_server

int shishi_ticket_server (*Shishi* * *handle*, *Shishi_asn1* *ticket*,   [Function]
     char ** *server*, *size_t* * *serverlen*)

> *handle*: Shishi library handle create by `shishi_init()`.

ticket: ASN.1 Ticket variable to get server name from.

server: pointer to newly allocated zero terminated string containing principal name. May be NULL (to only populate `serverlen`).

serverlen: pointer to length of `server` on output, excluding terminating zero. May be NULL (to only populate `server`).

Represent server principal name in Ticket as zero-terminated string. The string is allocate by this function, and it is the responsibility of the caller to deallocate it. Note that the output length `serverlen` does not include the terminating zero.

Return value: Returns SHISHI_OK iff successful.

shishi_ticket_sname_set

int shishi_ticket_sname_set (*Shishi* * `handle`, *Shishi_asn1* `ticket`,   [Function]
    Shishi_name_type `name_type`, *char* * [] `sname`)
handle: shishi handle as allocated by `shishi_init()`.

ticket: Ticket variable to set server name field in.

name_type: type of principial, see Shishi_name_type, usually SHISHI_NT_UNKNOWN.

sname: input array with principal name.

Set the server name field in the Ticket.

Return value: Returns SHISHI_OK iff successful.

shishi_ticket_get_enc_part_etype

int shishi_ticket_get_enc_part_etype (*Shishi* * `handle`,   [Function]
    Shishi_asn1 `ticket`, *int32_t* * `etype`)
handle: shishi handle as allocated by `shishi_init()`.

ticket: Ticket variable to get value from.

etype: output variable that holds the value.

Extract Ticket.enc-part.etype.

Return value: Returns SHISHI_OK iff successful.

shishi_ticket_set_enc_part

int shishi_ticket_set_enc_part (*Shishi* * `handle`, *Shishi_asn1*   [Function]
    `ticket`, *int32_t* `etype`, *uint32_t* `kvno`, *const char* * `buf`, *size_t* `buflen`)
handle: shishi handle as allocated by `shishi_init()`.

ticket: Ticket to add enc-part field to.

etype: encryption type used to encrypt enc-part.

kvno: key version number.

buf: input array with encrypted enc-part.

buflen: size of input array with encrypted enc-part.

Set the encrypted enc-part field in the Ticket. The encrypted data is usually created by calling `shishi_encrypt()` on the DER encoded enc-part. To save time, you may want to use `shishi_ticket_add_enc_part()` instead, which calculates the encrypted data and calls this function in one step.

Return value: Returns SHISHI_OK iff successful.

shishi_ticket_add_enc_part

int shishi_ticket_add_enc_part (*Shishi* * **handle**, *Shishi_asn1*   [Function]
     ticket, *Shishi_key* * **key**, *Shishi_asn1* **encticketpart**)
> *handle*: shishi handle as allocated by `shishi_init()`.
>
> *ticket*: Ticket to add enc-part field to.
>
> *key*: key used to encrypt enc-part.
>
> *encticketpart*: EncTicketPart to add.
>
> Encrypts DER encoded EncTicketPart using key and stores it in the Ticket.
>
> **Return value:** Returns `SHISHI_OK` iff successful.

shishi_encticketpart_get_key

int shishi_encticketpart_get_key (*Shishi* * **handle**, *Shishi_asn1*   [Function]
     encticketpart, *Shishi_key* ** **key**)
> *handle*: shishi handle as allocated by `shishi_init()`.
>
> *encticketpart*: input EncTicketPart variable.
>
> *key*: newly allocated key.
>
> Extract the session key in the Ticket.
>
> **Return value:** Returns `SHISHI_OK` iff successful.

shishi_encticketpart_key_set

int shishi_encticketpart_key_set (*Shishi* * **handle**, *Shishi_asn1*   [Function]
     encticketpart, *Shishi_key* * **key**)
> *handle*: shishi handle as allocated by `shishi_init()`.
>
> *encticketpart*: input EncTicketPart variable.
>
> *key*: key handle with information to store in encticketpart.
>
> Set the EncTicketPart.key field to key type and value of supplied key.
>
> **Return value:** Returns `SHISHI_OK` iff successful.

shishi_encticketpart_flags_set

int shishi_encticketpart_flags_set (*Shishi* * **handle**, *Shishi_asn1*   [Function]
     encticketpart, *int* **flags**)
> *handle*: shishi handle as allocated by `shishi_init()`.
>
> *encticketpart*: input EncTicketPart variable.
>
> *flags*: flags to set in encticketpart.
>
> Set the EncTicketPart.flags to supplied value.
>
> **Return value:** Returns `SHISHI_OK` iff successful.

shishi_encticketpart_crealm_set

int shishi_encticketpart_crealm_set (*Shishi* * *handle*,   [Function]
    Shishi_asn1 **encticketpart**, *const char* * **realm**)
    handle: shishi handle as allocated by shishi_init().

    encticketpart: input EncTicketPart variable.

    realm: input array with name of realm.

    Set the realm field in the KDC-REQ.

    Return value: Returns SHISHI_OK iff successful.

shishi_encticketpart_cname_set

int shishi_encticketpart_cname_set (*Shishi* * *handle*, *Shishi_asn1*   [Function]
    encticketpart, *Shishi_name_type* **name_type**, *const char* * **principal**)
    handle: shishi handle as allocated by shishi_init().

    encticketpart: input EncTicketPart variable.

    name_type: type of principial, see Shishi_name_type, usually SHISHI_NT_UNKNOWN.

    principal: input array with principal name.

    Set the client name field in the EncTicketPart.

    Return value: Returns SHISHI_OK iff successful.

shishi_encticketpart_transited_set

int shishi_encticketpart_transited_set (*Shishi* * *handle*,   [Function]
    Shishi_asn1 **encticketpart**, *int32_t* **trtype**, *const char* * **trdata**, *size_t*
    trdatalen)
    handle: shishi handle as allocated by shishi_init().

    encticketpart: input EncTicketPart variable.

    trtype: transitedencoding type, e.g. SHISHI_TR_DOMAIN_X500_COMPRESS.

    trdata: actual transited realm data.

    trdatalen: length of actual transited realm data.

    Set the EncTicketPart.transited field to supplied value.

    Return value: Returns SHISHI_OK iff successful.

shishi_encticketpart_authtime_set

int shishi_encticketpart_authtime_set (*Shishi* * *handle*,   [Function]
    Shishi_asn1 **encticketpart**, *const char* * **authtime**)
    handle: shishi handle as allocated by shishi_init().

    encticketpart: input EncTicketPart variable.

    authtime: character buffer containing a generalized time string.

    Set the EncTicketPart.authtime to supplied value.

    Return value: Returns SHISHI_OK iff successful.

shishi_encticketpart_endtime_set

int shishi_encticketpart_endtime_set (*Shishi* * `handle`,   [Function]
    Shishi_asn1 `encticketpart`, *const char* * `endtime`)
> *handle*: shishi handle as allocated by `shishi_init()`.

> *encticketpart*: input EncTicketPart variable.

> *endtime*: character buffer containing a generalized time string.

> Set the EncTicketPart.endtime to supplied value.

> **Return value:** Returns `SHISHI_OK` iff successful.

shishi_encticketpart_client

int shishi_encticketpart_client (*Shishi* * `handle`, *Shishi_asn1*   [Function]
    `encticketpart`, *char* ** `client`, *size_t* * `clientlen`)
> *handle*: Shishi library handle create by `shishi_init()`.

> *encticketpart*: EncTicketPart variable to get client name from.

> *client*: pointer to newly allocated zero terminated string containing principal name. May be `NULL` (to only populate `clientlen`).

> *clientlen*: pointer to length of `client` on output, excluding terminating zero. May be `NULL` (to only populate `client`).

> Represent client principal name in EncTicketPart as zero-terminated string. The string is allocate by this function, and it is the responsibility of the caller to deallocate it. Note that the output length `clientlen` does not include the terminating zero.

> **Return value:** Returns SHISHI_OK iff successful.

shishi_encticketpart_clientrealm

int shishi_encticketpart_clientrealm (*Shishi* * `handle`,   [Function]
    Shishi_asn1 `encticketpart`, *char* ** `client`, *size_t* * `clientlen`)
> *handle*: Shishi library handle create by `shishi_init()`.

> *encticketpart*: EncTicketPart variable to get client name and realm from.

> *client*: pointer to newly allocated zero terminated string containing principal name and realm. May be `NULL` (to only populate `clientlen`).

> *clientlen*: pointer to length of `client` on output, excluding terminating zero. May be `NULL` (to only populate `client`).

> Convert cname and realm fields from EncTicketPart to printable principal name format. The string is allocate by this function, and it is the responsibility of the caller to deallocate it. Note that the output length `clientlen` does not include the terminating zero.

> **Return value:** Returns SHISHI_OK iff successful.

5.10 AS/TGS Functions

The Authentication Service (AS) is used to get an initial ticket using e.g. your password. The Ticket Granting Service (TGS) is used to get subsequent tickets using other tickets. Protocol wise the procedures are very similar, which is the reason they are described together. The following illustrates the AS-REQ, TGS-REQ and AS-REP, TGS-REP ASN.1 structures. Most of the functions use the mnemonic "KDC" instead of either AS or TGS, which means the function operates on both AS and TGS types. Only where the distinction between AS and TGS is important are the AS and TGS names used. Remember, these are low-level functions, and normal applications will likely be satisfied with the AS (see Section 5.7 [AS Functions], page 113) and TGS (see Section 5.8 [TGS Functions], page 118) interfaces, or the even more high-level Ticket Set (see Section 5.3 [Ticket Set Functions], page 64) interface.

```
-- Request --

AS-REQ            ::= KDC-REQ {10}
TGS-REQ           ::= KDC-REQ {12}

KDC-REQ {INTEGER:tagnum}        ::= [APPLICATION tagnum] SEQUENCE {
        pvno          [1] INTEGER (5) -- first tag is [1], not [0] --,
        msg-type      [2] INTEGER (tagnum),
        padata        [3] SEQUENCE OF PA-DATA OPTIONAL,
        req-body      [4] KDC-REQ-BODY
}

KDC-REQ-BODY      ::= SEQUENCE {
        kdc-options               [0] KDCOptions,
        cname                     [1] PrincipalName OPTIONAL
                                      -- Used only in AS-REQ --,
        realm                     [2] Realm
                                      -- Server's realm
                                      -- Also client's in AS-REQ --,
        sname                     [3] PrincipalName OPTIONAL,
        from                      [4] KerberosTime OPTIONAL,
        till                      [5] KerberosTime,
        rtime                     [6] KerberosTime OPTIONAL,
        nonce                     [7] UInt32,
        etype                     [8] SEQUENCE OF Int32 -- EncryptionType
                                      -- in preference order --,
        addresses                 [9] HostAddresses OPTIONAL,
        enc-authorization-data    [10] EncryptedData {
                                          AuthorizationData,
                                          { keyuse-TGSReqAuthData-sesskey
                                            | keyuse-TGSReqAuthData-subkey }
                                      } OPTIONAL,
        additional-tickets        [11] SEQUENCE OF Ticket OPTIONAL
}
```

```
-- Reply --

AS-REP             ::= KDC-REP {11, EncASRepPart, {keyuse-EncASRepPart}}
TGS-REP            ::= KDC-REP {13, EncTGSRepPart,
                        { keyuse-EncTGSRepPart-sesskey
                          | keyuse-EncTGSRepPart-subkey }}

KDC-REP {INTEGER:tagnum,
         TypeToEncrypt,
         UInt32:KeyUsages}        ::= [APPLICATION tagnum] SEQUENCE {
        pvno            [0] INTEGER (5),
        msg-type        [1] INTEGER (tagnum),
        padata          [2] SEQUENCE OF PA-DATA OPTIONAL,
        crealm          [3] Realm,
        cname           [4] PrincipalName,
        ticket          [5] Ticket,
        enc-part        [6] EncryptedData {TypeToEncrypt, KeyUsages}
}

EncASRepPart    ::= [APPLICATION 25] EncKDCRepPart
EncTGSRepPart   ::= [APPLICATION 26] EncKDCRepPart

EncKDCRepPart    ::= SEQUENCE {
        key             [0] EncryptionKey,
        last-req        [1] LastReq,
        nonce           [2] UInt32,
        key-expiration  [3] KerberosTime OPTIONAL,
        flags           [4] TicketFlags,
        authtime        [5] KerberosTime,
        starttime       [6] KerberosTime OPTIONAL,
        endtime         [7] KerberosTime,
        renew-till      [8] KerberosTime OPTIONAL,
        srealm          [9] Realm,
        sname           [10] PrincipalName,
        caddr           [11] HostAddresses OPTIONAL
}
```

shishi_as_derive_salt

int shishi_as_derive_salt (*Shishi * handle*, *Shishi_asn1* **asreq**,   [Function]
      Shishi_asn1 **asrep**, *char ** **salt**, *size_t ** **saltlen**)

   handle: shishi handle as allocated by shishi_init().

   asreq: input AS-REQ variable.

   asrep: input AS-REP variable.

   salt: newly allocated output array with salt.

   saltlen: holds actual size of output array with salt.

Derive the salt that should be used when deriving a key via `shishi_string_to_key()` for an AS exchange. Currently this searches for PA-DATA of type SHISHI_PA_PW_SALT in the AS-REP and returns it if found, otherwise the salt is derived from the client name and realm in AS-REQ.

Return value: Returns SHISHI_OK iff successful.

shishi_kdc_copy_crealm

int shishi_kdc_copy_crealm (*Shishi* * *handle*, *Shishi_asn1* *kdcrep*,   [Function]
            Shishi_asn1 *encticketpart*)

handle: shishi handle as allocated by `shishi_init()`.

kdcrep: KDC-REP to read crealm from.

encticketpart: EncTicketPart to set crealm in.

Set crealm in KDC-REP to value in EncTicketPart.

Return value: Returns SHISHI_OK if successful.

shishi_as_check_crealm

int shishi_as_check_crealm (*Shishi* * *handle*, *Shishi_asn1* *asreq*,   [Function]
            Shishi_asn1 *asrep*)

handle: shishi handle as allocated by `shishi_init()`.

asreq: AS-REQ to compare realm field in.

asrep: AS-REP to compare realm field in.

Verify that AS-REQ.req-body.realm and AS-REP.crealm fields matches. This is one of the steps that has to be performed when processing a AS-REQ and AS-REP exchange, see `shishi_kdc_process()`.

Return value: Returns SHISHI_OK if successful, SHISHI_REALM_MISMATCH if the values differ, or an error code.

shishi_kdc_copy_cname

int shishi_kdc_copy_cname (*Shishi* * *handle*, *Shishi_asn1* *kdcrep*,   [Function]
            Shishi_asn1 *encticketpart*)

handle: shishi handle as allocated by `shishi_init()`.

kdcrep: KDC-REQ to read cname from.

encticketpart: EncTicketPart to set cname in.

Set cname in KDC-REP to value in EncTicketPart.

Return value: Returns SHISHI_OK if successful.

shishi_as_check_cname

int shishi_as_check_cname (*Shishi* * *handle*, *Shishi_asn1* *asreq*,   [Function]
            Shishi_asn1 *asrep*)

handle: shishi handle as allocated by `shishi_init()`.

asreq: AS-REQ to compare client name field in.

asrep: AS-REP to compare client name field in.

Verify that AS-REQ.req-body.realm and AS-REP.crealm fields matches. This is one of the steps that has to be performed when processing a AS-REQ and AS-REP exchange, see `shishi_kdc_process()`.

Return value: Returns SHISHI_OK if successful, SHISHI_CNAME_MISMATCH if the values differ, or an error code.

shishi_kdc_copy_nonce

int **shishi_kdc_copy_nonce** (*Shishi* * `handle`, *Shishi_asn1* `kdcreq`,   [Function]
    Shishi_asn1 `enckdcreppart`)

handle: shishi handle as allocated by `shishi_init()`.

kdcreq: KDC-REQ to read nonce from.

enckdcreppart: EncKDCRepPart to set nonce in.

Set nonce in EncKDCRepPart to value in KDC-REQ.

Return value: Returns SHISHI_OK if successful.

shishi_kdc_check_nonce

int **shishi_kdc_check_nonce** (*Shishi* * `handle`, *Shishi_asn1* `kdcreq`,   [Function]
    Shishi_asn1 `enckdcreppart`)

handle: shishi handle as allocated by `shishi_init()`.

kdcreq: KDC-REQ to compare nonce field in.

enckdcreppart: Encrypted KDC-REP part to compare nonce field in.

Verify that KDC-REQ.req-body.nonce and EncKDCRepPart.nonce fields matches. This is one of the steps that has to be performed when processing a KDC-REQ and KDC-REP exchange.

Return value: Returns SHISHI_OK if successful, SHISHI_NONCE_LENGTH_MISMATCH if the nonces have different lengths (usually indicates that buggy server truncated nonce to 4 bytes), SHISHI_NONCE_MISMATCH if the values differ, or an error code.

shishi_tgs_process

int **shishi_tgs_process** (*Shishi* * `handle`, *Shishi_asn1* `tgsreq`,   [Function]
    Shishi_asn1 `tgsrep`, *Shishi_asn1* `authenticator`, *Shishi_asn1*
    `oldenckdcreppart`, *Shishi_asn1* * `enckdcreppart`)

handle: shishi handle as allocated by `shishi_init()`.

tgsreq: input variable that holds the sent KDC-REQ.

tgsrep: input variable that holds the received KDC-REP.

authenticator: input variable with Authenticator from AP-REQ in KDC-REQ.

oldenckdcreppart: input variable with EncKDCRepPart used in request.

enckdcreppart: output variable that holds new EncKDCRepPart.

Process a TGS client exchange and output decrypted EncKDCRepPart which holds details for the new ticket received. This function simply derives the encryption key from the ticket used to construct the TGS request and calls `shishi_kdc_process()`, which see.

Return value: Returns SHISHI_OK iff the TGS client exchange was successful.

shishi_as_process

`int shishi_as_process` (*Shishi * **handle**, *Shishi_asn1* **asreq**,   [Function]
        Shishi_asn1 **asrep**, *const char * **string**, *Shishi_asn1 * **enckdcreppart**)
handle: shishi handle as allocated by `shishi_init()`.

asreq: input variable that holds the sent KDC-REQ.

asrep: input variable that holds the received KDC-REP.

string: input variable with zero terminated password.

enckdcreppart: output variable that holds new EncKDCRepPart.

Process an AS client exchange and output decrypted EncKDCRepPart which holds details for the new ticket received. This function simply derives the encryption key from the password and calls `shishi_kdc_process()`, which see.

Return value: Returns SHISHI_OK iff the AS client exchange was successful.

shishi_kdc_process

`int shishi_kdc_process` (*Shishi * **handle**, *Shishi_asn1* **kdcreq**,   [Function]
        Shishi_asn1 **kdcrep**, *Shishi_key * **key**, *int* **keyusage**, *Shishi_asn1 ***
        enckdcreppart)
handle: shishi handle as allocated by `shishi_init()`.

kdcreq: input variable that holds the sent KDC-REQ.

kdcrep: input variable that holds the received KDC-REP.

key: input array with key to decrypt encrypted part of KDC-REP with.

keyusage: kereros key usage value.

enckdcreppart: output variable that holds new EncKDCRepPart.

Process a KDC client exchange and output decrypted EncKDCRepPart which holds details for the new ticket received. Use `shishi_kdcrep_get_ticket()` to extract the ticket. This function verifies the various conditions that must hold if the response is to be considered valid, specifically it compares nonces (`shishi_kdc_check_nonce()`) and if the exchange was a AS exchange, it also compares cname and crealm (`shishi_as_check_cname()` and `shishi_as_check_crealm()`).

Usually the `shishi_as_process()` and `shishi_tgs_process()` functions should be used instead, since they simplify the decryption key computation.

Return value: Returns SHISHI_OK iff the KDC client exchange was successful.

shishi_asreq

`Shishi_asn1 shishi_asreq` (*Shishi * **handle**)   [Function]
        handle: shishi handle as allocated by `shishi_init()`.

This function creates a new AS-REQ, populated with some default values.

Return value: Returns the AS-REQ or NULL on failure.

shishi_tgsreq

Shishi_asn1 shishi_tgsreq (*Shishi * `handle`*)   [Function]
> *handle*: shishi handle as allocated by `shishi_init()`.
>
> This function creates a new TGS-REQ, populated with some default values.
>
> **Return value:** Returns the TGS-REQ or NULL on failure.

shishi_kdcreq_print

int shishi_kdcreq_print (*Shishi * `handle`*, *FILE * `fh`*, *Shishi_asn1*   [Function]
    `kdcreq`)
> *handle*: shishi handle as allocated by `shishi_init()`.
>
> *fh*: file handle open for writing.
>
> *kdcreq*: KDC-REQ to print.
>
> Print ASCII armored DER encoding of KDC-REQ to file.
>
> **Return value:** Returns SHISHI_OK iff successful.

shishi_kdcreq_save

int shishi_kdcreq_save (*Shishi * `handle`*, *FILE * `fh`*, *Shishi_asn1*   [Function]
    `kdcreq`)
> *handle*: shishi handle as allocated by `shishi_init()`.
>
> *fh*: file handle open for writing.
>
> *kdcreq*: KDC-REQ to save.
>
> Print DER encoding of KDC-REQ to file.
>
> **Return value:** Returns SHISHI_OK iff successful.

shishi_kdcreq_to_file

int shishi_kdcreq_to_file (*Shishi * `handle`*, *Shishi_asn1 `kdcreq`*,   [Function]
    int `filetype`, *const char * `filename`*)
> *handle*: shishi handle as allocated by `shishi_init()`.
>
> *kdcreq*: KDC-REQ to save.
>
> *filetype*: input variable specifying type of file to be written, see Shishi_filetype.
>
> *filename*: input variable with filename to write to.
>
> Write KDC-REQ to file in specified TYPE. The file will be truncated if it exists.
>
> **Return value:** Returns SHISHI_OK iff successful.

shishi_kdcreq_parse

int shishi_kdcreq_parse (*Shishi * `handle`*, *FILE * `fh`*, *Shishi_asn1 **   [Function]
    `kdcreq`)
> *handle*: shishi handle as allocated by `shishi_init()`.
>
> *fh*: file handle open for reading.
>
> *kdcreq*: output variable with newly allocated KDC-REQ.
>
> Read ASCII armored DER encoded KDC-REQ from file and populate given variable.
>
> **Return value:** Returns SHISHI_OK iff successful.

shishi_kdcreq_read

int shishi_kdcreq_read (*Shishi* * **handle**, *FILE* * **fh**, *Shishi_asn1* *   [Function]
    kdcreq)
> *handle*: shishi handle as allocated by `shishi_init()`.
>
> *fh*: file handle open for reading.
>
> *kdcreq*: output variable with newly allocated KDC-REQ.
>
> Read DER encoded KDC-REQ from file and populate given variable.
>
> **Return value:** Returns SHISHI_OK iff successful.

shishi_kdcreq_from_file

int shishi_kdcreq_from_file (*Shishi* * **handle**, *Shishi_asn1* *   [Function]
    kdcreq, *int* **filetype**, *const char* * **filename**)
> *handle*: shishi handle as allocated by `shishi_init()`.
>
> *kdcreq*: output variable with newly allocated KDC-REQ.
>
> *filetype*: input variable specifying type of file to be read, see Shishi_filetype.
>
> *filename*: input variable with filename to read from.
>
> Read KDC-REQ from file in specified TYPE.
>
> **Return value:** Returns SHISHI_OK iff successful.

shishi_kdcreq_nonce_set

int shishi_kdcreq_nonce_set (*Shishi* * **handle**, *Shishi_asn1* **kdcreq**,   [Function]
    uint32_t **nonce**)
> *handle*: shishi handle as allocated by `shishi_init()`.
>
> *kdcreq*: KDC-REQ variable to set client name field in.
>
> *nonce*: integer nonce to store in KDC-REQ.
>
> Store nonce number field in KDC-REQ.
>
> **Return value:** Returns `SHISHI_OK` iff successful.

shishi_kdcreq_set_cname

int shishi_kdcreq_set_cname (*Shishi* * **handle**, *Shishi_asn1* **kdcreq**,   [Function]
    Shishi_name_type **name_type**, *const char* * **principal**)
> *handle*: shishi handle as allocated by `shishi_init()`.
>
> *kdcreq*: KDC-REQ variable to set client name field in.
>
> *name_type*: type of principial, see Shishi_name_type, usually SHISHI_NT_UNKNOWN.
>
> *principal*: input array with principal name.
>
> Set the client name field in the KDC-REQ.
>
> **Return value:** Returns SHISHI_OK iff successful.

shishi_kdcreq_client

int shishi_kdcreq_client (*Shishi * handle*, *Shishi_asn1* kdcreq,   [Function]
    char ** client, *size_t ** clientlen)

  handle: Shishi library handle create by shishi_init().

  kdcreq: KDC-REQ variable to get client name from.

  client: pointer to newly allocated zero terminated string containing principal name. May be NULL (to only populate clientlen).

  clientlen: pointer to length of client on output, excluding terminating zero. May be NULL (to only populate client).

  Represent client principal name in KDC-REQ as zero-terminated string. The string is allocate by this function, and it is the responsibility of the caller to deallocate it. Note that the output length clientlen does not include the terminating zero.

  Return value: Returns SHISHI_OK iff successful.

shishi_asreq_clientrealm

int shishi_asreq_clientrealm (*Shishi * handle*, *Shishi_asn1* asreq,   [Function]
    char ** client, *size_t ** clientlen)

  handle: Shishi library handle create by shishi_init().

  asreq: AS-REQ variable to get client name and realm from.

  client: pointer to newly allocated zero terminated string containing principal name and realm. May be NULL (to only populate clientlen).

  clientlen: pointer to length of client on output, excluding terminating zero. May be NULL (to only populate client).

  Convert cname and realm fields from AS-REQ to printable principal name format. The string is allocate by this function, and it is the responsibility of the caller to deallocate it. Note that the output length clientlen does not include the terminating zero.

  Return value: Returns SHISHI_OK iff successful.

shishi_kdcreq_realm

int shishi_kdcreq_realm (*Shishi * handle*, *Shishi_asn1* kdcreq, *char*   [Function]
    ** realm, *size_t ** realmlen)

  handle: Shishi library handle create by shishi_init().

  kdcreq: KDC-REQ variable to get client name from.

  realm: pointer to newly allocated zero terminated string containing realm. May be NULL (to only populate realmlen).

  realmlen: pointer to length of realm on output, excluding terminating zero. May be NULL (to only populate realmlen).

  Get realm field in KDC-REQ as zero-terminated string. The string is allocate by this function, and it is the responsibility of the caller to deallocate it. Note that the output length realmlen does not include the terminating zero.

  Return value: Returns SHISHI_OK iff successful.

shishi_kdcreq_set_realm

int shishi_kdcreq_set_realm (*Shishi* * **handle**, *Shishi_asn1* **kdcreq**,   [Function]
        const char * **realm**)
handle: shishi handle as allocated by shishi_init().

kdcreq: KDC-REQ variable to set realm field in.

realm: input array with name of realm.

Set the realm field in the KDC-REQ.

Return value: Returns SHISHI_OK iff successful.

shishi_kdcreq_server

int shishi_kdcreq_server (*Shishi* * **handle**, *Shishi_asn1* **kdcreq**,   [Function]
        char ** **server**, *size_t* * **serverlen**)
handle: Shishi library handle create by shishi_init().

kdcreq: KDC-REQ variable to get server name from.

server: pointer to newly allocated zero terminated string containing principal name.
May be NULL (to only populate serverlen).

serverlen: pointer to length of server on output, excluding terminating zero. May
be NULL (to only populate server).

Represent server principal name in KDC-REQ as zero-terminated string. The string
is allocate by this function, and it is the responsibility of the caller to deallocate it.
Note that the output length serverlen does not include the terminating zero.

Return value: Returns SHISHI_OK iff successful.

shishi_kdcreq_set_sname

int shishi_kdcreq_set_sname (*Shishi* * **handle**, *Shishi_asn1* **kdcreq**,   [Function]
        Shishi_name_type **name_type**, *const char* * [] **sname**)
handle: shishi handle as allocated by shishi_init().

kdcreq: KDC-REQ variable to set server name field in.

name_type: type of principial, see Shishi_name_type, usually SHISHI_NT_UNKNOWN.

sname: input array with principal name.

Set the server name field in the KDC-REQ.

Return value: Returns SHISHI_OK iff successful.

shishi_kdcreq_till

int shishi_kdcreq_till (*Shishi* * **handle**, *Shishi_asn1* **kdcreq**, *char*   [Function]
        ** **till**, *size_t* * **tilllen**)
handle: Shishi library handle create by shishi_init().

kdcreq: KDC-REQ variable to get client name from.

till: pointer to newly allocated zero terminated string containing "till" field with
generalized time. May be NULL (to only populate realmlen).

tilllen: pointer to length of `till` on output, excluding terminating zero. May be `NULL` (to only populate `tilllen`).

Get "till" field (i.e. "endtime") in KDC-REQ, as zero-terminated string. The string is typically 15 characters long. The string is allocated by this function, and it is the responsibility of the caller to deallocate it. Note that the output length `realmlen` does not include the terminating zero.

Return value: Returns SHISHI_OK iff successful.

shishi_kdcreq_tillc

time_t **shishi_kdcreq_tillc** (*Shishi* * **handle**, *Shishi_asn1* **kdcreq**)   [Function]
    handle: Shishi library handle create by `shishi_init()`.

    kdcreq: KDC-REQ variable to get till field from.

    Extract C time corresponding to the "till" field.

    Return value: Returns C time interpretation of the "till" field in KDC-REQ.

shishi_kdcreq_etype

int **shishi_kdcreq_etype** (*Shishi* * **handle**, *Shishi_asn1* **kdcreq**,   [Function]
    int32_t * **etype**, *int* **netype**)
    handle: shishi handle as allocated by `shishi_init()`.

    kdcreq: KDC-REQ variable to get etype field from.

    etype: output encryption type.

    netype: element number to return.

    Return the netype: th encryption type from KDC-REQ. The first etype is number 1.

    Return value: Returns SHISHI_OK iff etype successful set.

shishi_kdcreq_set_etype

int **shishi_kdcreq_set_etype** (*Shishi* * **handle**, *Shishi_asn1* **kdcreq**,   [Function]
    int32_t * **etype**, *int* **netype**)
    handle: shishi handle as allocated by `shishi_init()`.

    kdcreq: KDC-REQ variable to set etype field in.

    etype: input array with encryption types.

    netype: number of elements in input array with encryption types.

    Set the list of supported or wanted encryption types in the request. The list should be sorted in priority order.

    Return value: Returns SHISHI_OK iff successful.

shishi_kdcreq_options

int **shishi_kdcreq_options** (*Shishi* * **handle**, *Shishi_asn1* **kdcreq**,   [Function]
    uint32_t * **flags**)
    handle: shishi handle as allocated by `shishi_init()`.

    kdcreq: KDC-REQ variable to get kdc-options field from.

flags: pointer to output integer with flags.

Extract KDC-Options from KDC-REQ.

Return value: Returns SHISHI_OK iff successful.

shishi_kdcreq_forwardable_p

int **shishi_kdcreq_forwardable_p** (*Shishi * handle*, *Shishi_asn1*   [Function]
    kdcreq)
handle: shishi handle as allocated by `shishi_init()`.

kdcreq: KDC-REQ variable to get kdc-options field from.

Determine if KDC-Option forwardable flag is set.

The FORWARDABLE option indicates that the ticket to be issued is to have its forwardable flag set. It may only be set on the initial request, or in a subsequent request if the ticket-granting ticket on which it is based is also forwardable.

Return value: Returns non-0 iff forwardable flag is set in KDC-REQ.

shishi_kdcreq_forwarded_p

int **shishi_kdcreq_forwarded_p** (*Shishi * handle*, *Shishi_asn1*   [Function]
    kdcreq)
handle: shishi handle as allocated by `shishi_init()`.

kdcreq: KDC-REQ variable to get kdc-options field from.

Determine if KDC-Option forwarded flag is set.

The FORWARDED option is only specified in a request to the ticket-granting server and will only be honored if the ticket-granting ticket in the request has its FOR-WARDABLE bit set. This option indicates that this is a request for forwarding. The address(es) of the host from which the resulting ticket is to be valid are included in the addresses field of the request.

Return value: Returns non-0 iff forwarded flag is set in KDC-REQ.

shishi_kdcreq_proxiable_p

int **shishi_kdcreq_proxiable_p** (*Shishi * handle*, *Shishi_asn1*   [Function]
    kdcreq)
handle: shishi handle as allocated by `shishi_init()`.

kdcreq: KDC-REQ variable to get kdc-options field from.

Determine if KDC-Option proxiable flag is set.

The PROXIABLE option indicates that the ticket to be issued is to have its proxiable flag set. It may only be set on the initial request, or in a subsequent request if the ticket-granting ticket on which it is based is also proxiable.

Return value: Returns non-0 iff proxiable flag is set in KDC-REQ.

shishi_kdcreq_proxy_p

int shishi_kdcreq_proxy_p (*Shishi * handle*, *Shishi_asn1 kdcreq*)   [Function]

handle: shishi handle as allocated by shishi_init().

kdcreq: KDC-REQ variable to get kdc-options field from.

Determine if KDC-Option proxy flag is set.

The PROXY option indicates that this is a request for a proxy. This option will only be honored if the ticket-granting ticket in the request has its PROXIABLE bit set. The address(es) of the host from which the resulting ticket is to be valid are included in the addresses field of the request.

Return value: Returns non-0 iff proxy flag is set in KDC-REQ.

shishi_kdcreq_allow_postdate_p

int shishi_kdcreq_allow_postdate_p (*Shishi * handle*, *Shishi_asn1*   [Function]
kdcreq)

handle: shishi handle as allocated by shishi_init().

kdcreq: KDC-REQ variable to get kdc-options field from.

Determine if KDC-Option allow-postdate flag is set.

The ALLOW-POSTDATE option indicates that the ticket to be issued is to have its MAY-POSTDATE flag set. It may only be set on the initial request, or in a subsequent request if the ticket-granting ticket on which it is based also has its MAY-POSTDATE flag set.

Return value: Returns non-0 iff allow-postdate flag is set in KDC-REQ.

shishi_kdcreq_postdated_p

int shishi_kdcreq_postdated_p (*Shishi * handle*, *Shishi_asn1*   [Function]
kdcreq)

handle: shishi handle as allocated by shishi_init().

kdcreq: KDC-REQ variable to get kdc-options field from.

Determine if KDC-Option postdated flag is set.

The POSTDATED option indicates that this is a request for a postdated ticket. This option will only be honored if the ticket-granting ticket on which it is based has its MAY-POSTDATE flag set. The resulting ticket will also have its INVALID flag set, and that flag may be reset by a subsequent request to the KDC after the starttime in the ticket has been reached.

Return value: Returns non-0 iff postdated flag is set in KDC-REQ.

shishi_kdcreq_renewable_p

int shishi_kdcreq_renewable_p (*Shishi * handle*, *Shishi_asn1*   [Function]
kdcreq)

handle: shishi handle as allocated by shishi_init().

kdcreq: KDC-REQ variable to get kdc-options field from.

Determine if KDC-Option renewable flag is set.

The RENEWABLE option indicates that the ticket to be issued is to have its RENEW-ABLE flag set. It may only be set on the initial request, or when the ticket-granting ticket on which the request is based is also renewable. If this option is requested, then the rtime field in the request contains the desired absolute expiration time for the ticket.

Return value: Returns non-0 iff renewable flag is set in KDC-REQ.

shishi_kdcreq_disable_transited_check_p

int shishi_kdcreq_disable_transited_check_p (*Shishi* * `handle`,   [Function]
     Shishi_asn1 `kdcreq`)

handle: shishi handle as allocated by `shishi_init()`.

kdcreq: KDC-REQ variable to get kdc-options field from.

Determine if KDC-Option disable-transited-check flag is set.

By default the KDC will check the transited field of a ticket-granting-ticket against the policy of the local realm before it will issue derivative tickets based on the ticket-granting ticket. If this flag is set in the request, checking of the transited field is disabled. Tickets issued without the performance of this check will be noted by the reset (0) value of the TRANSITED-POLICY-CHECKED flag, indicating to the application server that the tranisted field must be checked locally. KDCs are encouraged but not required to honor the DISABLE-TRANSITED-CHECK option.

This flag is new since RFC 1510

Return value: Returns non-0 iff disable-transited-check flag is set in KDC-REQ.

shishi_kdcreq_renewable_ok_p

int shishi_kdcreq_renewable_ok_p (*Shishi* * `handle`, *Shishi_asn1*   [Function]
     `kdcreq`)

handle: shishi handle as allocated by `shishi_init()`.

kdcreq: KDC-REQ variable to get kdc-options field from.

Determine if KDC-Option renewable-ok flag is set.

The RENEWABLE-OK option indicates that a renewable ticket will be acceptable if a ticket with the requested life cannot otherwise be provided. If a ticket with the requested life cannot be provided, then a renewable ticket may be issued with a renew-till equal to the requested endtime. The value of the renew-till field may still be limited by local limits, or limits selected by the individual principal or server.

Return value: Returns non-0 iff renewable-ok flag is set in KDC-REQ.

shishi_kdcreq_enc_tkt_in_skey_p

int shishi_kdcreq_enc_tkt_in_skey_p (*Shishi* * `handle`,   [Function]
     Shishi_asn1 `kdcreq`)

handle: shishi handle as allocated by `shishi_init()`.

kdcreq: KDC-REQ variable to get kdc-options field from.

Determine if KDC-Option enc-tkt-in-skey flag is set.

This option is used only by the ticket-granting service. The ENC-TKT-IN-SKEY option indicates that the ticket for the end server is to be encrypted in the session key from the additional ticket-granting ticket provided.

Return value: Returns non-0 iff enc-tkt-in-skey flag is set in KDC-REQ.

shishi_kdcreq_renew_p

int shishi_kdcreq_renew_p (*Shishi* * **handle**, *Shishi_asn1* **kdcreq**)   [Function]
handle: shishi handle as allocated by shishi_init().

kdcreq: KDC-REQ variable to get kdc-options field from.

Determine if KDC-Option renew flag is set.

This option is used only by the ticket-granting service. The RENEW option indicates that the present request is for a renewal. The ticket provided is encrypted in the secret key for the server on which it is valid. This option will only be honored if the ticket to be renewed has its RENEWABLE flag set and if the time in its renew-till field has not passed. The ticket to be renewed is passed in the padata field as part of the authentication header.

Return value: Returns non-0 iff renew flag is set in KDC-REQ.

shishi_kdcreq_validate_p

int shishi_kdcreq_validate_p (*Shishi* * **handle**, *Shishi_asn1*   [Function]
    kdcreq)
handle: shishi handle as allocated by shishi_init().

kdcreq: KDC-REQ variable to get kdc-options field from.

Determine if KDC-Option validate flag is set.

This option is used only by the ticket-granting service. The VALIDATE option indicates that the request is to validate a postdated ticket. It will only be honored if the ticket presented is postdated, presently has its INVALID flag set, and would be otherwise usable at this time. A ticket cannot be validated before its starttime. The ticket presented for validation is encrypted in the key of the server for which it is valid and is passed in the padata field as part of the authentication header.

Return value: Returns non-0 iff validate flag is set in KDC-REQ.

shishi_kdcreq_options_set

int shishi_kdcreq_options_set (*Shishi* * **handle**, *Shishi_asn1*   [Function]
    kdcreq, *uint32_t* **options**)
handle: shishi handle as allocated by shishi_init().

kdcreq: KDC-REQ variable to set etype field in.

options: integer with flags to store in KDC-REQ.

Set options in KDC-REQ. Note that this reset any already existing flags.

Return value: Returns SHISHI_OK iff successful.

shishi_kdcreq_options_add

int shishi_kdcreq_options_add (*Shishi * handle*, *Shishi_asn1*   [Function]
      kdcreq, *uint32_t option*)
> *handle*: shishi handle as allocated by shishi_init().
>
> *kdcreq*: KDC-REQ variable to set etype field in.
>
> *option*: integer with options to add in KDC-REQ.
>
> Add KDC-Option to KDC-REQ. This preserves all existing options.
>
> **Return value:** Returns SHISHI_OK iff successful.

shishi_kdcreq_clear_padata

int shishi_kdcreq_clear_padata (*Shishi * handle*, *Shishi_asn1*   [Function]
      kdcreq)
> *handle*: shishi handle as allocated by shishi_init().
>
> *kdcreq*: KDC-REQ to remove PA-DATA from.
>
> Remove the padata field from KDC-REQ.
>
> **Return value:** Returns SHISHI_OK iff successful.

shishi_kdcreq_get_padata

int shishi_kdcreq_get_padata (*Shishi * handle*, *Shishi_asn1*   [Function]
      kdcreq, *Shishi_padata_type padatatype*, *char ** out*, *size_t * outlen*)
> *handle*: shishi handle as allocated by shishi_init().
>
> *kdcreq*: KDC-REQ to get PA-DATA from.
>
> *padatatype*: type of PA-DATA, see Shishi_padata_type.
>
> *out*: output array with newly allocated PA-DATA value.
>
> *outlen*: size of output array with PA-DATA value.
>
> Get pre authentication data (PA-DATA) from KDC-REQ. Pre authentication data is used to pass various information to KDC, such as in case of a SHISHI_PA_TGS_REQ padatatype the AP-REQ that authenticates the user to get the ticket.
>
> **Return value:** Returns SHISHI_OK iff successful.

shishi_kdcreq_get_padata_tgs

int shishi_kdcreq_get_padata_tgs (*Shishi * handle*, *Shishi_asn1*   [Function]
      kdcreq, *Shishi_asn1 * apreq*)
> *handle*: shishi handle as allocated by shishi_init().
>
> *kdcreq*: KDC-REQ to get PA-TGS-REQ from.
>
> *apreq*: Output variable with newly allocated AP-REQ.
>
> Extract TGS pre-authentication data from KDC-REQ. The data is an AP-REQ that authenticates the request. This function call shishi_kdcreq_get_padata() with a SHISHI_PA_TGS_REQ padatatype and DER decode the result (if any).
>
> **Return value:** Returns SHISHI_OK iff successful.

shishi_kdcreq_add_padata

int shishi_kdcreq_add_padata (*Shishi* * handle, *Shishi_asn1*   [Function]
    kdcreq, *int* padatatype, *const char* * data, *size_t* datalen)
> *handle*: shishi handle as allocated by shishi_init().
>
> *kdcreq*: KDC-REQ to add PA-DATA to.
>
> *padatatype*: type of PA-DATA, see Shishi_padata_type.
>
> *data*: input array with PA-DATA value.
>
> *datalen*: size of input array with PA-DATA value.
>
> Add new pre authentication data (PA-DATA) to KDC-REQ. This is used to pass various information to KDC, such as in case of a SHISHI_PA_TGS_REQ padatatype the AP-REQ that authenticates the user to get the ticket. (But also see shishi_kdcreq_add_padata_tgs() which takes an AP-REQ directly.)
>
> **Return value:** Returns SHISHI_OK iff successful.

shishi_kdcreq_add_padata_tgs

int shishi_kdcreq_add_padata_tgs (*Shishi* * handle, *Shishi_asn1*   [Function]
    kdcreq, *Shishi_asn1* apreq)
> *handle*: shishi handle as allocated by shishi_init().
>
> *kdcreq*: KDC-REQ to add PA-DATA to.
>
> *apreq*: AP-REQ to add as PA-DATA.
>
> Add TGS pre-authentication data to KDC-REQ. The data is an AP-REQ that authenticates the request. This functions simply DER encodes the AP-REQ and calls shishi_kdcreq_add_padata() with a SHISHI_PA_TGS_REQ padatatype.
>
> **Return value:** Returns SHISHI_OK iff successful.

shishi_kdcreq_add_padata_preauth

int shishi_kdcreq_add_padata_preauth (*Shishi* * handle,   [Function]
    Shishi_asn1 kdcreq, *Shishi_key* * key)
> *handle*: shishi handle as allocated by shishi_init().
>
> *kdcreq*: KDC-REQ to add pre-authentication data to.
>
> *key*: Key used to encrypt pre-auth data.
>
> Add pre-authentication data to KDC-REQ.
>
> **Return value:** Returns SHISHI_OK iff successful.

shishi_asrep

Shishi_asn1 shishi_asrep (*Shishi* * handle)   [Function]
> *handle*: shishi handle as allocated by shishi_init().
>
> This function creates a new AS-REP, populated with some default values.
>
> **Return value:** Returns the AS-REP or NULL on failure.

shishi_tgsrep

Shishi_asn1 shishi_tgsrep (*Shishi* * `handle`)   [Function]
> *handle*: shishi handle as allocated by `shishi_init()`.
>
> This function creates a new TGS-REP, populated with some default values.
>
> **Return value:** Returns the TGS-REP or NULL on failure.

shishi_kdcrep_print

int shishi_kdcrep_print (*Shishi* * `handle`, *FILE* * `fh`, *Shishi_asn1*   [Function]
> `kdcrep`)
> *handle*: shishi handle as allocated by `shishi_init()`.
>
> *fh*: file handle open for writing.
>
> *kdcrep*: KDC-REP to print.
>
> Print ASCII armored DER encoding of KDC-REP to file.
>
> **Return value:** Returns SHISHI_OK iff successful.

shishi_kdcrep_save

int shishi_kdcrep_save (*Shishi* * `handle`, *FILE* * `fh`, *Shishi_asn1*   [Function]
> `kdcrep`)
> *handle*: shishi handle as allocated by `shishi_init()`.
>
> *fh*: file handle open for writing.
>
> *kdcrep*: KDC-REP to save.
>
> Print DER encoding of KDC-REP to file.
>
> **Return value:** Returns SHISHI_OK iff successful.

shishi_kdcrep_to_file

int shishi_kdcrep_to_file (*Shishi* * `handle`, *Shishi_asn1* `kdcrep`,   [Function]
> *int* `filetype`, *const char* * `filename`)
> *handle*: shishi handle as allocated by `shishi_init()`.
>
> *kdcrep*: KDC-REP to save.
>
> *filetype*: input variable specifying type of file to be written, see Shishi_filetype.
>
> *filename*: input variable with filename to write to.
>
> Write KDC-REP to file in specified TYPE. The file will be truncated if it exists.
>
> **Return value:** Returns SHISHI_OK iff successful.

shishi_kdcrep_parse

int shishi_kdcrep_parse (*Shishi* * `handle`, *FILE* * `fh`, *Shishi_asn1* *   [Function]
> `kdcrep`)
> *handle*: shishi handle as allocated by `shishi_init()`.
>
> *fh*: file handle open for reading.
>
> *kdcrep*: output variable with newly allocated KDC-REP.
>
> Read ASCII armored DER encoded KDC-REP from file and populate given variable.
>
> **Return value:** Returns SHISHI_OK iff successful.

shishi_kdcrep_read

int shishi_kdcrep_read (*Shishi * handle, FILE * fh, Shishi_asn1 *   [Function]
       kdcrep*)

handle: shishi handle as allocated by shishi_init().

fh: file handle open for reading.

kdcrep: output variable with newly allocated KDC-REP.

Read DER encoded KDC-REP from file and populate given variable.

Return value: Returns SHISHI_OK iff successful.

shishi_kdcrep_from_file

int shishi_kdcrep_from_file (*Shishi * handle, Shishi_asn1 *   [Function]
       kdcrep, int filetype, const char * filename*)

handle: shishi handle as allocated by shishi_init().

kdcrep: output variable with newly allocated KDC-REP.

filetype: input variable specifying type of file to be read, see Shishi_filetype.

filename: input variable with filename to read from.

Read KDC-REP from file in specified TYPE.

Return value: Returns SHISHI_OK iff successful.

shishi_kdcrep_crealm_set

int shishi_kdcrep_crealm_set (*Shishi * handle, Shishi_asn1   [Function]
       kdcrep, const char * crealm*)

handle: shishi handle as allocated by shishi_init().

kdcrep: Kdcrep variable to set realm field in.

crealm: input array with name of realm.

Set the client realm field in the KDC-REP.

Return value: Returns SHISHI_OK iff successful.

shishi_kdcrep_cname_set

int shishi_kdcrep_cname_set (*Shishi * handle, Shishi_asn1 kdcrep,   [Function]
       Shishi_name_type name_type, const char * [] cname*)

handle: shishi handle as allocated by shishi_init().

kdcrep: Kdcrep variable to set server name field in.

name_type: type of principial, see Shishi_name_type, usually SHISHI_NT_UNKNOWN.

cname: input array with principal name.

Set the client name field in the KDC-REP.

Return value: Returns SHISHI_OK iff successful.

shishi_kdcrep_client_set

int **shishi_kdcrep_client_set** (*Shishi* * **handle**, *Shishi_asn1*   [Function]
    kdcrep, *const char* * **client**)
    handle: shishi handle as allocated by `shishi_init()`.

    kdcrep: Kdcrep variable to set server name field in.

    client: zero-terminated string with principal name on RFC 1964 form.

    Set the client name field in the KDC-REP.

    Return value: Returns SHISHI_OK iff successful.

shishi_kdcrep_get_enc_part_etype

int **shishi_kdcrep_get_enc_part_etype** (*Shishi* * **handle**,   [Function]
    Shishi_asn1 **kdcrep**, *int32_t* * **etype**)
    handle: shishi handle as allocated by `shishi_init()`.

    kdcrep: KDC-REP variable to get value from.

    etype: output variable that holds the value.

    Extract KDC-REP.enc-part.etype.

    Return value: Returns SHISHI_OK iff successful.

shishi_kdcrep_get_ticket

int **shishi_kdcrep_get_ticket** (*Shishi* * **handle**, *Shishi_asn1*   [Function]
    kdcrep, *Shishi_asn1* * **ticket**)
    handle: shishi handle as allocated by `shishi_init()`.

    kdcrep: KDC-REP variable to get ticket from.

    ticket: output variable to hold extracted ticket.

    Extract ticket from KDC-REP.

    Return value: Returns SHISHI_OK iff successful.

shishi_kdcrep_set_ticket

int **shishi_kdcrep_set_ticket** (*Shishi* * **handle**, *Shishi_asn1*   [Function]
    kdcrep, *Shishi_asn1* **ticket**)
    handle: shishi handle as allocated by `shishi_init()`.

    kdcrep: KDC-REP to add ticket field to.

    ticket: input ticket to copy into KDC-REP ticket field.

    Copy ticket into KDC-REP.

    Return value: Returns SHISHI_OK iff successful.

shishi_kdcrep_set_enc_part

int shishi_kdcrep_set_enc_part (*Shishi * handle, Shishi_asn1*   [Function]
      *kdcrep, int32_t etype, uint32_t kvno, const char * buf, size_t buflen*)

handle: shishi handle as allocated by shishi_init().

kdcrep: KDC-REP to add enc-part field to.

etype: encryption type used to encrypt enc-part.

kvno: key version number.

buf: input array with encrypted enc-part.

buflen: size of input array with encrypted enc-part.

Set the encrypted enc-part field in the KDC-REP. The encrypted data is usually created by calling shishi_encrypt() on the DER encoded enc-part. To save time, you may want to use shishi_kdcrep_add_enc_part() instead, which calculates the encrypted data and calls this function in one step.

Return value: Returns SHISHI_OK iff successful.

shishi_kdcrep_add_enc_part

int shishi_kdcrep_add_enc_part (*Shishi * handle, Shishi_asn1*   [Function]
      *kdcrep, Shishi_key * key, int keyusage, Shishi_asn1 enckdcreppart*)

handle: shishi handle as allocated by shishi_init().

kdcrep: KDC-REP to add enc-part field to.

key: key used to encrypt enc-part.

keyusage: key usage to use, normally SHISHI_KEYUSAGE_ENCASREPPART, SHISHI_KEYUSAGE_ENCTGSREPPART_SESSION_KEY or SHISHI_KEYUSAGE_ENCTGSREPPA

enckdcreppart: EncKDCRepPart to add.

Encrypts DER encoded EncKDCRepPart using key and stores it in the KDC-REP.

Return value: Returns SHISHI_OK iff successful.

shishi_kdcrep_clear_padata

int shishi_kdcrep_clear_padata (*Shishi * handle, Shishi_asn1*   [Function]
      kdcrep)

handle: shishi handle as allocated by shishi_init().

kdcrep: KDC-REP to remove PA-DATA from.

Remove the padata field from KDC-REP.

Return value: Returns SHISHI_OK iff successful.

shishi_enckdcreppart_get_key

int shishi_enckdcreppart_get_key (*Shishi * handle, Shishi_asn1*   [Function]
      *enckdcreppart, Shishi_key ** key*)

handle: shishi handle as allocated by shishi_init().

enckdcreppart: input EncKDCRepPart variable.

key: newly allocated encryption key handle.

Extract the key to use with the ticket sent in the KDC-REP associated with the EncKDCRepPart input variable.

Return value: Returns `SHISHI_OK` iff successful.

shishi_enckdcreppart_key_set

int shishi_enckdcreppart_key_set (*Shishi* * `handle`, *Shishi_asn1*   [Function]
    `enckdcreppart`, *Shishi_key* * `key`)

handle: shishi handle as allocated by `shishi_init()`.

enckdcreppart: input EncKDCRepPart variable.

key: key handle with information to store in enckdcreppart.

Set the EncKDCRepPart.key field to key type and value of supplied key.

Return value: Returns `SHISHI_OK` iff successful.

shishi_enckdcreppart_nonce_set

int shishi_enckdcreppart_nonce_set (*Shishi* * `handle`, *Shishi_asn1*   [Function]
    `enckdcreppart`, *uint32_t* `nonce`)

handle: shishi handle as allocated by `shishi_init()`.

enckdcreppart: input EncKDCRepPart variable.

nonce: nonce to set in EncKDCRepPart.

Set the EncKDCRepPart.nonce field.

Return value: Returns `SHISHI_OK` iff successful.

shishi_enckdcreppart_flags_set

int shishi_enckdcreppart_flags_set (*Shishi* * `handle`, *Shishi_asn1*   [Function]
    `enckdcreppart`, *int* `flags`)

handle: shishi handle as allocated by `shishi_init()`.

enckdcreppart: input EncKDCRepPart variable.

flags: flags to set in EncKDCRepPart.

Set the EncKDCRepPart.flags field.

Return value: Returns `SHISHI_OK` iff successful.

shishi_enckdcreppart_authtime_set

int shishi_enckdcreppart_authtime_set (*Shishi* * `handle`,   [Function]
    Shishi_asn1 `enckdcreppart`, *const char* * `authtime`)

handle: shishi handle as allocated by `shishi_init()`.

enckdcreppart: input EncKDCRepPart variable.

authtime: character buffer containing a generalized time string.

Set the EncTicketPart.authtime to supplied value.

Return value: Returns `SHISHI_OK` iff successful.

shishi_enckdcreppart_starttime_set

int **shishi_enckdcreppart_starttime_set** (*Shishi * handle*,   [Function]
    Shishi_asn1 enckdcreppart, *const char * starttime*)

handle: shishi handle as allocated by `shishi_init()`.

enckdcreppart: input EncKDCRepPart variable.

starttime: character buffer containing a generalized time string.

Set the EncTicketPart.starttime to supplied value. Use a NULL value for `starttime` to remove the field.

Return value: Returns `SHISHI_OK` iff successful.

shishi_enckdcreppart_endtime_set

int **shishi_enckdcreppart_endtime_set** (*Shishi * handle*,   [Function]
    Shishi_asn1 enckdcreppart, *const char * endtime*)

handle: shishi handle as allocated by `shishi_init()`.

enckdcreppart: input EncKDCRepPart variable.

endtime: character buffer containing a generalized time string.

Set the EncTicketPart.endtime to supplied value.

Return value: Returns `SHISHI_OK` iff successful.

shishi_enckdcreppart_renew_till_set

int **shishi_enckdcreppart_renew_till_set** (*Shishi * handle*,   [Function]
    Shishi_asn1 enckdcreppart, *const char * renew_till*)

handle: shishi handle as allocated by `shishi_init()`.

enckdcreppart: input EncKDCRepPart variable.

renew_till: character buffer containing a generalized time string.

Set the EncTicketPart.renew-till to supplied value. Use a NULL value for `renew_till` to remove the field.

Return value: Returns `SHISHI_OK` iff successful.

shishi_enckdcreppart_srealm_set

int **shishi_enckdcreppart_srealm_set** (*Shishi * handle*,   [Function]
    Shishi_asn1 enckdcreppart, *const char * srealm*)

handle: shishi handle as allocated by `shishi_init()`.

enckdcreppart: EncKDCRepPart variable to set realm field in.

srealm: input array with name of realm.

Set the server realm field in the EncKDCRepPart.

Return value: Returns `SHISHI_OK` iff successful.

shishi_enckdcreppart_sname_set

int shishi_enckdcreppart_sname_set (*Shishi * handle*, *Shishi_asn1*   [Function]
      enckdcreppart, *Shishi_name_type name_type*, *char * [] sname*)

handle: shishi handle as allocated by `shishi_init()`.

enckdcreppart: EncKDCRepPart variable to set server name field in.

name_type: type of principial, see Shishi_name_type, usually SHISHI_NT_UNKNOWN.

sname: input array with principal name.

Set the server name field in the EncKDCRepPart.

Return value: Returns SHISHI_OK iff successful.

shishi_enckdcreppart_populate_encticketpart

int shishi_enckdcreppart_populate_encticketpart (*Shishi **   [Function]
      handle, *Shishi_asn1 enckdcreppart*, *Shishi_asn1 encticketpart*)

handle: shishi handle as allocated by `shishi_init()`.

enckdcreppart: input EncKDCRepPart variable.

encticketpart: input EncTicketPart variable.

Set the flags, authtime, starttime, endtime, renew-till and caddr fields of the EncK-DCRepPart to the corresponding values in the EncTicketPart.

Return value: Returns `SHISHI_OK` iff successful.

5.11 Authenticator Functions

An "Authenticator" is an ASN.1 structure that work as a proof that an entity owns a ticket. It is usually embedded in the AP-REQ structure (see Section 5.4 [AP-REQ and AP-REP Functions], page 70), and you most likely want to use an AP-REQ instead of a Authenticator in normal applications. The following illustrates the Authenticator ASN.1 structure.

```
Authenticator   ::= [APPLICATION 2] SEQUENCE  {
        authenticator-vno     [0] INTEGER (5),
        crealm                [1] Realm,
        cname                 [2] PrincipalName,
        cksum                 [3] Checksum OPTIONAL,
        cusec                 [4] Microseconds,
        ctime                 [5] KerberosTime,
        subkey                [6] EncryptionKey OPTIONAL,
        seq-number            [7] UInt32 OPTIONAL,
        authorization-data    [8] AuthorizationData OPTIONAL
}
```

shishi_authenticator

Shishi_asn1 shishi_authenticator (*Shishi * handle*)   [Function]
      handle: shishi handle as allocated by `shishi_init()`.

This function creates a new Authenticator, populated with some default values. It uses the current time as returned by the system for the ctime and cusec fields.

Return value: Returns the authenticator or NULL on failure.

shishi_authenticator_subkey

Shishi_asn1 shishi_authenticator_subkey (*Shishi* * `handle`)   [Function]
    handle: shishi handle as allocated by `shishi_init`().

This function creates a new Authenticator, populated with some default values. It uses the current time as returned by the system for the ctime and cusec fields. It adds a random subkey.

Return value: Returns the authenticator or NULL on failure.

shishi_authenticator_print

int shishi_authenticator_print (*Shishi* * `handle`, *FILE* * `fh`,   [Function]
    Shishi_asn1 `authenticator`)
    handle: shishi handle as allocated by `shishi_init`().

fh: file handle open for writing.

authenticator: authenticator as allocated by `shishi_authenticator`().

Print ASCII armored DER encoding of authenticator to file.

Return value: Returns SHISHI_OK iff successful.

shishi_authenticator_save

int shishi_authenticator_save (*Shishi* * `handle`, *FILE* * `fh`,   [Function]
    Shishi_asn1 `authenticator`)
    handle: shishi handle as allocated by `shishi_init`().

fh: file handle open for writing.

authenticator: authenticator as allocated by `shishi_authenticator`().

Save DER encoding of authenticator to file.

Return value: Returns SHISHI_OK iff successful.

shishi_authenticator_to_file

int shishi_authenticator_to_file (*Shishi* * `handle`, *Shishi_asn1*   [Function]
    `authenticator`, *int* `filetype`, *const char* * `filename`)
    handle: shishi handle as allocated by `shishi_init`().

authenticator: Authenticator to save.

filetype: input variable specifying type of file to be written, see Shishi_filetype.

filename: input variable with filename to write to.

Write Authenticator to file in specified TYPE. The file will be truncated if it exists.

Return value: Returns SHISHI_OK iff successful.

shishi_authenticator_parse

int shishi_authenticator_parse (*Shishi* * `handle`, *FILE* * `fh`,   [Function]
    Shishi_asn1 * `authenticator`)

handle: shishi handle as allocated by `shishi_init()`.

fh: file handle open for reading.

authenticator: output variable with newly allocated authenticator.

Read ASCII armored DER encoded authenticator from file and populate given authenticator variable.

Return value: Returns SHISHI_OK iff successful.

shishi_authenticator_read

int shishi_authenticator_read (*Shishi* * `handle`, *FILE* * `fh`,   [Function]
    Shishi_asn1 * `authenticator`)

handle: shishi handle as allocated by `shishi_init()`.

fh: file handle open for reading.

authenticator: output variable with newly allocated authenticator.

Read DER encoded authenticator from file and populate given authenticator variable.

Return value: Returns SHISHI_OK iff successful.

shishi_authenticator_from_file

int shishi_authenticator_from_file (*Shishi* * `handle`, *Shishi_asn1*   [Function]
    * `authenticator`, *int* `filetype`, *const char* * `filename`)

handle: shishi handle as allocated by `shishi_init()`.

authenticator: output variable with newly allocated Authenticator.

filetype: input variable specifying type of file to be read, see Shishi_filetype.

filename: input variable with filename to read from.

Read Authenticator from file in specified TYPE.

Return value: Returns SHISHI_OK iff successful.

shishi_authenticator_set_crealm

int shishi_authenticator_set_crealm (*Shishi* * `handle`,   [Function]
    Shishi_asn1 `authenticator`, *const char* * `crealm`)

handle: shishi handle as allocated by `shishi_init()`.

authenticator: authenticator as allocated by `shishi_authenticator()`.

crealm: input array with realm.

Set realm field in authenticator to specified value.

Return value: Returns SHISHI_OK iff successful.

shishi_authenticator_set_cname

int **shishi_authenticator_set_cname** (*Shishi * handle*, *Shishi_asn1*   [Function]
    authenticator, *Shishi_name_type* **name_type**, *const char * []* **cname**)

handle: shishi handle as allocated by `shishi_init()`.

authenticator: authenticator as allocated by `shishi_authenticator()`.

name_type: type of principial, see Shishi_name_type, usually SHISHI_NT_UNKNOWN.

cname: input array with principal name.

Set principal field in authenticator to specified value.

Return value: Returns SHISHI_OK iff successful.

shishi_authenticator_client_set

int **shishi_authenticator_client_set** (*Shishi * handle*,   [Function]
    Shishi_asn1 **authenticator**, *const char * client*)

handle: shishi handle as allocated by `shishi_init()`.

authenticator: Authenticator to set client name field in.

client: zero-terminated string with principal name on RFC 1964 form.

Set the client name field in the Authenticator.

Return value: Returns SHISHI_OK iff successful.

shishi_authenticator_ctime

int **shishi_authenticator_ctime** (*Shishi * handle*, *Shishi_asn1*   [Function]
    authenticator, *char ** t*)

handle: shishi handle as allocated by `shishi_init()`.

authenticator: Authenticator as allocated by `shishi_authenticator()`.

t: newly allocated zero-terminated character array with client time.

Extract client time from Authenticator.

Return value: Returns SHISHI_OK iff successful.

shishi_authenticator_ctime_set

int **shishi_authenticator_ctime_set** (*Shishi * handle*, *Shishi_asn1*   [Function]
    authenticator, *const char * t*)

handle: shishi handle as allocated by `shishi_init()`.

authenticator: Authenticator as allocated by `shishi_authenticator()`.

t: string with generalized time value to store in Authenticator.

Store client time in Authenticator.

Return value: Returns SHISHI_OK iff successful.

shishi_authenticator_cusec_get

int shishi_authenticator_cusec_get (*Shishi * handle*, *Shishi_asn1*   [Function]
    authenticator, *uint32_t * cusec*)
  handle: shishi handle as allocated by shishi_init().

  authenticator: Authenticator as allocated by shishi_authenticator().

  cusec: output integer with client microseconds field.

  Extract client microseconds field from Authenticator.

  Return value: Returns SHISHI_OK iff successful.

shishi_authenticator_cusec_set

int shishi_authenticator_cusec_set (*Shishi * handle*, *Shishi_asn1*   [Function]
    authenticator, *uint32_t cusec*)
  handle: shishi handle as allocated by shishi_init().

  authenticator: authenticator as allocated by shishi_authenticator().

  cusec: client microseconds to set in authenticator, 0-999999.

  Set the cusec field in the Authenticator.

  Return value: Returns SHISHI_OK iff successful.

shishi_authenticator_seqnumber_get

int shishi_authenticator_seqnumber_get (*Shishi * handle*,   [Function]
    Shishi_asn1 authenticator, *uint32_t * seqnumber*)
  handle: shishi handle as allocated by shishi_init().

  authenticator: authenticator as allocated by shishi_authenticator().

  seqnumber: output integer with sequence number field.

  Extract sequence number field from Authenticator.

  Return value: Returns SHISHI_OK iff successful.

shishi_authenticator_seqnumber_remove

int shishi_authenticator_seqnumber_remove (*Shishi * handle*,   [Function]
    Shishi_asn1 authenticator)
  handle: shishi handle as allocated by shishi_init().

  authenticator: authenticator as allocated by shishi_authenticator().

  Remove sequence number field in Authenticator.

  Return value: Returns SHISHI_OK iff successful.

shishi_authenticator_seqnumber_set

int shishi_authenticator_seqnumber_set (*Shishi * handle*,   [Function]
    Shishi_asn1 authenticator, *uint32_t seqnumber*)
  handle: shishi handle as allocated by shishi_init().

  authenticator: authenticator as allocated by shishi_authenticator().

seqnumber: integer with sequence number field to store in Authenticator.

Store sequence number field in Authenticator.

Return value: Returns `SHISHI_OK` iff successful.

shishi_authenticator_client

int shishi_authenticator_client (*Shishi * handle*, *Shishi_asn1*   [Function]
    authenticator, *char ** client*, *size_t * clientlen*)
handle: Shishi library handle create by `shishi_init()`.

authenticator: Authenticator variable to get client name from.

client: pointer to newly allocated zero terminated string containing principal name. May be `NULL` (to only populate `clientlen`).

clientlen: pointer to length of `client` on output, excluding terminating zero. May be `NULL` (to only populate `client`).

Represent client principal name in Authenticator as zero-terminated string. The string is allocate by this function, and it is the responsibility of the caller to deallocate it. Note that the output length `clientlen` does not include the terminating zero.

Return value: Returns SHISHI_OK iff successful.

shishi_authenticator_clientrealm

int shishi_authenticator_clientrealm (*Shishi * handle*,   [Function]
    Shishi_asn1 **authenticator**, *char ** client*, *size_t * clientlen*)
handle: Shishi library handle create by `shishi_init()`.

authenticator: Authenticator variable to get client name and realm from.

client: pointer to newly allocated zero terminated string containing principal name and realm. May be `NULL` (to only populate `clientlen`).

clientlen: pointer to length of `client` on output, excluding terminating zero. May be `NULL` (to only populate `client`).

Convert cname and realm fields from Authenticator to printable principal name format. The string is allocate by this function, and it is the responsibility of the caller to deallocate it. Note that the output length `clientlen` does not include the terminating zero.

Return value: Returns SHISHI_OK iff successful.

shishi_authenticator_cksum

int shishi_authenticator_cksum (*Shishi * handle*, *Shishi_asn1*   [Function]
    authenticator, *int32_t * cksumtype*, *char ** cksum*, *size_t * cksumlen*)
handle: shishi handle as allocated by `shishi_init()`.

authenticator: authenticator as allocated by `shishi_authenticator()`.

cksumtype: output checksum type.

cksum: newly allocated output checksum data from authenticator.

cksumlen: on output, actual size of allocated output checksum data buffer.

Read checksum value from authenticator. `cksum` is allocated by this function, and it is the responsibility of caller to deallocate it.

Return value: Returns SHISHI_OK iff successful.

shishi_authenticator_set_cksum

int shishi_authenticator_set_cksum (*Shishi * handle, Shishi_asn1*   [Function]
      authenticator, *int32_t cksumtype, char * cksum, size_t cksumlen*)

handle: shishi handle as allocated by `shishi_init()`.

authenticator: authenticator as allocated by `shishi_authenticator()`.

cksumtype: input checksum type to store in authenticator.

cksum: input checksum data to store in authenticator.

cksumlen: size of input checksum data to store in authenticator.

Store checksum value in authenticator. A checksum is usually created by calling `shishi_checksum()` on some application specific data using the key from the ticket that is being used. To save time, you may want to use `shishi_authenticator_add_cksum()` instead, which calculates the checksum and calls this function in one step.

Return value: Returns SHISHI_OK iff successful.

shishi_authenticator_add_cksum

int shishi_authenticator_add_cksum (*Shishi * handle, Shishi_asn1*   [Function]
      authenticator, *Shishi_key * key, int keyusage, char * data, size_t*
      datalen)

handle: shishi handle as allocated by `shishi_init()`.

authenticator: authenticator as allocated by `shishi_authenticator()`.

key: key to to use for encryption.

keyusage: cryptographic key usage value to use in encryption.

data: input array with data to calculate checksum on.

datalen: size of input array with data to calculate checksum on.

Calculate checksum for data and store it in the authenticator.

Return value: Returns SHISHI_OK iff successful.

shishi_authenticator_add_cksum_type

int shishi_authenticator_add_cksum_type (*Shishi * handle,*   [Function]
      Shishi_asn1 authenticator, *Shishi_key * key, int keyusage, int*
      cksumtype, *char * data, size_t datalen*)

handle: shishi handle as allocated by `shishi_init()`.

authenticator: authenticator as allocated by `shishi_authenticator()`.

key: key to to use for encryption.

keyusage: cryptographic key usage value to use in encryption.

cksumtype: checksum to type to calculate checksum.

data: input array with data to calculate checksum on.

datalen: size of input array with data to calculate checksum on.

Calculate checksum for data and store it in the authenticator.

Return value: Returns SHISHI_OK iff successful.

shishi_authenticator_clear_authorizationdata

int shishi_authenticator_clear_authorizationdata (*Shishi **   [Function]
    `handle`, *Shishi_asn1* `authenticator`)
handle: shishi handle as allocated by `shishi_init()`.

authenticator: Authenticator as allocated by `shishi_authenticator()`.

Remove the authorization-data field from Authenticator.

Return value: Returns SHISHI_OK iff successful.

shishi_authenticator_add_authorizationdata

int shishi_authenticator_add_authorizationdata (*Shishi **   [Function]
    `handle`, *Shishi_asn1* `authenticator`, *int32_t* `adtype`, *const char ** `addata`,
    size_t `addatalen`)
handle: shishi handle as allocated by `shishi_init()`.

authenticator: authenticator as allocated by `shishi_authenticator()`.

adtype: input authorization data type to add.

addata: input authorization data to add.

addatalen: size of input authorization data to add.

Add authorization data to authenticator.

Return value: Returns SHISHI_OK iff successful.

shishi_authenticator_authorizationdata

int shishi_authenticator_authorizationdata (*Shishi * handle*,   [Function]
    Shishi_asn1 `authenticator`, *int32_t ** `adtype`, *char *** `addata`, *size_t **
    `addatalen`, *size_t* `nth`)
handle: shishi handle as allocated by `shishi_init()`.

authenticator: authenticator as allocated by `shishi_authenticator()`.

adtype: output authorization data type.

addata: newly allocated output authorization data.

addatalen: on output, actual size of newly allocated authorization data.

nth: element number of authorization-data to extract.

Extract n: th authorization data from authenticator. The first field is 1.

Return value: Returns SHISHI_OK iff successful.

shishi_authenticator_remove_subkey

int shishi_authenticator_remove_subkey (*Shishi * handle*,   [Function]
        Shishi_asn1 authenticator)

handle: shishi handle as allocated by shishi_init().

authenticator: authenticator as allocated by shishi_authenticator().

Remove subkey from the authenticator.

Return value: Returns SHISHI_OK iff successful.

shishi_authenticator_get_subkey

int shishi_authenticator_get_subkey (*Shishi * handle*,   [Function]
        Shishi_asn1 authenticator, *Shishi_key ** subkey*)

handle: shishi handle as allocated by shishi_init().

authenticator: authenticator as allocated by shishi_authenticator().

subkey: output newly allocated subkey from authenticator.

Read subkey value from authenticator.

Return value: Returns SHISHI_OK if successful or SHISHI_ASN1_NO_ELEMENT
if subkey is not present.

shishi_authenticator_set_subkey

int shishi_authenticator_set_subkey (*Shishi * handle*,   [Function]
        Shishi_asn1 authenticator, *int32_t* subkeytype, *const char * subkey*,
        size_t subkeylen)

handle: shishi handle as allocated by shishi_init().

authenticator: authenticator as allocated by shishi_authenticator().

subkeytype: input subkey type to store in authenticator.

subkey: input subkey data to store in authenticator.

subkeylen: size of input subkey data to store in authenticator.

Store subkey value in authenticator. A subkey is usually created by calling shishi_
key_random() using the default encryption type of the key from the ticket that is being used. To save time, you may want to use shishi_authenticator_add_subkey()
instead, which calculates the subkey and calls this function in one step.

Return value: Returns SHISHI_OK iff successful.

shishi_authenticator_add_random_subkey

int shishi_authenticator_add_random_subkey (*Shishi * handle*,   [Function]
        Shishi_asn1 authenticator)

handle: shishi handle as allocated by shishi_init().

authenticator: authenticator as allocated by shishi_authenticator().

Generate random subkey, of the default encryption type from configuration, and store
it in the authenticator.

Return value: Returns SHISHI_OK iff successful.

shishi_authenticator_add_random_subkey_etype

int shishi_authenticator_add_random_subkey_etype (*Shishi **   [Function]
       `handle`, *Shishi_asn1* `authenticator`, *int* `etype`)

handle: shishi handle as allocated by `shishi_init()`.

authenticator: authenticator as allocated by `shishi_authenticator()`.

etype: encryption type of random key to generate.

Generate random subkey of indicated encryption type, and store it in the authenticator.

Return value: Returns SHISHI_OK iff successful.

shishi_authenticator_add_subkey

int shishi_authenticator_add_subkey (*Shishi ** `handle`,   [Function]
       Shishi_asn1 `authenticator`, *Shishi_key ** `subkey`)

handle: shishi handle as allocated by `shishi_init()`.

authenticator: authenticator as allocated by `shishi_authenticator()`.

subkey: subkey to add to authenticator.

Store subkey in the authenticator.

Return value: Returns SHISHI_OK iff successful.

5.12 KRB-ERROR Functions

The "KRB-ERROR" is an ASN.1 structure that can be returned, instead of, e.g., KDC-REP or AP-REP, to indicate various error conditions. Unfortunately, the semantics of several of the fields are ill specified, so the typically procedure is to extract "e-text" and/or "e-data" and show it to the user. The following illustrates the KRB-ERROR ASN.1 structure.

```
KRB-ERROR       ::= [APPLICATION 30] SEQUENCE {
        pvno            [0] INTEGER (5),
        msg-type        [1] INTEGER (30),
        ctime           [2] KerberosTime OPTIONAL,
        cusec           [3] Microseconds OPTIONAL,
        stime           [4] KerberosTime,
        susec           [5] Microseconds,
        error-code      [6] Int32,
        crealm          [7] Realm OPTIONAL,
        cname           [8] PrincipalName OPTIONAL,
        realm           [9] Realm -- service realm --,
        sname           [10] PrincipalName -- service name --,
        e-text          [11] KerberosString OPTIONAL,
        e-data          [12] OCTET STRING OPTIONAL
}
```

shishi_krberror

Shishi_asn1 shishi_krberror (*Shishi ** `handle`)   [Function]
       handle: shishi handle as allocated by `shishi_init()`.

This function creates a new KRB-ERROR, populated with some default values.

Return value: Returns the KRB-ERROR or NULL on failure.

shishi_krberror_print

int **shishi_krberror_print** (*Shishi* * `handle`, *FILE* * `fh`, *Shishi_asn1*   [Function]
      `krberror`)

handle: shishi handle as allocated by `shishi_init()`.

fh: file handle open for writing.

krberror: KRB-ERROR to print.

Print ASCII armored DER encoding of KRB-ERROR to file.

Return value: Returns SHISHI_OK iff successful.

shishi_krberror_save

int **shishi_krberror_save** (*Shishi* * `handle`, *FILE* * `fh`, *Shishi_asn1*   [Function]
      `krberror`)

handle: shishi handle as allocated by `shishi_init()`.

fh: file handle open for writing.

krberror: KRB-ERROR to save.

Save DER encoding of KRB-ERROR to file.

Return value: Returns SHISHI_OK iff successful.

shishi_krberror_to_file

int **shishi_krberror_to_file** (*Shishi* * `handle`, *Shishi_asn1*   [Function]
      `krberror`, *int* `filetype`, *const char* * `filename`)

handle: shishi handle as allocated by `shishi_init()`.

krberror: KRB-ERROR to save.

filetype: input variable specifying type of file to be written, see Shishi_filetype.

filename: input variable with filename to write to.

Write KRB-ERROR to file in specified TYPE. The file will be truncated if it exists.

Return value: Returns SHISHI_OK iff successful.

shishi_krberror_parse

int **shishi_krberror_parse** (*Shishi* * `handle`, *FILE* * `fh`, *Shishi_asn1*   [Function]
      * `krberror`)

handle: shishi handle as allocated by `shishi_init()`.

fh: file handle open for reading.

krberror: output variable with newly allocated KRB-ERROR.

Read ASCII armored DER encoded KRB-ERROR from file and populate given variable.

Return value: Returns SHISHI_OK iff successful.

shishi_krberror_read

int shishi_krberror_read (*Shishi * handle*, *FILE * fh*, *Shishi_asn1 *   [Function]
    krberror*)

handle: shishi handle as allocated by shishi_init().

fh: file handle open for reading.

krberror: output variable with newly allocated KRB-ERROR.

Read DER encoded KRB-ERROR from file and populate given variable.

Return value: Returns SHISHI_OK iff successful.

shishi_krberror_from_file

int shishi_krberror_from_file (*Shishi * handle*, *Shishi_asn1 *   [Function]
    krberror*, *int filetype*, *const char * filename*)

handle: shishi handle as allocated by shishi_init().

krberror: output variable with newly allocated KRB-ERROR.

filetype: input variable specifying type of file to be read, see Shishi_filetype.

filename: input variable with filename to read from.

Read KRB-ERROR from file in specified TYPE.

Return value: Returns SHISHI_OK iff successful.

shishi_krberror_build

int shishi_krberror_build (*Shishi * handle*, *Shishi_asn1 krberror*)   [Function]
    handle: shishi handle as allocated by shishi_init().

krberror: krberror as allocated by shishi_krberror().

Finish KRB-ERROR, called before e.g. shishi_krberror_der. This function removes
empty but OPTIONAL fields (such as cname), and

Return value: Returns SHISHI_OK iff successful.

shishi_krberror_der

int shishi_krberror_der (*Shishi * handle*, *Shishi_asn1 krberror*,   [Function]
    *char ** out*, *size_t * outlen*)

handle: shishi handle as allocated by shishi_init().

krberror: krberror as allocated by shishi_krberror().

out: output array with newly allocated DER encoding of KRB-ERROR.

outlen: length of output array with DER encoding of KRB-ERROR.

DER encode KRB-ERROR. The caller must deallocate the OUT buffer.

Return value: Returns SHISHI_OK iff successful.

shishi_krberror_crealm

int **shishi_krberror_crealm** (*Shishi * handle*, *Shishi_asn1*   [Function]
   krberror, *char ** realm*, *size_t * realmlen*)

   handle: shishi handle as allocated by `shishi_init()`.

   krberror: krberror as allocated by `shishi_krberror()`.

   realm: output array with newly allocated name of realm in KRB-ERROR.

   realmlen: size of output array.

   Extract client realm from KRB-ERROR.

   Return value: Returns SHISHI_OK iff successful.

shishi_krberror_remove_crealm

int **shishi_krberror_remove_crealm** (*Shishi * handle*, *Shishi_asn1*   [Function]
   krberror)

   handle: shishi handle as allocated by `shishi_init()`.

   krberror: krberror as allocated by `shishi_krberror()`.

   Remove client realm field in KRB-ERROR.

   Return value: Returns SHISHI_OK iff successful.

shishi_krberror_set_crealm

int **shishi_krberror_set_crealm** (*Shishi * handle*, *Shishi_asn1*   [Function]
   krberror, *const char * crealm*)

   handle: shishi handle as allocated by `shishi_init()`.

   krberror: krberror as allocated by `shishi_krberror()`.

   crealm: input array with realm.

   Set realm field in krberror to specified value.

   Return value: Returns SHISHI_OK iff successful.

shishi_krberror_client

int **shishi_krberror_client** (*Shishi * handle*, *Shishi_asn1*   [Function]
   krberror, *char ** client*, *size_t * clientlen*)

   handle: shishi handle as allocated by `shishi_init()`.

   krberror: krberror as allocated by `shishi_krberror()`.

   client: pointer to newly allocated zero terminated string containing principal name.
   May be `NULL` (to only populate `clientlen`).

   clientlen: pointer to length of `client` on output, excluding terminating zero. May be
   `NULL` (to only populate `client`).

   Return client principal name in KRB-ERROR.

   Return value: Returns SHISHI_OK iff successful.

shishi_krberror_set_cname

int shishi_krberror_set_cname (*Shishi * handle*, *Shishi_asn1*   [Function]
    krberror, *Shishi_name_type* name_type, *const char ** [] cname)
    handle: shishi handle as allocated by shishi_init().

    krberror: krberror as allocated by shishi_krberror().

    name_type: type of principial, see Shishi_name_type, usually SHISHI_NT_UNKNOWN.

    cname: input array with principal name.

    Set principal field in krberror to specified value.

    Return value: Returns SHISHI_OK iff successful.

shishi_krberror_remove_cname

int shishi_krberror_remove_cname (*Shishi * handle*, *Shishi_asn1*   [Function]
    krberror)
    handle: shishi handle as allocated by shishi_init().

    krberror: krberror as allocated by shishi_krberror().

    Remove client realm field in KRB-ERROR.

    Return value: Returns SHISHI_OK iff successful.

shishi_krberror_client_set

int shishi_krberror_client_set (*Shishi * handle*, *Shishi_asn1*   [Function]
    krberror, *const char ** client)
    handle: shishi handle as allocated by shishi_init().

    krberror: Krberror to set client name field in.

    client: zero-terminated string with principal name on RFC 1964 form.

    Set the client name field in the Krberror.

    Return value: Returns SHISHI_OK iff successful.

shishi_krberror_realm

int shishi_krberror_realm (*Shishi * handle*, *Shishi_asn1 krberror*,   [Function]
    char ** realm, *size_t ** realmlen)
    handle: shishi handle as allocated by shishi_init().

    krberror: krberror as allocated by shishi_krberror().

    realm: output array with newly allocated name of realm in KRB-ERROR.

    realmlen: size of output array.

    Extract (server) realm from KRB-ERROR.

    Return value: Returns SHISHI_OK iff successful.

shishi_krberror_set_realm

int shishi_krberror_set_realm (*Shishi * handle*, *Shishi_asn1*   [Function]
    krberror, *const char * realm*)

handle: shishi handle as allocated by shishi_init().

krberror: krberror as allocated by shishi_krberror().

realm: input array with (server) realm.

Set (server) realm field in krberror to specified value.

Return value: Returns SHISHI_OK iff successful.

shishi_krberror_server

int shishi_krberror_server (*Shishi * handle*, *Shishi_asn1*   [Function]
    krberror, *char ** server*, *size_t * serverlen*)

handle: shishi handle as allocated by shishi_init().

krberror: krberror as allocated by shishi_krberror().

server: pointer to newly allocated zero terminated string containing server name.
May be NULL (to only populate serverlen).

serverlen: pointer to length of server on output, excluding terminating zero. May
be NULL (to only populate server).

Return server principal name in KRB-ERROR.

Return value: Returns SHISHI_OK iff successful.

shishi_krberror_remove_sname

int shishi_krberror_remove_sname (*Shishi * handle*, *Shishi_asn1*   [Function]
    krberror)

handle: shishi handle as allocated by shishi_init().

krberror: Krberror to set server name field in.

Remove server name field in KRB-ERROR. (Since it is not marked OPTIONAL in
the ASN.1 profile, what is done is to set the name-type to UNKNOWN and make
sure the name-string sequence is empty.)

Return value: Returns SHISHI_OK iff successful.

shishi_krberror_set_sname

int shishi_krberror_set_sname (*Shishi * handle*, *Shishi_asn1*   [Function]
    krberror, *Shishi_name_type name_type*, *const char * [] sname*)

handle: shishi handle as allocated by shishi_init().

krberror: krberror as allocated by shishi_krberror().

name_type: type of principial, see Shishi_name_type, usually SHISHI_NT_UNKNOWN.

sname: input array with principal name.

Set principal field in krberror to specified value.

Return value: Returns SHISHI_OK iff successful.

shishi_krberror_server_set

int shishi_krberror_server_set (*Shishi * handle, Shishi_asn1*   [Function]
    ***krberror**, *const char * server*)

> *handle*: shishi handle as allocated by `shishi_init()`.
>
> *krberror*: Krberror to set server name field in.
>
> *server*: zero-terminated string with principal name on RFC 1964 form.
>
> Set the server name field in the Krberror.
>
> **Return value:** Returns SHISHI_OK iff successful.

shishi_krberror_ctime

int shishi_krberror_ctime (*Shishi * handle, Shishi_asn1 **krberror**,*   [Function]
    *char ** t*)

> *handle*: shishi handle as allocated by `shishi_init()`.
>
> *krberror*: Krberror to set client name field in.
>
> *t*: newly allocated zero-terminated output array with client time.
>
> Extract client time from KRB-ERROR.
>
> **Return value:** Returns SHISHI_OK iff successful.

shishi_krberror_ctime_set

int shishi_krberror_ctime_set (*Shishi * handle, Shishi_asn1*   [Function]
    ***krberror**, *const char * t*)

> *handle*: shishi handle as allocated by `shishi_init()`.
>
> *krberror*: Krberror as allocated by `shishi_krberror()`.
>
> *t*: string with generalized time value to store in Krberror.
>
> Store client time in Krberror.
>
> **Return value:** Returns SHISHI_OK iff successful.

shishi_krberror_remove_ctime

int shishi_krberror_remove_ctime (*Shishi * handle, Shishi_asn1*   [Function]
    krberror)

> *handle*: shishi handle as allocated by `shishi_init()`.
>
> *krberror*: Krberror as allocated by `shishi_krberror()`.
>
> Remove client time field in Krberror.
>
> **Return value:** Returns SHISHI_OK iff successful.

shishi_krberror_cusec

int shishi_krberror_cusec (*Shishi * handle, Shishi_asn1 **krberror**,*   [Function]
    *uint32_t * cusec*)

> *handle*: shishi handle as allocated by `shishi_init()`.
>
> *krberror*: Krberror as allocated by `shishi_krberror()`.

cusec: output integer with client microseconds field.

Extract client microseconds field from Krberror.

Return value: Returns SHISHI_OK iff successful.

shishi_krberror_cusec_set

int shishi_krberror_cusec_set (*Shishi * handle*, *Shishi_asn1*   [Function]
          krberror, *uint32_t cusec*)
handle: shishi handle as allocated by shishi_init().

krberror: krberror as allocated by shishi_krberror().

cusec: client microseconds to set in krberror, 0-999999.

Set the cusec field in the Krberror.

Return value: Returns SHISHI_OK iff successful.

shishi_krberror_remove_cusec

int shishi_krberror_remove_cusec (*Shishi * handle*, *Shishi_asn1*   [Function]
          krberror)
handle: shishi handle as allocated by shishi_init().

krberror: Krberror as allocated by shishi_krberror().

Remove client usec field in Krberror.

Return value: Returns SHISHI_OK iff successful.

shishi_krberror_stime

int shishi_krberror_stime (*Shishi * handle*, *Shishi_asn1 krberror*,   [Function]
          char ** t)
handle: shishi handle as allocated by shishi_init().

krberror: Krberror to set client name field in.

t: newly allocated zero-terminated output array with server time.

Extract server time from KRB-ERROR.

Return value: Returns SHISHI_OK iff successful.

shishi_krberror_stime_set

int shishi_krberror_stime_set (*Shishi * handle*, *Shishi_asn1*   [Function]
          krberror, *const char * t*)
handle: shishi handle as allocated by shishi_init().

krberror: Krberror as allocated by shishi_krberror().

t: string with generalized time value to store in Krberror.

Store server time in Krberror.

Return value: Returns SHISHI_OK iff successful.

shishi_krberror_susec

int shishi_krberror_susec (*Shishi* * `handle`, *Shishi_asn1* `krberror`,   [Function]
    uint32_t * `susec`)

    handle: shishi handle as allocated by `shishi_init()`.

    krberror: Krberror as allocated by `shishi_krberror()`.

    susec: output integer with server microseconds field.

    Extract server microseconds field from Krberror.

    Return value: Returns SHISHI_OK iff successful.

shishi_krberror_susec_set

int shishi_krberror_susec_set (*Shishi* * `handle`, *Shishi_asn1*   [Function]
    `krberror`, *uint32_t* `susec`)

    handle: shishi handle as allocated by `shishi_init()`.

    krberror: krberror as allocated by `shishi_krberror()`.

    susec: server microseconds to set in krberror, 0-999999.

    Set the susec field in the Krberror.

    Return value: Returns SHISHI_OK iff successful.

shishi_krberror_errorcode

int shishi_krberror_errorcode (*Shishi* * `handle`, *Shishi_asn1*   [Function]
    `krberror`, *int32_t* * `errorcode`)

    handle: shishi handle as allocated by `shishi_init()`.

    krberror: KRB-ERROR structure with error code.

    errorcode: output integer KRB-ERROR error code.

    Extract error code from KRB-ERROR.

    Return value: Returns SHISHI_OK iff successful.

shishi_krberror_errorcode_fast

int shishi_krberror_errorcode_fast (*Shishi* * `handle`, *Shishi_asn1*   [Function]
    `krberror`)

    handle: shishi handle as allocated by `shishi_init()`.

    krberror: KRB-ERROR structure with error code.

    Get error code from KRB-ERROR, without error checking.

    Return value: Return error code (see `shishi_krberror_errorcode()`) directly, or
    -1 on error.

shishi_krberror_errorcode_set

int shishi_krberror_errorcode_set (*Shishi* * `handle`, *Shishi_asn1*   [Function]
    `krberror`, *int* `errorcode`)

    handle: shishi handle as allocated by `shishi_init()`.

krberror: KRB-ERROR structure with error code to set.

errorcode: new error code to set in krberror.

Set the error-code field to a new error code.

Return value: Returns SHISHI_OK iff successful.

shishi_krberror_etext

int shishi_krberror_etext (*Shishi * handle*, *Shishi_asn1 krberror*,   [Function]
    char ** etext, *size_t * etextlen*)

handle: shishi handle as allocated by shishi_init().

krberror: KRB-ERROR structure with error code.

etext: output array with newly allocated error text.

etextlen: output length of error text.

Extract additional error text from server (possibly empty).

Return value: Returns SHISHI_OK iff successful.

shishi_krberror_set_etext

int shishi_krberror_set_etext (*Shishi * handle*, *Shishi_asn1*   [Function]
    krberror, *const char * etext*)

handle: shishi handle as allocated by shishi_init().

krberror: krberror as allocated by shishi_krberror().

etext: input array with error text to set.

Set error text (e-text) field in KRB-ERROR to specified value.

Return value: Returns SHISHI_OK iff successful.

shishi_krberror_remove_etext

int shishi_krberror_remove_etext (*Shishi * handle*, *Shishi_asn1*   [Function]
    krberror)

handle: shishi handle as allocated by shishi_init().

krberror: krberror as allocated by shishi_krberror().

Remove error text (e-text) field in KRB-ERROR.

Return value: Returns SHISHI_OK iff successful.

shishi_krberror_edata

int shishi_krberror_edata (*Shishi * handle*, *Shishi_asn1 krberror*,   [Function]
    char ** edata, *size_t * edatalen*)

handle: shishi handle as allocated by shishi_init().

krberror: KRB-ERROR structure with error code.

edata: output array with newly allocated error data.

edatalen: output length of error data.

Extract additional error data from server (possibly empty).

Return value: Returns SHISHI_OK iff successful.

shishi_krberror_methoddata

int **shishi_krberror_methoddata** (*Shishi * `handle`, *Shishi_asn1*   [Function]
    `krberror`, *Shishi_asn1* * `methoddata`)
handle: shishi handle as allocated by `shishi_init()`.

krberror: KRB-ERROR structure with error code.

methoddata: output ASN.1 METHOD-DATA.

Extract METHOD-DATA ASN.1 object from the e-data field. The e-data field
will only contain a METHOD-DATA if the krberror error code is `SHISHI_KDC_ERR_`
`PREAUTH_REQUIRED`.

Return value: Returns SHISHI_OK iff successful.

shishi_krberror_set_edata

int **shishi_krberror_set_edata** (*Shishi * `handle`, *Shishi_asn1*   [Function]
    `krberror`, *const char* * `edata`)
handle: shishi handle as allocated by `shishi_init()`.

krberror: krberror as allocated by `shishi_krberror()`.

edata: input array with error text to set.

Set error text (e-data) field in KRB-ERROR to specified value.

Return value: Returns SHISHI_OK iff successful.

shishi_krberror_remove_edata

int **shishi_krberror_remove_edata** (*Shishi * `handle`, *Shishi_asn1*   [Function]
    `krberror`)
handle: shishi handle as allocated by `shishi_init()`.

krberror: krberror as allocated by `shishi_krberror()`.

Remove error text (e-data) field in KRB-ERROR.

Return value: Returns SHISHI_OK iff successful.

shishi_krberror_pretty_print

int **shishi_krberror_pretty_print** (*Shishi * `handle`, *FILE* * `fh`,   [Function]
    Shishi_asn1 `krberror`)
handle: shishi handle as allocated by `shishi_init()`.

fh: file handle opened for writing.

krberror: KRB-ERROR structure with error code.

Print KRB-ERROR error condition and some explanatory text to file descriptor.

Return value: Returns SHISHI_OK iff successful.

shishi_krberror_errorcode_message

const char * shishi_krberror_errorcode_message (*Shishi* *   [Function]
     handle, *int* errorcode)

     handle: shishi handle as allocated by shishi_init().

     errorcode: integer KRB-ERROR error code.

     Get human readable string describing KRB-ERROR code.

     Return value: Return a string describing error code. This function will always return a string even if the error code isn't known.

shishi_krberror_message

const char * shishi_krberror_message (*Shishi* * handle,   [Function]
     Shishi_asn1 krberror)

     handle: shishi handle as allocated by shishi_init().

     krberror: KRB-ERROR structure with error code.

     Extract error code (see shishi_krberror_errorcode_fast()) and return error message (see shishi_krberror_errorcode_message()).

     Return value: Return a string describing error code. This function will always return a string even if the error code isn't known.

5.13 Cryptographic Functions

Underneath the high-level functions described earlier, cryptographic operations are happening. If you need to access these cryptographic primitives directly, this section describes the functions available.

Most cryptographic operations need keying material, and cryptographic keys have been isolated into it's own data structure Shishi_key. The following illustrates it's contents, but note that you cannot access it's elements directly but must use the accessor functions described below.

```
struct Shishi_key
{
  int type;    /* RFC 1510 encryption integer type */
  char *value; /* Cryptographic key data */
  int version; /* RFC 1510 ''kvno'' */
};
```

     All functions that operate on this data structure are described now.

shishi_key_principal

const char * shishi_key_principal (*const Shishi_key* * key)   [Function]
     key: structure that holds key information

     Get the principal part of the key owner principal name, i.e., except the realm.

     Return value: Returns the principal owning the key. (Not a copy of it, so don't modify or deallocate it.)

shishi_key_principal_set

void shishi_key_principal_set (*Shishi_key* * `key`, *const char* *   [Function]
    `principal`)

key: structure that holds key information

principal: string with new principal name.

Set the principal owning the key. The string is copied into the key, so you can dispose of the variable immediately after calling this function.

shishi_key_realm

const char * shishi_key_realm (*const Shishi_key* * `key`)   [Function]

key: structure that holds key information

Get the realm part of the key owner principal name.

Return value: Returns the realm for the principal owning the key. (Not a copy of it, so don't modify or deallocate it.)

shishi_key_realm_set

void shishi_key_realm_set (*Shishi_key* * `key`, *const char* * `realm`)   [Function]

key: structure that holds key information

realm: string with new realm name.

Set the realm for the principal owning the key. The string is copied into the key, so you can dispose of the variable immediately after calling this function.

shishi_key_type

int shishi_key_type (*const Shishi_key* * `key`)   [Function]

key: structure that holds key information

Get key type.

Return value: Returns the type of key as an integer as described in the standard.

shishi_key_type_set

void shishi_key_type_set (*Shishi_key* * `key`, *int32_t* `type`)   [Function]

key: structure that holds key information

type: type to set in key.

Set the type of key in key structure.

shishi_key_value

const char * shishi_key_value (*const Shishi_key* * `key`)   [Function]

key: structure that holds key information

Get the raw key bytes.

Return value: Returns the key value as a pointer which is valid throughout the lifetime of the key structure.

shishi_key_value_set

void shishi_key_value_set (*Shishi_key* * **key**, *const char* * **value**)   [Function]
  key: structure that holds key information

  value: input array with key data.

  Set the key value and length in key structure. The value is copied into the key (in other words, you can deallocate **value** right after calling this function without modifying the value inside the key).

shishi_key_version

uint32_t shishi_key_version (*const Shishi_key* * **key**)   [Function]
  key: structure that holds key information

  Get the "kvno" (key version) of key. It will be UINT32_MAX if the key is not long-lived.

  Return value: Returns the version of key ("kvno").

shishi_key_version_set

void shishi_key_version_set (*Shishi_key* * **key**, *uint32_t kvno*)   [Function]
  key: structure that holds key information

  kvno: new version integer.

  Set the version of key ("kvno") in key structure. Use UINT32_MAX for non-ptermanent keys.

shishi_key_timestamp

time_t shishi_key_timestamp (*const Shishi_key* * **key**)   [Function]
  key: structure that holds key information

  Get the time the key was established. Typically only present when the key was imported from a keytab format.

  Return value: Returns the time the key was established, or (time_t)-1 if not available.

  Since: 0.0.42

shishi_key_timestamp_set

void shishi_key_timestamp_set (*Shishi_key* * **key**, *time_t* **timestamp**)   [Function]
  key: structure that holds key information

  timestamp: new timestamp.

  Set the time the key was established. Typically only relevant when exporting the key to keytab format.

  Since: 0.0.42

shishi_key_name

const char * shishi_key_name (*Shishi_key* * **key**)   [Function]
> *key*: structure that holds key information
>
> Calls shishi_cipher_name for key type.
>
> **Return value:** Return name of key.

shishi_key_length

size_t shishi_key_length (*const Shishi_key* * **key**)   [Function]
> *key*: structure that holds key information
>
> Calls shishi_cipher_keylen for key type.
>
> **Return value:** Returns the length of the key value.

shishi_key

int shishi_key (*Shishi* * **handle**, *Shishi_key* ** **key**)   [Function]
> *handle*: Shishi library handle create by shishi_init().
>
> *key*: pointer to structure that will hold newly created key information
>
> Create a new Key information structure.
>
> **Return value:** Returns SHISHI_OK iff successful.

shishi_key_done

void shishi_key_done (*Shishi_key* * **key**)   [Function]
> *key*: pointer to structure that holds key information.
>
> Deallocates key information structure.

shishi_key_copy

void shishi_key_copy (*Shishi_key* * **dstkey**, *Shishi_key* * **srckey**)   [Function]
> *dstkey*: structure that holds destination key information
>
> *srckey*: structure that holds source key information
>
> Copies source key into existing allocated destination key.

shishi_key_from_value

int shishi_key_from_value (*Shishi* * **handle**, *int32_t* **type**, const   [Function]
        char * **value**, *Shishi_key* ** **key**)
> *handle*: Shishi library handle create by shishi_init().
>
> *type*: type of key.
>
> *value*: input array with key value, or NULL.
>
> *key*: pointer to structure that will hold newly created key information
>
> Create a new Key information structure, and set the key type and key value. KEY contains a newly allocated structure only if this function is successful.
>
> **Return value:** Returns SHISHI_OK iff successful.

shishi_key_from_base64

int shishi_key_from_base64 (*Shishi * handle*, *int32_t type*, *const*   [Function]
     char * value, *Shishi_key ** key*)
> *handle*: Shishi library handle create by shishi_init().
>
> *type*: type of key.
>
> *value*: input string with base64 encoded key value, or NULL.
>
> *key*: pointer to structure that will hold newly created key information
>
> Create a new Key information structure, and set the key type and key value. KEY contains a newly allocated structure only if this function is successful.
>
> **Return value:** Returns SHISHI_INVALID_KEY if the base64 encoded key length doesn't match the key type, and SHISHI_OK on success.

shishi_key_random

int shishi_key_random (*Shishi * handle*, *int32_t type*, *Shishi_key ***   [Function]
     key)
> *handle*: Shishi library handle create by shishi_init().
>
> *type*: type of key.
>
> *key*: pointer to structure that will hold newly created key information
>
> Create a new Key information structure for the key type and some random data. KEY contains a newly allocated structure only if this function is successful.
>
> **Return value:** Returns SHISHI_OK iff successful.

shishi_key_from_random

int shishi_key_from_random (*Shishi * handle*, *int32_t type*, *const*   [Function]
     char * rnd, *size_t rndlen*, *Shishi_key ** outkey*)
> *handle*: Shishi library handle create by shishi_init().
>
> *type*: type of key.
>
> *rnd*: random data.
>
> *rndlen*: length of random data.
>
> *outkey*: pointer to structure that will hold newly created key information
>
> Create a new Key information structure, and set the key type and key value using shishi_random_to_key(). KEY contains a newly allocated structure only if this function is successful.
>
> **Return value:** Returns SHISHI_OK iff successful.

shishi_key_from_string

int shishi_key_from_string (*Shishi * handle*, *int32_t type*, *const*   [Function]
     char * password, *size_t passwordlen*, *const char * salt*, *size_t saltlen*,
     const char * parameter, *Shishi_key ** outkey*)
> *handle*: Shishi library handle create by shishi_init().
>
> *type*: type of key.

password: input array containing password.

passwordlen: length of input array containing password.

salt: input array containing salt.

saltlen: length of input array containing salt.

parameter: input array with opaque encryption type specific information.

outkey: pointer to structure that will hold newly created key information

Create a new Key information structure, and set the key type and key value using `shishi_string_to_key()`. KEY contains a newly allocated structure only if this function is successful.

Return value: Returns SHISHI_OK iff successful.

shishi_key_from_name

int **shishi_key_from_name** (*Shishi * **handle**, *int32_t* **type**, *const char*   [Function]
      * **name**, *const char * **password**, *size_t* **passwordlen**, *const char * *
      parameter, *Shishi_key ** **outkey**)
      handle: Shishi library handle create by `shishi_init()`.

type: type of key.

name: principal name of user.

password: input array containing password.

passwordlen: length of input array containing password.

parameter: input array with opaque encryption type specific information.

outkey: pointer to structure that will hold newly created key information

Create a new Key information structure, and derive the key from principal name and password using `shishi_key_from_name()`. The salt is derived from the principal name by concatenating the decoded realm and principal.

Return value: Returns SHISHI_OK iff successful.

Applications that run uninteractively may need keying material. In these cases, the keys are stored in a file, a file that is normally stored on the local host. The file should be protected from unauthorized access. The file is in ASCII format and contains keys as outputed by `shishi_key_print`. All functions that handle these keys sets are described now.

shishi_keys

int **shishi_keys** (*Shishi * **handle**, *Shishi_keys ** **keys**)   [Function]
      handle: shishi handle as allocated by `shishi_init()`.

keys: output pointer to newly allocated keys handle.

Get a new key set handle.

Return value: Returns `SHISHI_OK` iff successful.

shishi_keys_done

void shishi_keys_done (*Shishi_keys* ** *keys*)   [Function]

> *keys*: key set handle as allocated by shishi_keys().

> Deallocates all resources associated with key set. The key set handle must not be used in calls to other shishi_keys_*() functions after this.

shishi_keys_size

int shishi_keys_size (*Shishi_keys* * *keys*)   [Function]

> *keys*: key set handle as allocated by shishi_keys().

> Get size of key set.

> **Return value:** Returns number of keys stored in key set.

shishi_keys_nth

const Shishi_key * shishi_keys_nth (*Shishi_keys* * *keys*, *int*   [Function]
    keyno)

> *keys*: key set handle as allocated by shishi_keys().

> *keyno*: integer indicating requested key in key set.

> **Get the n:** th ticket in key set.

> **Return value:** Returns a key handle to the keyno:th key in the key set, or NULL if keys is invalid or keyno is out of bounds. The first key is keyno 0, the second key keyno 1, and so on.

shishi_keys_remove

void shishi_keys_remove (*Shishi_keys* * *keys*, *int keyno*)   [Function]

> *keys*: key set handle as allocated by shishi_keys().

> *keyno*: key number of key in the set to remove. The first key is key number 0.

> Remove a key, indexed by keyno, in given key set.

shishi_keys_add

int shishi_keys_add (*Shishi_keys* * *keys*, *Shishi_key* * *key*) [Function]

> *keys*: key set handle as allocated by shishi_keys().

> *key*: key to be added to key set.

> Add a key to the key set. A deep copy of the key is stored, so changing key, or deallocating it, will not modify the value stored in the key set.

> **Return value:** Returns SHISHI_OK iff successful.

shishi_keys_print

int shishi_keys_print (*Shishi_keys* * *keys*, *FILE* * *fh*)   [Function]

> *keys*: key set to print.

> *fh*: file handle, open for writing, to print keys to.

> Print all keys in set using shishi_key_print.

> **Returns:** Returns SHISHI_OK on success.

shishi_keys_to_file

int shishi_keys_to_file (*Shishi* * `handle`, *const char* * `filename`,   [Function]
    Shishi_keys * `keys`)

handle: shishi handle as allocated by `shishi_init()`.

filename: filename to append key to.

keys: set of keys to print.

Print an ASCII representation of a key structure to a file, for each key in the key set.
The file is appended to if it exists. See `shishi_key_print()` for the format of the
output.

Return value: Returns `SHISHI_OK` iff successful.

shishi_keys_from_file

int shishi_keys_from_file (*Shishi_keys* * `keys`, *const char* *   [Function]
    `filename`)

keys: key set handle as allocated by `shishi_keys()`.

filename: filename to read keys from.

Read zero or more keys from file `filename` and append them to the keyset `keys`. See
`shishi_key_print()` for the format of the input.

Return value: Returns `SHISHI_OK` iff successful.

Since: 0.0.42

shishi_keys_for_serverrealm_in_file

Shishi_key * shishi_keys_for_serverrealm_in_file (*Shishi* *   [Function]
    `handle`, *const char* * `filename`, *const char* * `server`, *const char* * `realm`)

handle: Shishi library handle create by `shishi_init()`.

filename: file to read keys from.

server: server name to get key for.

realm: realm of server to get key for.

Get keys that match specified `server` and `realm` from the key set file `filename`.

Return value: Returns the key for specific server and realm, read from the indicated
file, or NULL if no key could be found or an error encountered.

shishi_keys_for_server_in_file

Shishi_key * shishi_keys_for_server_in_file (*Shishi* * `handle`,   [Function]
    const char * `filename`, *const char* * `server`)

handle: Shishi library handle create by `shishi_init()`.

filename: file to read keys from.

server: server name to get key for.

Get key for specified `server` from `filename`.

Return value: Returns the key for specific server, read from the indicated file, or
NULL if no key could be found or an error encountered.

shishi_keys_for_localservicerealm_in_file

Shishi_key * shishi_keys_for_localservicerealm_in_file   [Function]
    (*Shishi* * `handle`, *const char* * `filename`, *const char* * `service`, *const char* *
    `realm`)

    handle: Shishi library handle create by `shishi_init()`.

    filename: file to read keys from.

    service: service to get key for.

    realm: realm of server to get key for, or NULL for default realm.

    Get key for specified `service` and `realm` from `filename`.

    Return value: Returns the key for the server "SERVICE/HOSTNAMEREALM" (where
    HOSTNAME is the current system's hostname), read from the default host keys file
    (see `shishi_hostkeys_default_file()`), or NULL if no key could be found or an
    error encountered.

The previous functions require that the filename is known. For some applications,
servers, it makes sense to provide a system default. These key sets used by server applications are known as "hostkeys". Here are the functions that operate on hostkeys (they
are mostly wrappers around generic key sets).

shishi_hostkeys_default_file

const char * shishi_hostkeys_default_file (*Shishi* * `handle`)   [Function]
    handle: Shishi library handle create by `shishi_init()`.

    Get file name of default host key file.

    Return value: Returns the default host key filename used in the library. (Not a copy
    of it, so don't modify or deallocate it.)

shishi_hostkeys_default_file_set

void shishi_hostkeys_default_file_set (*Shishi* * `handle`, *const*   [Function]
    char * `hostkeysfile`)

    handle: Shishi library handle create by `shishi_init()`.

    hostkeysfile: string with new default hostkeys file name, or NULL to reset to default.

    Set the default host key filename used in the library. The string is copied into the
    library, so you can dispose of the variable immediately after calling this function.

shishi_hostkeys_for_server

Shishi_key * shishi_hostkeys_for_server (*Shishi* * `handle`, *const*   [Function]
    char * `server`)

    handle: Shishi library handle create by `shishi_init()`.

    server: server name to get key for

    Get host key for `server`.

    Return value: Returns the key for specific server, read from the default host keys file
    (see `shishi_hostkeys_default_file()`), or NULL if no key could be found or an
    error encountered.

shishi_hostkeys_for_serverrealm

Shishi_key * shishi_hostkeys_for_serverrealm (*Shishi * *   [Function]
    handle, *const char * * **server**, *const char * * **realm**)
> *handle*: Shishi library handle create by `shishi_init()`.
>
> *server*: server name to get key for
>
> *realm*: realm of server to get key for.
>
> Get host key for `server` in `realm`.
>
> **Return value:** Returns the key for specific server and realm, read from the default host keys file (see `shishi_hostkeys_default_file()`), or NULL if no key could be found or an error encountered.

shishi_hostkeys_for_localservicerealm

Shishi_key * shishi_hostkeys_for_localservicerealm (*Shishi * *   [Function]
    handle, *const char * * **service**, *const char * * **realm**)
> *handle*: Shishi library handle create by `shishi_init()`.
>
> *service*: service to get key for.
>
> *realm*: realm of server to get key for, or NULL for default realm.
>
> Get host key for `service` on current host in `realm`.
>
> **Return value:** Returns the key for the server "SERVICE/HOSTNAMEREALM" (where HOSTNAME is the current system's hostname), read from the default host keys file (see `shishi_hostkeys_default_file()`), or NULL if no key could be found or an error encountered.

shishi_hostkeys_for_localservice

Shishi_key * shishi_hostkeys_for_localservice (*Shishi * *   [Function]
    handle, *const char * * **service**)
> *handle*: Shishi library handle create by `shishi_init()`.
>
> *service*: service to get key for.
>
> Get host key for `service` on current host in default realm.
>
> **Return value:** Returns the key for the server "SERVICE/HOSTNAME" (where HOSTNAME is the current system's hostname), read from the default host keys file (see `shishi_hostkeys_default_file()`), or NULL if no key could be found or an error encountered.

After creating the key structure, it can be used to encrypt and decrypt data, calculate checksum on data etc. All available functions are described now.

shishi_cipher_supported_p

int shishi_cipher_supported_p (*int32_t* **type**)   [Function]
> *type*: encryption type, see Shishi_etype.
>
> Find out if cipher is supported.
>
> **Return value:** Return 0 iff cipher is unsupported.

shishi_cipher_name

const char * shishi_cipher_name (*int32_t type*)   [Function]
> *type*: encryption type, see Shishi_etype.
>
> Read humanly readable string for cipher.
>
> **Return value:** Return name of encryption type, e.g. "des3-cbc-sha1-kd", as defined in the standards.

shishi_cipher_blocksize

int shishi_cipher_blocksize (*int32_t type*)   [Function]
> *type*: encryption type, see Shishi_etype.
>
> Get block size for cipher.
>
> **Return value:** Return block size for encryption type, as defined in the standards.

shishi_cipher_confoundersize

int shishi_cipher_confoundersize (*int32_t type*)   [Function]
> *type*: encryption type, see Shishi_etype.
>
> Get length of confounder for cipher.
>
> **Return value:** Returns the size of the confounder (random data) for encryption type, as defined in the standards, or (size_t)-1 on error (e.g., unsupported encryption type).

shishi_cipher_keylen

size_t shishi_cipher_keylen (*int32_t type*)   [Function]
> *type*: encryption type, see Shishi_etype.
>
> Get key length for cipher.
>
> **Return value:** Return length of key used for the encryption type, as defined in the standards.

shishi_cipher_randomlen

size_t shishi_cipher_randomlen (*int32_t type*)   [Function]
> *type*: encryption type, see Shishi_etype.
>
> Get length of random data for cipher.
>
> **Return value:** Return length of random used for the encryption type, as defined in the standards, or (size_t)-1 on error (e.g., unsupported encryption type).

shishi_cipher_defaultcksumtype

int shishi_cipher_defaultcksumtype (*int32_t type*)   [Function]
> *type*: encryption type, see Shishi_etype.
>
> Get the default checksum associated with cipher.
>
> **Return value:** Return associated checksum mechanism for the encryption type, as defined in the standards.

shishi_cipher_parse

int shishi_cipher_parse (*const char* * `cipher`)   [Function]

    cipher: name of encryption type, e.g. "des3-cbc-sha1-kd".

    Get cipher number by parsing string.

    Return value: Return encryption type corresponding to a string.

shishi_checksum_supported_p

int shishi_checksum_supported_p (*int32_t* `type`)   [Function]

    type: checksum type, see Shishi_cksumtype.

    Find out whether checksum is supported.

    Return value: Return 0 iff checksum is unsupported.

shishi_checksum_name

const char * shishi_checksum_name (*int32_t* `type`)   [Function]

    type: checksum type, see Shishi_cksumtype.

    Get name of checksum.

    Return value: Return name of checksum type, e.g. "hmac-sha1-96-aes256", as defined in the standards.

shishi_checksum_cksumlen

size_t shishi_checksum_cksumlen (*int32_t* `type`)   [Function]

    type: checksum type, see Shishi_cksumtype.

    Get length of checksum output.

    Return value: Return length of checksum used for the checksum type, as defined in the standards.

shishi_checksum_parse

int shishi_checksum_parse (*const char* * `checksum`)   [Function]

    checksum: name of checksum type, e.g. "hmac-sha1-96-aes256".

    Get checksum number by parsing a string.

    Return value: Return checksum type, see Shishi_cksumtype, corresponding to a string.

shishi_string_to_key

int shishi_string_to_key (*Shishi* * `handle`, *int32_t* `keytype`, *const*   [Function]
    char * `password`, *size_t* `passwordlen`, *const char* * `salt`, *size_t* `saltlen`,
    const char * `parameter`, *Shishi_key* * `outkey`)

    handle: shishi handle as allocated by `shishi_init`().

    keytype: cryptographic encryption type, see Shishi_etype.

    password: input array with password.

passwordlen: length of input array with password.

salt: input array with salt.

saltlen: length of input array with salt.

parameter: input array with opaque encryption type specific information.

outkey: allocated key handle that will contain new key.

Derive key from a string (password) and salt (commonly concatenation of realm and principal) for specified key type, and set the type and value in the given key to the computed values. The parameter value is specific for each keytype, and can be set if the parameter information is not available.

Return value: Returns `SHISHI_OK` iff successful.

shishi_random_to_key

int **shishi_random_to_key** (*Shishi* * **handle**, *int32_t* **keytype**, *const*   [Function]
    char * **rnd**, *size_t* **rndlen**, *Shishi_key* * **outkey**)
handle: shishi handle as allocated by `shishi_init()`.

keytype: cryptographic encryption type, see Shishi_etype.

rnd: input array with random data.

rndlen: length of input array with random data.

outkey: allocated key handle that will contain new key.

Derive key from random data for specified key type, and set the type and value in the given key to the computed values.

Return value: Returns `SHISHI_OK` iff successful.

shishi_checksum

int **shishi_checksum** (*Shishi* * **handle**, *Shishi_key* * **key**, *int*   [Function]
    keyusage, *int* **cksumtype**, *const char* * **in**, *size_t* **inlen**, *char* ** **out**, *size_t* *
    outlen)
handle: shishi handle as allocated by `shishi_init()`.

key: key to compute checksum with.

keyusage: integer specifying what this key is used for.

cksumtype: the checksum algorithm to use.

in: input array with data to integrity protect.

inlen: size of input array with data to integrity protect.

out: output array with newly allocated integrity protected data.

outlen: output variable with length of output array with checksum.

Integrity protect data using key, possibly altered by supplied key usage. If key usage is 0, no key derivation is used. The OUT buffer must be deallocated by the caller.

Return value: Returns `SHISHI_OK` iff successful.

shishi_verify

int shishi_verify (*Shishi* * *handle*, *Shishi_key* * *key*, *int* keyusage,   [Function]
     int cksumtype, *const char* * in, *size_t* inlen, *const char* * cksum, *size_t*
     cksumlen)
> *handle*: shishi handle as allocated by shishi_init().
>
> *key*: key to verify checksum with.
>
> *keyusage*: integer specifying what this key is used for.
>
> *cksumtype*: the checksum algorithm to use.
>
> *in*: input array with data that was integrity protected.
>
> *inlen*: size of input array with data that was integrity protected.
>
> *cksum*: input array with alleged checksum of data.
>
> *cksumlen*: size of input array with alleged checksum of data.
>
> Verify checksum of data using key, possibly altered by supplied key usage. If key usage is 0, no key derivation is used.
>
> **Return value:** Returns SHISHI_OK iff successful.

shishi_encrypt_ivupdate_etype

int shishi_encrypt_ivupdate_etype (*Shishi* * *handle*, *Shishi_key* *   [Function]
     key, *int* keyusage, *int32_t* etype, *const char* * iv, *size_t* ivlen, *char* **
     ivout, *size_t* * ivoutlen, *const char* * in, *size_t* inlen, *char* ** out, *size_t* *
     outlen)
> *handle*: shishi handle as allocated by shishi_init().
>
> *key*: key to encrypt with.
>
> *keyusage*: integer specifying what this key is encrypting.
>
> *etype*: integer specifying what cipher to use.
>
> *iv*: input array with initialization vector
>
> *ivlen*: size of input array with initialization vector.
>
> *ivout*: output array with newly allocated updated initialization vector.
>
> *ivoutlen*: size of output array with updated initialization vector.
>
> *in*: input array with data to encrypt.
>
> *inlen*: size of input array with data to encrypt.
>
> *out*: output array with newly allocated encrypted data.
>
> *outlen*: output variable with size of newly allocated output array.
>
> Encrypts data as per encryption method using specified initialization vector and key. The key actually used is derived using the key usage. If key usage is 0, no key derivation is used. The OUT buffer must be deallocated by the caller. If IVOUT or IVOUTLEN is NULL, the updated IV is not saved anywhere.
>
> Note that DECRYPT(ENCRYPT(data)) does not necessarily yield data exactly. Some encryption types add pad to make the data fit into the block size of the encryption algorithm. Furthermore, the pad is not guaranteed to look in any special

way, although existing implementations often pad with the zero byte. This means that you may have to "frame" data, so it is possible to infer the original length after decryption. Compare ASN.1 DER which contains such information.

Return value: Returns `SHISHI_OK` iff successful.

shishi_encrypt_iv_etype

int shishi_encrypt_iv_etype (*Shishi* * `handle`, *Shishi_key* * `key`, *int*   [Function]
    `keyusage`, *int32_t* `etype`, *const char* * `iv`, *size_t* `ivlen`, *const char* * `in`,
    size_t `inlen`, *char* ** `out`, *size_t* * `outlen`)

handle: shishi handle as allocated by `shishi_init()`.

key: key to encrypt with.

keyusage: integer specifying what this key is encrypting.

etype: integer specifying what cipher to use.

iv: input array with initialization vector

ivlen: size of input array with initialization vector.

in: input array with data to encrypt.

inlen: size of input array with data to encrypt.

out: output array with newly allocated encrypted data.

outlen: output variable with size of newly allocated output array.

Encrypts data as per encryption method using specified initialization vector and key. The key actually used is derived using the key usage. If key usage is 0, no key derivation is used. The OUT buffer must be deallocated by the caller. The next IV is lost, see shishi_encrypt_ivupdate_etype if you need it.

Note that DECRYPT(ENCRYPT(data)) does not necessarily yield data exactly. Some encryption types add pad to make the data fit into the block size of the encryption algorithm. Furthermore, the pad is not guaranteed to look in any special way, although existing implementations often pad with the zero byte. This means that you may have to "frame" data, so it is possible to infer the original length after decryption. Compare ASN.1 DER which contains such information.

Return value: Returns `SHISHI_OK` iff successful.

shishi_encrypt_etype

int shishi_encrypt_etype (*Shishi* * `handle`, *Shishi_key* * `key`, *int*   [Function]
    `keyusage`, *int32_t* `etype`, *const char* * `in`, *size_t* `inlen`, *char* ** `out`, *size_t* *
    `outlen`)

handle: shishi handle as allocated by `shishi_init()`.

key: key to encrypt with.

keyusage: integer specifying what this key is encrypting.

etype: integer specifying what cipher to use.

in: input array with data to encrypt.

inlen: size of input array with data to encrypt.

out: output array with newly allocated encrypted data.

outlen: output variable with size of newly allocated output array.

Encrypts data as per encryption method using specified initialization vector and key. The key actually used is derived using the key usage. If key usage is 0, no key derivation is used. The OUT buffer must be deallocated by the caller. The default IV is used, see shishi_encrypt_iv_etype if you need to alter it. The next IV is lost, see shishi_encrypt_ivupdate_etype if you need it.

Note that DECRYPT(ENCRYPT(data)) does not necessarily yield data exactly. Some encryption types add pad to make the data fit into the block size of the encryption algorithm. Furthermore, the pad is not guaranteed to look in any special way, although existing implementations often pad with the zero byte. This means that you may have to "frame" data, so it is possible to infer the original length after decryption. Compare ASN.1 DER which contains such information.

Return value: Returns `SHISHI_OK` iff successful.

shishi_encrypt_ivupdate

int shishi_encrypt_ivupdate (*Shishi* * `handle`, *Shishi_key* * `key`, *int*   [Function]
    `keyusage`, *const char* * `iv`, *size_t* `ivlen`, *char* ** `ivout`, *size_t* * `ivoutlen`,
    const char * `in`, *size_t* `inlen`, *char* ** `out`, *size_t* * `outlen`)
handle: shishi handle as allocated by `shishi_init()`.

key: key to encrypt with.

keyusage: integer specifying what this key is encrypting.

iv: input array with initialization vector

ivlen: size of input array with initialization vector.

ivout: output array with newly allocated updated initialization vector.

ivoutlen: size of output array with updated initialization vector.

in: input array with data to encrypt.

inlen: size of input array with data to encrypt.

out: output array with newly allocated encrypted data.

outlen: output variable with size of newly allocated output array.

Encrypts data using specified initialization vector and key. The key actually used is derived using the key usage. If key usage is 0, no key derivation is used. The OUT buffer must be deallocated by the caller. If IVOUT or IVOUTLEN is NULL, the updated IV is not saved anywhere.

Note that DECRYPT(ENCRYPT(data)) does not necessarily yield data exactly. Some encryption types add pad to make the data fit into the block size of the encryption algorithm. Furthermore, the pad is not guaranteed to look in any special way, although existing implementations often pad with the zero byte. This means that you may have to "frame" data, so it is possible to infer the original length after decryption. Compare ASN.1 DER which contains such information.

Return value: Returns `SHISHI_OK` iff successful.

shishi_encrypt_iv

int **shishi_encrypt_iv** (*Shishi* * `handle`, *Shishi_key* * `key`, *int*   [Function]
    keyusage, *const char* * `iv`, *size_t* `ivlen`, *const char* * `in`, *size_t* `inlen`, *char*
    ** `out`, *size_t* * `outlen`)

handle: shishi handle as allocated by `shishi_init()`.

key: key to encrypt with.

keyusage: integer specifying what this key is encrypting.

iv: input array with initialization vector

ivlen: size of input array with initialization vector.

in: input array with data to encrypt.

inlen: size of input array with data to encrypt.

out: output array with newly allocated encrypted data.

outlen: output variable with size of newly allocated output array.

Encrypts data using specified initialization vector and key. The key actually used is derived using the key usage. If key usage is 0, no key derivation is used. The OUT buffer must be deallocated by the caller. The next IV is lost, see shishi_encrypt_ivupdate if you need it.

Note that DECRYPT(ENCRYPT(data)) does not necessarily yield data exactly. Some encryption types add pad to make the data fit into the block size of the encryption algorithm. Furthermore, the pad is not guaranteed to look in any special way, although existing implementations often pad with the zero byte. This means that you may have to "frame" data, so it is possible to infer the original length after decryption. Compare ASN.1 DER which contains such information.

Return value: Returns `SHISHI_OK` iff successful.

shishi_encrypt

int **shishi_encrypt** (*Shishi* * `handle`, *Shishi_key* * `key`, *int* `keyusage`,   [Function]
    char * `in`, *size_t* `inlen`, *char* ** `out`, *size_t* * `outlen`)

handle: shishi handle as allocated by `shishi_init()`.

key: key to encrypt with.

keyusage: integer specifying what this key is encrypting.

in: input array with data to encrypt.

inlen: size of input array with data to encrypt.

out: output array with newly allocated encrypted data.

outlen: output variable with size of newly allocated output array.

Encrypts data using specified key. The key actually used is derived using the key usage. If key usage is 0, no key derivation is used. The OUT buffer must be deallocated by the caller. The default IV is used, see shishi_encrypt_iv if you need to alter it. The next IV is lost, see shishi_encrypt_ivupdate if you need it.

Note that DECRYPT(ENCRYPT(data)) does not necessarily yield data exactly. Some encryption types add pad to make the data fit into the block size of the encryption algorithm. Furthermore, the pad is not guaranteed to look in any special way, although existing implementations often pad with the zero byte. This means that you may have to "frame" data, so it is possible to infer the original length after decryption. Compare ASN.1 DER which contains such information.

Return value: Returns `SHISHI_OK` iff successful.

shishi_decrypt_ivupdate_etype

`int shishi_decrypt_ivupdate_etype` (*Shishi* * `handle`, *Shishi_key* *   [Function] `key`, *int* `keyusage`, *int32_t* `etype`, *const char* * `iv`, *size_t* `ivlen`, *char* ** `ivout`, *size_t* * `ivoutlen`, *const char* * `in`, *size_t* `inlen`, *char* ** `out`, *size_t* * `outlen`)

handle: shishi handle as allocated by `shishi_init()`.

key: key to decrypt with.

keyusage: integer specifying what this key is decrypting.

etype: integer specifying what cipher to use.

iv: input array with initialization vector

ivlen: size of input array with initialization vector.

ivout: output array with newly allocated updated initialization vector.

ivoutlen: size of output array with updated initialization vector.

in: input array with data to decrypt.

inlen: size of input array with data to decrypt.

out: output array with newly allocated decrypted data.

outlen: output variable with size of newly allocated output array.

Decrypts data as per encryption method using specified initialization vector and key. The key actually used is derived using the key usage. If key usage is 0, no key derivation is used. The OUT buffer must be deallocated by the caller. If IVOUT or IVOUTLEN is NULL, the updated IV is not saved anywhere.

Note that DECRYPT(ENCRYPT(data)) does not necessarily yield data exactly. Some encryption types add pad to make the data fit into the block size of the encryption algorithm. Furthermore, the pad is not guaranteed to look in any special way, although existing implementations often pad with the zero byte. This means that you may have to "frame" data, so it is possible to infer the original length after decryption. Compare ASN.1 DER which contains such information.

Return value: Returns `SHISHI_OK` iff successful.

shishi_decrypt_iv_etype

`int shishi_decrypt_iv_etype` (*Shishi* * `handle`, *Shishi_key* * `key`, *int*   [Function] `keyusage`, *int32_t* `etype`, *const char* * `iv`, *size_t* `ivlen`, *const char* * `in`, *size_t* `inlen`, *char* ** `out`, *size_t* * `outlen`)

handle: shishi handle as allocated by `shishi_init()`.

key: key to decrypt with.

keyusage: integer specifying what this key is decrypting.

etype: integer specifying what cipher to use.

iv: input array with initialization vector

ivlen: size of input array with initialization vector.

in: input array with data to decrypt.

inlen: size of input array with data to decrypt.

out: output array with newly allocated decrypted data.

outlen: output variable with size of newly allocated output array.

Decrypts data as per encryption method using specified initialization vector and key. The key actually used is derived using the key usage. If key usage is 0, no key derivation is used. The OUT buffer must be deallocated by the caller. The next IV is lost, see shishi_decrypt_ivupdate_etype if you need it.

Note that DECRYPT(ENCRYPT(data)) does not necessarily yield data exactly. Some encryption types add pad to make the data fit into the block size of the encryption algorithm. Furthermore, the pad is not guaranteed to look in any special way, although existing implementations often pad with the zero byte. This means that you may have to "frame" data, so it is possible to infer the original length after decryption. Compare ASN.1 DER which contains such information.

Return value: Returns `SHISHI_OK` iff successful.

shishi_decrypt_etype

int shishi_decrypt_etype (*Shishi * `handle`, Shishi_key * `key`, int*   [Function]
    `keyusage`, *int32_t* `etype`, *const char * `in`, size_t `inlen`, char ** `out`, size_t *
    `outlen`)

handle: shishi handle as allocated by `shishi_init()`.

key: key to decrypt with.

keyusage: integer specifying what this key is decrypting.

etype: integer specifying what cipher to use.

in: input array with data to decrypt.

inlen: size of input array with data to decrypt.

out: output array with newly allocated decrypted data.

outlen: output variable with size of newly allocated output array.

Decrypts data as per encryption method using specified key. The key actually used is derived using the key usage. If key usage is 0, no key derivation is used. The OUT buffer must be deallocated by the caller. The default IV is used, see shishi_decrypt_iv_etype if you need to alter it. The next IV is lost, see shishi_decrypt_ivupdate_etype if you need it.

Note that DECRYPT(ENCRYPT(data)) does not necessarily yield data exactly. Some encryption types add pad to make the data fit into the block size of the encryption algorithm. Furthermore, the pad is not guaranteed to look in any special way, although existing implementations often pad with the zero byte. This means that you may have to "frame" data, so it is possible to infer the original length after decryption. Compare ASN.1 DER which contains such information.

Return value: Returns `SHISHI_OK` iff successful.

shishi_decrypt_ivupdate

int shishi_decrypt_ivupdate (*Shishi* * `handle`, *Shishi_key* * `key`, *int*   [Function]
     `keyusage`, *const char* * `iv`, *size_t* `ivlen`, *char* ** `ivout`, *size_t* * `ivoutlen`,
     const char * `in`, *size_t* `inlen`, *char* ** `out`, *size_t* * `outlen`)

handle: shishi handle as allocated by `shishi_init()`.

key: key to decrypt with.

keyusage: integer specifying what this key is decrypting.

iv: input array with initialization vector

ivlen: size of input array with initialization vector.

ivout: output array with newly allocated updated initialization vector.

ivoutlen: size of output array with updated initialization vector.

in: input array with data to decrypt.

inlen: size of input array with data to decrypt.

out: output array with newly allocated decrypted data.

outlen: output variable with size of newly allocated output array.

Decrypts data using specified initialization vector and key. The key actually used is derived using the key usage. If key usage is 0, no key derivation is used. The OUT buffer must be deallocated by the caller. If IVOUT or IVOUTLEN is NULL, the updated IV is not saved anywhere.

Note that DECRYPT(ENCRYPT(data)) does not necessarily yield data exactly. Some encryption types add pad to make the data fit into the block size of the encryption algorithm. Furthermore, the pad is not guaranteed to look in any special way, although existing implementations often pad with the zero byte. This means that you may have to "frame" data, so it is possible to infer the original length after decryption. Compare ASN.1 DER which contains such information.

Return value: Returns `SHISHI_OK` iff successful.

shishi_decrypt_iv

int shishi_decrypt_iv (*Shishi* * `handle`, *Shishi_key* * `key`, *int*   [Function]
     `keyusage`, *const char* * `iv`, *size_t* `ivlen`, *const char* * `in`, *size_t* `inlen`, *char*
     ** `out`, *size_t* * `outlen`)

handle: shishi handle as allocated by `shishi_init()`.

key: key to decrypt with.

keyusage: integer specifying what this key is decrypting.

iv: input array with initialization vector

ivlen: size of input array with initialization vector.

in: input array with data to decrypt.

inlen: size of input array with data to decrypt.

out: output array with newly allocated decrypted data.

outlen: output variable with size of newly allocated output array.

Decrypts data using specified initialization vector and key. The key actually used is derived using the key usage. If key usage is 0, no key derivation is used. The OUT buffer must be deallocated by the caller. The next IV is lost, see shishi_decrypt_ivupdate_etype if you need it.

Note that DECRYPT(ENCRYPT(data)) does not necessarily yield data exactly. Some encryption types add pad to make the data fit into the block size of the encryption algorithm. Furthermore, the pad is not guaranteed to look in any special way, although existing implementations often pad with the zero byte. This means that you may have to "frame" data, so it is possible to infer the original length after decryption. Compare ASN.1 DER which contains such information.

Return value: Returns `SHISHI_OK` iff successful.

shishi_decrypt

int **shishi_decrypt** (*Shishi* * `handle`, *Shishi_key* * `key`, *int* `keyusage`,   [Function]
      const char * `in`, *size_t* `inlen`, *char* ** `out`, *size_t* * `outlen`)
handle: shishi handle as allocated by `shishi_init()`.

key: key to decrypt with.

keyusage: integer specifying what this key is decrypting.

in: input array with data to decrypt.

inlen: size of input array with data to decrypt.

out: output array with newly allocated decrypted data.

outlen: output variable with size of newly allocated output array.

Decrypts data specified key. The key actually used is derived using the key usage. If key usage is 0, no key derivation is used. The OUT buffer must be deallocated by the caller. The default IV is used, see shishi_decrypt_iv if you need to alter it. The next IV is lost, see shishi_decrypt_ivupdate if you need it.

Note that DECRYPT(ENCRYPT(data)) does not necessarily yield data exactly. Some encryption types add pad to make the data fit into the block size of the encryption algorithm. Furthermore, the pad is not guaranteed to look in any special way, although existing implementations often pad with the zero byte. This means that you may have to "frame" data, so it is possible to infer the original length after decryption. Compare ASN.1 DER which contains such information.

Return value: Returns `SHISHI_OK` iff successful.

shishi_n_fold

int **shishi_n_fold** (*Shishi* * `handle`, *const char* * `in`, *size_t* `inlen`,   [Function]
      char * `out`, *size_t* `outlen`)
handle: shishi handle as allocated by `shishi_init()`.

in: input array with data to decrypt.

inlen: size of input array with data to decrypt ("M").

out: output array with decrypted data.

outlen: size of output array ("N").

Fold data into a fixed length output array, with the intent to give each input bit approximately equal weight in determining the value of each output bit.

The algorithm is from "A Better Key Schedule For DES-like Ciphers" by Uri Blumenthal and Steven M. Bellovin, http://www.research.att.com/~smb/papers/ides.pdf, although the sample vectors provided by the paper are incorrect.

Return value: Returns `SHISHI_OK` iff successful.

shishi_dr

`int shishi_dr` (*Shishi* * **handle**, *Shishi_key* * **key**, *const char* *   [Function]
    prfconstant, *size_t* **prfconstantlen**, *char* * **derivedrandom**, *size_t*
    derivedrandomlen)
handle: shishi handle as allocated by `shishi_init()`.

key: input array with cryptographic key to use.

prfconstant: input array with the constant string.

prfconstantlen: size of input array with the constant string.

derivedrandom: output array with derived random data.

derivedrandomlen: size of output array with derived random data.

Derive "random" data from a key and a constant thusly: DR(KEY, PRFCONSTANT) = TRUNCATE(DERIVEDRANDOMLEN, SHISHI_ENCRYPT(KEY, PRFCONSTANT)).

Return value: Returns `SHISHI_OK` iff successful.

shishi_dk

`int shishi_dk` (*Shishi* * **handle**, *Shishi_key* * **key**, *const char* *   [Function]
    prfconstant, *size_t* **prfconstantlen**, *Shishi_key* * **derivedkey**)
handle: shishi handle as allocated by `shishi_init()`.

key: input cryptographic key to use.

prfconstant: input array with the constant string.

prfconstantlen: size of input array with the constant string.

derivedkey: pointer to derived key (allocated by caller).

Derive a key from a key and a constant thusly: DK(KEY, PRFCONSTANT) = SHISHI_RANDOM-TO-KEY(SHISHI_DR(KEY, PRFCONSTANT)).

Return value: Returns `SHISHI_OK` iff successful.

An easier way to use encryption and decryption if your application repeatedly calls, e.g., `shishi_encrypt_ivupdate`, is to use the following functions. They store the key, initialization vector, etc, in a context, and the encryption and decryption operations update the IV within the context automatically.

shishi_crypto

Shishi_crypto * shishi_crypto (*Shishi * handle*, *Shishi_key * key*, [Function]
        int keyusage, *int32_t etype*, *const char * iv*, *size_t ivlen*)
handle: shishi handle as allocated by **shishi_init()**.

key: key to encrypt with.

keyusage: integer specifying what this key will encrypt/decrypt.

etype: integer specifying what cipher to use.

iv: input array with initialization vector

ivlen: size of input array with initialization vector.

Initialize a crypto context. This store a key, keyusage, encryption type and initialization vector in a "context", and the caller can then use this context to perform encryption via **shishi_crypto_encrypt()** and decryption via **shishi_crypto_encrypt()** without supplying all those details again. The functions also takes care of propagating the IV between calls.

When the application no longer need to use the context, it should deallocate resources associated with it by calling **shishi_crypto_close()**.

Return value: Return a newly allocated crypto context.

shishi_crypto_encrypt

int shishi_crypto_encrypt (*Shishi_crypto * ctx*, *const char * in*, [Function]
        size_t inlen, *char ** out*, *size_t * outlen*)
ctx: crypto context as returned by **shishi_crypto()**.

in: input array with data to encrypt.

inlen: size of input array with data to encrypt.

out: output array with newly allocated encrypted data.

outlen: output variable with size of newly allocated output array.

Encrypt data, using information (e.g., key and initialization vector) from context. The IV is updated inside the context after this call.

When the application no longer need to use the context, it should deallocate resources associated with it by calling **shishi_crypto_close()**.

Return value: Returns **SHISHI_OK** iff successful.

shishi_crypto_decrypt

int shishi_crypto_decrypt (*Shishi_crypto * ctx*, *const char * in*, [Function]
        size_t inlen, *char ** out*, *size_t * outlen*)
ctx: crypto context as returned by **shishi_crypto()**.

in: input array with data to decrypt.

inlen: size of input array with data to decrypt.

out: output array with newly allocated decrypted data.

outlen: output variable with size of newly allocated output array.

Decrypt data, using information (e.g., key and initialization vector) from context. The IV is updated inside the context after this call.

When the application no longer need to use the context, it should deallocate resources associated with it by calling `shishi_crypto_close()`.

Return value: Returns `SHISHI_OK` iff successful.

shishi_crypto_close

void **shishi_crypto_close** (*Shishi_crypto* * `ctx`)   [Function]
>   *ctx*: crypto context as returned by `shishi_crypto()`.
>
>   Deallocate resources associated with the crypto context.

Also included in Shishi is an interface to the really low-level cryptographic primitives. They map directly on the underlying cryptographic library used (i.e., Gnulib or Libgcrypt) and is used internally by Shishi.

shishi_randomize

int **shishi_randomize** (*Shishi* * `handle`, *int* `strong`, *void* * `data`,   [Function]
>   *size_t* `datalen`)
>   *handle*: shishi handle as allocated by `shishi_init()`.
>
>   *strong*: 0 iff operation should not block, non-0 for very strong randomness.
>
>   *data*: output array to be filled with random data.
>
>   *datalen*: size of output array.
>
>   Store cryptographically random data of given size in the provided buffer.
>
>   **Return value:** Returns `SHISHI_OK` iff successful.

shishi_crc

int **shishi_crc** (*Shishi* * `handle`, *const char* * `in`, *size_t* `inlen`, *char* *   [Function]
>   `out[4]`)
>   *handle*: shishi handle as allocated by `shishi_init()`.
>
>   *in*: input character array of data to checksum.
>
>   *inlen*: length of input character array of data to checksum.
>
>   Compute checksum of data using CRC32 modified according to RFC 1510. The `out` buffer must be deallocated by the caller.
>
>   The modifications compared to standard CRC32 is that no initial and final XOR is performed, and that the output is returned in LSB-first order.
>
>   **Return value:** Returns SHISHI_OK iff successful.

shishi_md4

int **shishi_md4** (*Shishi* * `handle`, *const char* * `in`, *size_t* `inlen`, *char* *   [Function]
>   `out[16]`)
>   *handle*: shishi handle as allocated by `shishi_init()`.
>
>   *in*: input character array of data to hash.

inlen: length of input character array of data to hash.

Compute hash of data using MD4. The `out` buffer must be deallocated by the caller.

Return value: Returns SHISHI_OK iff successful.

shishi_md5

int shishi_md5 (*Shishi * handle*, *const char * in*, *size_t inlen*, *char * *   [Function]
    out[16])
    handle: shishi handle as allocated by `shishi_init()`.

in: input character array of data to hash.

inlen: length of input character array of data to hash.

Compute hash of data using MD5. The `out` buffer must be deallocated by the caller.

Return value: Returns SHISHI_OK iff successful.

shishi_hmac_md5

int shishi_hmac_md5 (*Shishi * handle*, *const char * key*, *size_t*   [Function]
    keylen, *const char * in*, *size_t inlen*, *char * outhash[16]*)
    handle: shishi handle as allocated by `shishi_init()`.

key: input character array with key to use.

keylen: length of input character array with key to use.

in: input character array of data to hash.

inlen: length of input character array of data to hash.

Compute keyed checksum of data using HMAC-MD5. The `outhash` buffer must be deallocated by the caller.

Return value: Returns SHISHI_OK iff successful.

shishi_hmac_sha1

int shishi_hmac_sha1 (*Shishi * handle*, *const char * key*, *size_t*   [Function]
    keylen, *const char * in*, *size_t inlen*, *char * outhash[20]*)
    handle: shishi handle as allocated by `shishi_init()`.

key: input character array with key to use.

keylen: length of input character array with key to use.

in: input character array of data to hash.

inlen: length of input character array of data to hash.

Compute keyed checksum of data using HMAC-SHA1. The `outhash` buffer must be deallocated by the caller.

Return value: Returns SHISHI_OK iff successful.

shishi_des_cbc_mac

int shishi_des_cbc_mac (*Shishi * handle*, *const char* key[8], *const*   [Function]
    char iv[8], *const char * in*, *size_t* inlen, *char ** out[8])
> *handle*: shishi handle as allocated by shishi_init().
>
> *in*: input character array of data to hash.
>
> *inlen*: length of input character array of data to hash.
>
> Computed keyed checksum of data using DES-CBC-MAC. The out buffer must be deallocated by the caller.
>
> **Return value:** Returns SHISHI_OK iff successful.

shishi_arcfour

int shishi_arcfour (*Shishi * handle*, *int* decryptp, *const char * key*,   [Function]
    size_t keylen, *const char* iv[258], *char ** ivout[258], *const char * in*, *size_t*
    inlen, *char *** out)
> *handle*: shishi handle as allocated by shishi_init().
>
> *decryptp*: 0 to indicate encryption, non-0 to indicate decryption.
>
> *key*: input character array with key to use.
>
> *keylen*: length of input key array.
>
> *in*: input character array of data to encrypt/decrypt.
>
> *inlen*: length of input character array of data to encrypt/decrypt.
>
> *out*: newly allocated character array with encrypted/decrypted data.
>
> Encrypt or decrypt data (depending on decryptp) using ARCFOUR. The out buffer must be deallocated by the caller.
>
> The "initialization vector" used here is the concatenation of the sbox and i and j, and is thus always of size 256 + 1 + 1. This is a slight abuse of terminology, and assumes you know what you are doing. Don't use it if you can avoid to.
>
> **Return value:** Returns SHISHI_OK iff successful.

shishi_des

int shishi_des (*Shishi * handle*, *int* decryptp, *const char* key[8],   [Function]
    const char iv[8], *char ** ivout[8], *const char * in*, *size_t* inlen, *char *** out)
> *handle*: shishi handle as allocated by shishi_init().
>
> *decryptp*: 0 to indicate encryption, non-0 to indicate decryption.
>
> *in*: input character array of data to encrypt/decrypt.
>
> *inlen*: length of input character array of data to encrypt/decrypt.
>
> *out*: newly allocated character array with encrypted/decrypted data.
>
> Encrypt or decrypt data (depending on decryptp) using DES in CBC mode. The out buffer must be deallocated by the caller.
>
> **Return value:** Returns SHISHI_OK iff successful.

shishi_3des

int shishi_3des (*Shishi * handle*, *int decryptp*, *const char key*[*8*],   [Function]
    const char iv[*8*], *char * ivout*[*8*], *const char * in*, *size_t inlen*, *char ** out*)

handle: shishi handle as allocated by `shishi_init()`.

decryptp: 0 to indicate encryption, non-0 to indicate decryption.

in: input character array of data to encrypt/decrypt.

inlen: length of input character array of data to encrypt/decrypt.

out: newly allocated character array with encrypted/decrypted data.

Encrypt or decrypt data (depending on `decryptp`) using 3DES in CBC mode. The out buffer must be deallocated by the caller.

Return value: Returns SHISHI_OK iff successful.

shishi_aes_cts

int shishi_aes_cts (*Shishi * handle*, *int decryptp*, *const char * key*,   [Function]
    size_t keylen, *const char iv*[*16*], *char * ivout*[*16*], *const char * in*, *size_t*
    inlen, *char ** out*)

handle: shishi handle as allocated by `shishi_init()`.

decryptp: 0 to indicate encryption, non-0 to indicate decryption.

key: input character array with key to use.

keylen: length of input character array with key to use.

in: input character array of data to encrypt/decrypt.

inlen: length of input character array of data to encrypt/decrypt.

out: newly allocated character array with encrypted/decrypted data.

Encrypt or decrypt data (depending on `decryptp`) using AES in CBC-CTS mode. The length of the key, `keylen`, decide if AES 128 or AES 256 should be used. The out buffer must be deallocated by the caller.

Return value: Returns SHISHI_OK iff successful.

shishi_pbkdf2_sha1

int shishi_pbkdf2_sha1 (*Shishi * handle*, *const char * P*, *size_t Plen*,   [Function]
    *const char * S*, *size_t Slen*, *unsigned int c*, *unsigned int dkLen*, *char * DK*)

handle: shishi handle as allocated by `shishi_init()`.

P: input password, an octet string

Plen: length of password, an octet string

S: input salt, an octet string

Slen: length of salt, an octet string

c: iteration count, a positive integer

dkLen: intended length in octets of the derived key, a positive integer, at most $(2^{32} - 1) *$ hLen. The DK array must have room for this many characters.

DK: output derived key, a dkLen-octet string

Derive key using the PBKDF2 defined in PKCS5. PBKDF2 applies a pseudorandom function to derive keys. The length of the derived key is essentially unbounded. (However, the maximum effective search space for the derived key may be limited by the structure of the underlying pseudorandom function, which is this function is always SHA1.)

Return value: Returns SHISHI_OK iff successful.

5.14 X.509 Functions

The functions described in this section are used by the STARTTLS functionality, see Section 3.6 [Kerberos via TLS], page 26.

shishi_x509ca_default_file_guess

char * shishi_x509ca_default_file_guess (*Shishi * handle*)   [Function]
>   *handle*: Shishi library handle create by `shishi_init()`.

>   Guesses the default X.509 CA certificate filename; it is $HOME/.shishi/client.ca.

>   **Return value:** Returns default X.509 client certificate filename as a string that has to be deallocated with `free()` by the caller.

shishi_x509ca_default_file_set

void shishi_x509ca_default_file_set (*Shishi * handle, const char   [Function]
    * x509cafile*)
>   *handle*: Shishi library handle create by `shishi_init()`.

>   *x509cafile*: string with new default x509 client certificate file name, or NULL to reset to default.

>   Set the default X.509 CA certificate filename used in the library. The certificate is used during TLS connections with the KDC to authenticate the KDC. The string is copied into the library, so you can dispose of the variable immediately after calling this function.

shishi_x509ca_default_file

const char * shishi_x509ca_default_file (*Shishi * handle*)   [Function]
>   *handle*: Shishi library handle create by `shishi_init()`.

>   Get filename for default X.509 CA certificate.

>   **Return value:** Returns the default X.509 CA certificate filename used in the library. The certificate is used during TLS connections with the KDC to authenticate the KDC. The string is not a copy, so don't modify or deallocate it.

shishi_x509cert_default_file_guess

char * shishi_x509cert_default_file_guess (*Shishi * handle*)   [Function]
>   *handle*: Shishi library handle create by `shishi_init()`.

>   Guesses the default X.509 client certificate filename; it is $HOME/.shishi/client.certs.

>   **Return value:** Returns default X.509 client certificate filename as a string that has to be deallocated with `free()` by the caller.

shishi_x509cert_default_file_set

void shishi_x509cert_default_file_set (*Shishi* * *handle*, *const*   [Function]
    char * *x509certfile*)
>   *handle*: Shishi library handle create by shishi_init().

>   *x509certfile*: string with new default x509 client certificate file name, or NULL to reset to default.

>   Set the default X.509 client certificate filename used in the library. The certificate is used during TLS connections with the KDC to authenticate the client. The string is copied into the library, so you can dispose of the variable immediately after calling this function.

shishi_x509cert_default_file

const char * shishi_x509cert_default_file (*Shishi* * *handle*)   [Function]
>   *handle*: Shishi library handle create by shishi_init().

>   Get filename for default X.509 certificate.

>   **Return value:** Returns the default X.509 client certificate filename used in the library. The certificate is used during TLS connections with the KDC to authenticate the client. The string is not a copy, so don't modify or deallocate it.

shishi_x509key_default_file_guess

char * shishi_x509key_default_file_guess (*Shishi* * *handle*)   [Function]
>   *handle*: Shishi library handle create by shishi_init().

>   Guesses the default X.509 client key filename; it is $HOME/.shishi/client.key.

>   **Return value:** Returns default X.509 client key filename as a string that has to be deallocated with free() by the caller.

shishi_x509key_default_file_set

void shishi_x509key_default_file_set (*Shishi* * *handle*, *const*   [Function]
    char * *x509keyfile*)
>   *handle*: Shishi library handle create by shishi_init().

>   *x509keyfile*: string with new default x509 client key file name, or NULL to reset to default.

>   Set the default X.509 client key filename used in the library. The key is used during TLS connections with the KDC to authenticate the client. The string is copied into the library, so you can dispose of the variable immediately after calling this function.

shishi_x509key_default_file

const char * shishi_x509key_default_file (*Shishi* * *handle*)   [Function]
>   *handle*: Shishi library handle create by shishi_init().

>   Get filename for default X.509 key.

>   **Return value:** Returns the default X.509 client key filename used in the library. The key is used during TLS connections with the KDC to authenticate the client. The string is not a copy, so don't modify or deallocate it.

5.15 Utility Functions

shishi_realm_default_guess

char * shishi_realm_default_guess (*void*)   [Function]

 Guesses a realm based on getdomainname() (which really is NIS/YP domain, but if it is set it might be a good guess), or if it fails, based on gethostname(), or if it fails, the string "could-not-guess-default-realm". Note that the hostname is not trimmed off of the data returned by gethostname() to get the domain name and use that as the realm.

 Return value: Returns guessed realm for host as a string that has to be deallocated with free() by the caller.

shishi_realm_default

const char * shishi_realm_default (*Shishi * handle*)   [Function]

 handle: Shishi library handle create by shishi_init().

 Get name of default realm.

 Return value: Returns the default realm used in the library. (Not a copy of it, so don't modify or deallocate it.)

shishi_realm_default_set

void shishi_realm_default_set (*Shishi * handle*, *const char **   [Function]
       realm)

 handle: Shishi library handle create by shishi_init().

 realm: string with new default realm name, or NULL to reset to default.

 Set the default realm used in the library. The string is copied into the library, so you can dispose of the variable immediately after calling this function.

shishi_realm_for_server_file

char * shishi_realm_for_server_file (*Shishi * handle*, *char **   [Function]
       server)

 handle: Shishi library handle create by shishi_init().

 server: hostname to find realm for.

 Find realm for a host using configuration file.

 Return value: Returns realm for host, or NULL if not found.

shishi_realm_for_server_dns

char * shishi_realm_for_server_dns (*Shishi * handle*, *char **   [Function]
       server)

 handle: Shishi library handle create by shishi_init().

 server: hostname to find realm for.

 Find realm for a host using DNS lookups, according to draft-ietf-krb-wg-krb-dns-locate-03.txt. Since DNS lookups may be spoofed, relying on the realm information may result in a redirection attack. In a single-realm scenario, this only achieves a denial of service, but with cross-realm trust it may redirect you to a compromised realm. For this reason, Shishi prints a warning, suggesting that the user should add the proper 'server-realm' configuration tokens instead.

To illustrate the DNS information used, here is an extract from a zone file for the domain ASDF.COM:

_kerberos.asdf.com. IN TXT "ASDF.COM" _kerberos.mrkserver.asdf.com. IN TXT "MARKETING.ASDF.COM" _kerberos.salesserver.asdf.com. IN TXT "SALES.ASDF.COM"

Let us suppose that in this case, a client wishes to use a service on the host foo.asdf.com. It would first query:

_kerberos.foo.asdf.com. IN TXT

Finding no match, it would then query:

_kerberos.asdf.com. IN TXT

Return value: Returns realm for host, or NULL if not found.

shishi_realm_for_server

char * shishi_realm_for_server (*Shishi * handle*, *char * server*)   [Function]
handle: Shishi library handle create by `shishi_init()`.

server: hostname to find realm for.

Find realm for a host, using various methods. Currently this includes static configuration files (see `shishi_realm_for_server_file()`) and DNS (see `shishi_realm_for_server_dns()`).

Return value: Returns realm for host, or NULL if not found.

shishi_principal_default_guess

char * shishi_principal_default_guess (*void*)   [Function]
Guesses the principal name for the user, looking at environment variables SHISHI_USER, USER and LOGNAME, or if that fails, returns the string "user".

Return value: Returns guessed default principal for user as a string that has to be deallocated by the caller with `free()`.

shishi_principal_default

const char * shishi_principal_default (*Shishi * handle*)   [Function]
handle: Shishi library handle created by `shishi_init()`.

The default principal name is the name in the environment variable USER, or LOGNAME for some systems, but it can be overridden by specifying the environment variable SHISHI_USER.

Return value: Returns the default principal name used by the library. (Not a copy of it, so don't modify or deallocate it.)

shishi_principal_default_set

void shishi_principal_default_set (*Shishi * handle*, *const char *   [Function]
    principal*)

handle: Shishi library handle created by shishi_init().

principal: string with new default principal name, or NULL to reset to default.

Set the default principal used by the library. The string is copied into the library, so you can dispose of the variable immediately after calling this function.

shishi_parse_name

int shishi_parse_name (*Shishi * handle*, *const char *name*, *char ***   [Function]
    principal*, *char ** realm*)

handle: Shishi library handle created by shishi_init().

name: input principal name string, e.g. imap/mail.gnu.org\GNU.ORG.

principal: newly allocated output string with principal name.

realm: newly allocated output string with realm name.

Split principal name (e.g., "simon\JOSEFSSON.ORG") into two newly allocated strings, the principal ("simon"), and the realm ("JOSEFSSON.ORG"). If there is no realm part in name, realm is set to NULL.

Return value: Returns SHISHI_INVALID_PRINCIPAL_NAME if name is NULL or ends with the escape character "\", and SHISHI_OK if successful.

shishi_principal_name

int shishi_principal_name (*Shishi * handle*, *Shishi_asn1 namenode*,   [Function]
    *const char * namefield*, *char ** out*, *size_t * outlen*)

handle: Shishi library handle created by shishi_init().

namenode: ASN.1 structure with principal in namefield.

namefield: name of field in namenode containing principal name.

out: pointer to newly allocated, null terminated, string containing principal name. May be NULL (to only populate outlen).

outlen: pointer to length of out on output, excluding terminating null. May be NULL (to only populate out).

Represent principal name in ASN.1 structure as null-terminated string. The string is allocated by this function, and it is the responsibility of the caller to deallocate it. Note that the output length outlen does not include the terminating null.

Return value: Returns SHISHI_OK if successful.

shishi_principal_name_realm

int shishi_principal_name_realm (*Shishi * handle*, *Shishi_asn1*   [Function]
    namenode*, *const char * namefield*, *Shishi_asn1 realmnode*, *const char **
    realmfield*, *char ** out*, *size_t * outlen*)

handle: Shishi library handle created by shishi_init().

namenode: ASN.1 structure with principal name in `namefield`.

namefield: name of field in `namenode` containing principal name.

realmnode: ASN.1 structure with principal realm in `realmfield`.

realmfield: name of field in `realmnode` containing principal realm.

out: pointer to newly allocated null terminated string containing principal name. May be `NULL` (to only populate `outlen`).

outlen: pointer to length of `out` on output, excluding terminating null. May be `NULL` (to only populate `out`).

Represent principal name and realm in ASN.1 structure as null-terminated string. The string is allocated by this function. It is the responsibility of the caller to deallocate it. Note that the output length `outlen` does not include the terminating null character.

Return value: Returns SHISHI_OK if successful.

shishi_principal_name_set

int shishi_principal_name_set (*Shishi * handle*, *Shishi_asn1*   [Function]
  `namenode`, *const char * `namefield`*, *Shishi_name_type `name_type`*, *const char * [] `name`*)

handle: shishi handle as allocated by `shishi_init()`.

namenode: ASN.1 structure with principal in `namefield`.

namefield: name of field in `namenode` containing principal name.

name_type: type of principal, see Shishi_name_type, usually SHISHI_NT_UNKNOWN.

name: null-terminated input array with principal name.

Set the given principal name field to the given name.

Return value: Returns SHISHI_OK if successful.

shishi_principal_set

int shishi_principal_set (*Shishi * handle*, *Shishi_asn1 `namenode`*,   [Function]
  const char * `namefield`, *const char * `name`*)

handle: shishi handle as allocated by `shishi_init()`.

namenode: ASN.1 structure with principal in `namefield`.

namefield: name of field in `namenode` containing principal name.

name: null-terminated string with principal name in RFC 1964 form.

Set principal name field in an ASN.1 structure to the given name.

Return value: Returns SHISHI_OK if successful.

shishi_derive_default_salt

int shishi_derive_default_salt (*Shishi * handle*, *const char **   [Function]
  `name`, *char ** `salt`*)

handle: shishi handle as allocated by `shishi_init()`.

name: principal name of user.

salt: output variable with newly allocated salt string.

Derive the default salt from a principal. The default salt is the concatenation of the decoded realm and the principal.

Return value: Return SHISHI_OK if successful.

shishi_server_for_local_service

char * shishi_server_for_local_service (*Shishi* * `handle`, *const*   [Function]
    char * `service`)

handle: shishi handle as allocated by `shishi_init()`.

service: null terminated string with name of service, e.g., "host".

Construct a service principal (e.g., "imap/yxa.extuno.com") based on supplied service name (i.e., "imap") and the system's hostname as returned by `hostname()` (i.e., "yxa.extundo.com"). The string must be deallocated by the caller.

Return value: Return newly allocated service name string.

shishi_authorize_strcmp

int shishi_authorize_strcmp (*Shishi* * `handle`, *const char* *   [Function]
    `principal`, *const char* * `authzname`)

handle: shishi handle allocated by `shishi_init()`.

principal: string with desired principal name.

authzname: authorization name.

Authorization of `authzname` against desired `principal` according to "basic" authentication, i.e., testing for identical strings.

Return value: Returns 1 if `authzname` is authorized for services by the encrypted principal, and 0 otherwise.

shishi_authorize_k5login

int shishi_authorize_k5login (*Shishi* * `handle`, *const char* *   [Function]
    `principal`, *const char* * `authzname`)

handle: shishi handle allocated by `shishi_init()`.

principal: string with desired principal name and realm.

authzname: authorization name.

Authorization of `authzname` against desired `principal` in accordance with the MIT/Heimdal authorization method.

Return value: Returns 1 if `authzname` is authorized for services by `principal`, and returns 0 otherwise.

shishi_authorization_parse

int shishi_authorization_parse (*const char* * `authorization`)   [Function]
    authorization: name of authorization type, "basic" or "k5login".

Parse authorization type name.

Return value: Returns authorization type corresponding to a string.

shishi_authorized_p

int shishi_authorized_p (*Shishi * handle*, *Shishi_tkt * tkt, const*   [Function]
    *char * authzname*)

    handle: shishi handle allocated by `shishi_init()`.

    tkt: input variable with ticket info.

    authzname: authorization name.

    Simplistic authorization of `authzname` against encrypted client principal name inside ticket. For "basic" authentication type, the principal name must coincide with `authzname`. The "k5login" authentication type attempts the MIT/Heimdal method of parsing the file "~/.k5login" for additional equivalence names.

    Return value: Returns 1 if `authzname` is authorized for services by the encrypted principal, and 0 otherwise.

shishi_generalize_time

const char * shishi_generalize_time (*Shishi * handle*, *time_t t*)   [Function]
    handle: shishi handle as allocated by `shishi_init()`.

    t: C time to convert.

    Convert C time to KerberosTime. The string must not be deallocate by caller.

    Return value: Return a KerberosTime time string corresponding to C time t.

shishi_generalize_now

const char * shishi_generalize_now (*Shishi * handle*)   [Function]
    handle: shishi handle as allocated by `shishi_init()`.

    Convert current time to KerberosTime. The string must not be deallocate by caller.

    Return value: Return a KerberosTime time string corresponding to current time.

shishi_generalize_ctime

time_t shishi_generalize_ctime (*Shishi * handle*, *const char * t*)   [Function]
    handle: shishi handle as allocated by `shishi_init()`.

    t: KerberosTime to convert.

    Convert KerberosTime to C time.

    Return value: Returns C time corresponding to KerberosTime t.

shishi_time

int shishi_time (*Shishi * handle*, *Shishi_asn1 node*, *const char ***   [Function]
    field, *char ** t*)

    handle: shishi handle as allocated by `shishi_init()`.

    node: ASN.1 node to get time from.

    field: Name of field in ASN.1 node to get time from.

    t: newly allocated output array with zero terminated time string.

    Extract time from ASN.1 structure.

    Return value: Returns SHISHI_OK iff successful.

shishi_ctime

int shishi_ctime (*Shishi * handle*, *Shishi_asn1 node*, *const char *   [Function]
       field*, *time_t * t*)

handle: shishi handle as allocated by shishi_init().

node: ASN.1 variable to read field from.

field: name of field in node to read.

t: pointer to time field to set.

Extract time from ASN.1 structure.

Return value: Returns SHISHI_OK if successful, SHISHI_ASN1_NO_ELEMENT if
the element do not exist, SHISHI_ASN1_NO_VALUE if the field has no value, ot
SHISHI_ASN1_ERROR otherwise.

shishi_prompt_password_callback_set

void shishi_prompt_password_callback_set (*Shishi * handle*,   [Function]
       shishi_prompt_password_func cb)

handle: shishi handle as allocated by shishi_init().

cb: function pointer to application password callback, a shishi_prompt_password_
func type.

Set a callback function that will be used by shishi_prompt_password() to query the
user for a password. The function pointer can be retrieved using shishi_prompt_
password_callback_get().

The cb function should follow the shishi_prompt_password_func prototype:

int prompt_password (Shishi * handle, char **s, const char *format, va_list ap);

If the function returns 0, the s variable should contain a newly allocated string with
the password read from the user.

shishi_prompt_password_callback_get

shishi_prompt_password_func   [Function]
       shishi_prompt_password_callback_get (*Shishi * handle*)

handle: shishi handle as allocated by shishi_init().

Get the application password prompt function callback as set by shishi_prompt_
password_callback_set().

Returns: Returns the callback, a shishi_prompt_password_func type, or NULL.

shishi_prompt_password

int shishi_prompt_password (*Shishi * handle*, *char ** s*, *const char*   [Function]
       * format*, ...)

handle: shishi handle as allocated by shishi_init().

s: pointer to newly allocated output string with read password.

format: printf(3) style format string. ...: printf(3) style arguments.

Format and print a prompt, and read a password from user. The password is possibly converted (e.g., converted from Latin-1 to UTF-8, or processed using Stringprep profile) following any "stringprocess" keywords in configuration files.

Return value: Returns SHISHI_OK iff successful.

shishi_resolv

Shishi_dns shishi_resolv (*const char * zone, uint16_t querytype*)   [Function]
> *zone:* owner name of data, e.g. "EXAMPLE.ORG"
>
> *querytype:* type of data to query for, e.g., SHISHI_DNS_TXT.
>
> Query DNS resolver for data of type querytype at owner name zone. Currently TXT and SRV types are supported.
>
> **Return value:** Returns linked list of DNS records, or NULL if query failed.

shishi_resolv_free

void shishi_resolv_free (*Shishi_dns rrs*)   [Function]
> *rrs:* list of DNS RR as returned by shishi_resolv().
>
> Deallocate list of DNS RR as returned by shishi_resolv().

5.16 ASN.1 Functions

shishi_asn1_read_inline

int shishi_asn1_read_inline (*Shishi * handle, Shishi_asn1 node,*   [Function]
        *const char * field, char * data, size_t * datalen*)
> *handle:* shishi handle as allocated by shishi_init().
>
> *node:* ASN.1 variable to read field from.
>
> *field:* name of field in node to read.
>
> *data:* pre-allocated output buffer that will hold ASN.1 field data.
>
> *datalen:* on input, maximum size of output buffer, on output, actual size of output buffer.
>
> Extract data stored in a ASN.1 field into a fixed size buffer allocated by caller.
>
> Note that since it is difficult to predict the length of the field, it is often better to use shishi_asn1_read() instead.
>
> **Return value:** Returns SHISHI_OK if successful, SHISHI_ASN1_NO_ELEMENT if the element do not exist, SHISHI_ASN1_NO_VALUE if the field has no value, ot SHISHI_ASN1_ERROR otherwise.

shishi_asn1_read

int shishi_asn1_read (*Shishi * handle, Shishi_asn1 node, const char*   [Function]
        *field, char ** data, size_t * datalen*)
> *handle:* shishi handle as allocated by shishi_init().
>
> *node:* ASN.1 variable to read field from.

field: name of field in **node** to read.

data: newly allocated output buffer that will hold ASN.1 field data.

datalen: actual size of output buffer.

Extract data stored in a ASN.1 field into a newly allocated buffer. The buffer will always be zero terminated, even though **datalen** will not include the added zero.

Return value: Returns SHISHI_OK if successful, SHISHI_ASN1_NO_ELEMENT if the element do not exist, SHISHI_ASN1_NO_VALUE if the field has no value, ot SHISHI_ASN1_ERROR otherwise.

shishi_asn1_read_optional

int shishi_asn1_read_optional (*Shishi* * *handle*, *Shishi_asn1* *node*,   [Function]
    const char * *field*, *char* ** *data*, *size_t* * *datalen*)
    handle: shishi handle as allocated by **shishi_init**().

node: ASN.1 variable to read field from.

field: name of field in **node** to read.

data: newly allocated output buffer that will hold ASN.1 field data.

datalen: actual size of output buffer.

Extract data stored in a ASN.1 field into a newly allocated buffer. If the field does not exist (i.e., SHISHI_ASN1_NO_ELEMENT), this function set datalen to 0 and succeeds. Can be useful to read ASN.1 fields which are marked OPTIONAL in the grammar, if you want to avoid special error handling in your code.

Return value: Returns SHISHI_OK if successful, SHISHI_ASN1_NO_VALUE if the field has no value, ot SHISHI_ASN1_ERROR otherwise.

shishi_asn1_done

void shishi_asn1_done (*Shishi* * *handle*, *Shishi_asn1* *node*)   [Function]
    handle: shishi handle as allocated by **shishi_init**().

node: ASN.1 node to dellocate.

Deallocate resources associated with ASN.1 structure. Note that the node must not be used after this call.

shishi_asn1_pa_enc_ts_enc

Shishi_asn1 shishi_asn1_pa_enc_ts_enc (*Shishi* * *handle*)   [Function]
    handle: shishi handle as allocated by **shishi_init**().

Create new ASN.1 structure for PA-ENC-TS-ENC.

Return value: Returns ASN.1 structure.

shishi_asn1_encrypteddata

Shishi_asn1 shishi_asn1_encrypteddata (*Shishi* * *handle*)   [Function]
    handle: shishi handle as allocated by **shishi_init**().

Create new ASN.1 structure for EncryptedData

Return value: Returns ASN.1 structure.

shishi_asn1_padata

Shishi_asn1 shishi_asn1_padata (*Shishi* * `handle`)   [Function]
> *handle*: shishi handle as allocated by `shishi_init()`.
>
> Create new ASN.1 structure for PA-DATA.
>
> **Return value:** Returns ASN.1 structure.

shishi_asn1_methoddata

Shishi_asn1 shishi_asn1_methoddata (*Shishi* * `handle`)   [Function]
> *handle*: shishi handle as allocated by `shishi_init()`.
>
> Create new ASN.1 structure for METHOD-DATA.
>
> **Return value:** Returns ASN.1 structure.

shishi_asn1_etype_info

Shishi_asn1 shishi_asn1_etype_info (*Shishi* * `handle`)   [Function]
> *handle*: shishi handle as allocated by `shishi_init()`.
>
> Create new ASN.1 structure for ETYPE-INFO.
>
> **Return value:** Returns ASN.1 structure.

shishi_asn1_etype_info2

Shishi_asn1 shishi_asn1_etype_info2 (*Shishi* * `handle`)   [Function]
> *handle*: shishi handle as allocated by `shishi_init()`.
>
> Create new ASN.1 structure for ETYPE-INFO2.
>
> **Return value:** Returns ASN.1 structure.

shishi_asn1_asreq

Shishi_asn1 shishi_asn1_asreq (*Shishi* * `handle`)   [Function]
> *handle*: shishi handle as allocated by `shishi_init()`.
>
> Create new ASN.1 structure for AS-REQ.
>
> **Return value:** Returns ASN.1 structure.

shishi_asn1_asrep

Shishi_asn1 shishi_asn1_asrep (*Shishi* * `handle`)   [Function]
> *handle*: shishi handle as allocated by `shishi_init()`.
>
> Create new ASN.1 structure for AS-REP.
>
> **Return value:** Returns ASN.1 structure.

shishi_asn1_tgsreq

Shishi_asn1 shishi_asn1_tgsreq (*Shishi* * `handle`)   [Function]
> *handle*: shishi handle as allocated by `shishi_init()`.
>
> Create new ASN.1 structure for TGS-REQ.
>
> **Return value:** Returns ASN.1 structure.

shishi_asn1_tgsrep

Shishi_asn1 shishi_asn1_tgsrep (*Shishi* * `handle`)   [Function]
> *handle*: shishi handle as allocated by `shishi_init()`.
>
> Create new ASN.1 structure for TGS-REP.
>
> **Return value:** Returns ASN.1 structure.

shishi_asn1_apreq

Shishi_asn1 shishi_asn1_apreq (*Shishi* * `handle`)   [Function]
> *handle*: shishi handle as allocated by `shishi_init()`.
>
> Create new ASN.1 structure for AP-REQ.
>
> **Return value:** Returns ASN.1 structure.

shishi_asn1_aprep

Shishi_asn1 shishi_asn1_aprep (*Shishi* * `handle`)   [Function]
> *handle*: shishi handle as allocated by `shishi_init()`.
>
> Create new ASN.1 structure for AP-REP.
>
> **Return value:** Returns ASN.1 structure.

shishi_asn1_encapreppart

Shishi_asn1 shishi_asn1_encapreppart (*Shishi* * `handle`)   [Function]
> *handle*: shishi handle as allocated by `shishi_init()`.
>
> Create new ASN.1 structure for AP-REP.
>
> **Return value:** Returns ASN.1 structure.

shishi_asn1_ticket

Shishi_asn1 shishi_asn1_ticket (*Shishi* * `handle`)   [Function]
> *handle*: shishi handle as allocated by `shishi_init()`.
>
> Create new ASN.1 structure for Ticket.
>
> **Return value:** Returns ASN.1 structure.

shishi_asn1_encticketpart

Shishi_asn1 shishi_asn1_encticketpart (*Shishi* * `handle`)   [Function]
> *handle*: shishi handle as allocated by `shishi_init()`.
>
> Create new ASN.1 structure for EncTicketPart.
>
> **Return value:** Returns ASN.1 structure.

shishi_asn1_authenticator

Shishi_asn1 shishi_asn1_authenticator (*Shishi* * `handle`)   [Function]
> *handle*: shishi handle as allocated by `shishi_init()`.
>
> Create new ASN.1 structure for Authenticator.
>
> **Return value:** Returns ASN.1 structure.

shishi_asn1_enckdcreppart

Shishi_asn1 shishi_asn1_enckdcreppart (*Shishi* * *handle*)   [Function]
handle: shishi handle as allocated by `shishi_init()`.

Create new ASN.1 structure for EncKDCRepPart.

Return value: Returns ASN.1 structure.

shishi_asn1_encasreppart

Shishi_asn1 shishi_asn1_encasreppart (*Shishi* * *handle*)   [Function]
handle: shishi handle as allocated by `shishi_init()`.

Create new ASN.1 structure for EncASRepPart.

Return value: Returns ASN.1 structure.

shishi_asn1_krberror

Shishi_asn1 shishi_asn1_krberror (*Shishi* * *handle*)   [Function]
handle: shishi handle as allocated by `shishi_init()`.

Create new ASN.1 structure for KRB-ERROR.

Return value: Returns ASN.1 structure.

shishi_asn1_krbsafe

Shishi_asn1 shishi_asn1_krbsafe (*Shishi* * *handle*)   [Function]
handle: shishi handle as allocated by `shishi_init()`.

Create new ASN.1 structure for KRB-SAFE.

Return value: Returns ASN.1 structure.

shishi_asn1_priv

Shishi_asn1 shishi_asn1_priv (*Shishi* * *handle*)   [Function]
handle: shishi handle as allocated by `shishi_init()`.

Create new ASN.1 structure for KRB-PRIV.

Return value: Returns ASN.1 structure.

shishi_asn1_encprivpart

Shishi_asn1 shishi_asn1_encprivpart (*Shishi* * *handle*)   [Function]
handle: shishi handle as allocated by `shishi_init()`.

Create new ASN.1 structure for EncKrbPrivPart.

Return value: Returns ASN.1 structure.

shishi_asn1_to_der_field

int shishi_asn1_to_der_field (*Shishi * handle*, *Shishi_asn1 node*,   [Function]
        *const char * field*, *char ** der*, *size_t * len*)

handle: shishi handle as allocated by shishi_init().

node: ASN.1 data that have field to extract.

field: name of field in node to extract.

der: output array that holds DER encoding of field in node.

len: output variable with length of der output array.

Extract newly allocated DER representation of specified ASN.1 field.

Return value: Returns SHISHI_OK if successful, or SHISHI_ASN1_ERROR if DER encoding fails (common reasons for this is that the ASN.1 is missing required values).

shishi_asn1_to_der

int shishi_asn1_to_der (*Shishi * handle*, *Shishi_asn1 node*, *char ***   [Function]
        der, *size_t * len*)

handle: shishi handle as allocated by shishi_init().

node: ASN.1 data to convert to DER.

der: output array that holds DER encoding of node.

len: output variable with length of der output array.

Extract newly allocated DER representation of specified ASN.1 data.

Return value: Returns SHISHI_OK if successful, or SHISHI_ASN1_ERROR if DER encoding fails (common reasons for this is that the ASN.1 is missing required values).

shishi_asn1_msgtype

Shishi_msgtype shishi_asn1_msgtype (*Shishi * handle*, *Shishi_asn1*   [Function]
        node)

handle: shishi handle as allocated by shishi_init().

node: ASN.1 type to get msg type for.

Determine msg-type of ASN.1 type of a packet. Currently this uses the msg-type field instead of the APPLICATION tag, but this may be changed in the future.

Return value: Returns msg-type of ASN.1 type, 0 on failure.

shishi_der_msgtype

Shishi_msgtype shishi_der_msgtype (*Shishi * handle*, *const char **   [Function]
        der, *size_t derlen*)

handle: shishi handle as allocated by shishi_init().

der: input character array with DER encoding.

derlen: length of input character array with DER encoding.

Determine msg-type of DER coded data of a packet.

Return value: Returns msg-type of DER data, 0 on failure.

shishi_der2asn1

Shishi_asn1 shishi_der2asn1 (*Shishi* * **handle**, *const char* * **der**,   [Function]
     size_t **derlen**)

> *handle*: shishi handle as allocated by `shishi_init()`.
>
> *der*: input character array with DER encoding.
>
> *derlen*: length of input character array with DER encoding.
>
> Convert arbitrary DER data of a packet to a ASN.1 type.
>
> **Return value:** Returns newly allocate ASN.1 corresponding to DER data, or `NULL` on failure.

shishi_der2asn1_padata

Shishi_asn1 shishi_der2asn1_padata (*Shishi* * **handle**, *const char* *   [Function]
     der, *size_t* **derlen**)

> *handle*: shishi handle as allocated by `shishi_init()`.
>
> *der*: input character array with DER encoding.
>
> *derlen*: length of input character array with DER encoding.
>
> Decode DER encoding of PA-DATA and create a ASN.1 structure.
>
> **Return value:** Returns ASN.1 structure corresponding to DER data.

shishi_der2asn1_methoddata

Shishi_asn1 shishi_der2asn1_methoddata (*Shishi* * **handle**, *const*   [Function]
     char * **der**, *size_t* **derlen**)

> *handle*: shishi handle as allocated by `shishi_init()`.
>
> *der*: input character array with DER encoding.
>
> *derlen*: length of input character array with DER encoding.
>
> Decode DER encoding of METHOD-DATA and create a ASN.1 structure.
>
> **Return value:** Returns ASN.1 structure corresponding to DER data.

shishi_der2asn1_etype_info

Shishi_asn1 shishi_der2asn1_etype_info (*Shishi* * **handle**, *const*   [Function]
     char * **der**, *size_t* **derlen**)

> *handle*: shishi handle as allocated by `shishi_init()`.
>
> *der*: input character array with DER encoding.
>
> *derlen*: length of input character array with DER encoding.
>
> Decode DER encoding of ETYPE-INFO and create a ASN.1 structure.
>
> **Return value:** Returns ASN.1 structure corresponding to DER data.

shishi_der2asn1_etype_info2

Shishi_asn1 shishi_der2asn1_etype_info2 (*Shishi* * **handle**, *const*   [Function]
     char * **der**, *size_t* **derlen**)
> *handle*: shishi handle as allocated by shishi_init().
>
> *der*: input character array with DER encoding.
>
> *derlen*: length of input character array with DER encoding.
>
> Decode DER encoding of ETYPE-INFO2 and create a ASN.1 structure.
>
> **Return value:** Returns ASN.1 structure corresponding to DER data.

shishi_der2asn1_ticket

Shishi_asn1 shishi_der2asn1_ticket (*Shishi* * **handle**, *const char* *   [Function]
     der, *size_t* **derlen**)
> *handle*: shishi handle as allocated by shishi_init().
>
> *der*: input character array with DER encoding.
>
> *derlen*: length of input character array with DER encoding.
>
> Decode DER encoding of Ticket and create a ASN.1 structure.
>
> **Return value:** Returns ASN.1 structure corresponding to DER data.

shishi_der2asn1_encticketpart

Shishi_asn1 shishi_der2asn1_encticketpart (*Shishi* * **handle**,   [Function]
     const char * **der**, *size_t* **derlen**)
> *handle*: shishi handle as allocated by shishi_init().
>
> *der*: input character array with DER encoding.
>
> *derlen*: length of input character array with DER encoding.
>
> Decode DER encoding of EncTicketPart and create a ASN.1 structure.
>
> **Return value:** Returns ASN.1 structure corresponding to DER data.

shishi_der2asn1_asreq

Shishi_asn1 shishi_der2asn1_asreq (*Shishi* * **handle**, *const char* *   [Function]
     der, *size_t* **derlen**)
> *handle*: shishi handle as allocated by shishi_init().
>
> *der*: input character array with DER encoding.
>
> *derlen*: length of input character array with DER encoding.
>
> Decode DER encoding of AS-REQ and create a ASN.1 structure.
>
> **Return value:** Returns ASN.1 structure corresponding to DER data.

shishi_der2asn1_tgsreq

Shishi_asn1 shishi_der2asn1_tgsreq (*Shishi* * `handle`, *const char* *   [Function]
    `der`, *size_t* `derlen`)

    handle: shishi handle as allocated by `shishi_init()`.

    der: input character array with DER encoding.

    derlen: length of input character array with DER encoding.

    Decode DER encoding of TGS-REQ and create a ASN.1 structure.

    Return value: Returns ASN.1 structure corresponding to DER data.

shishi_der2asn1_asrep

Shishi_asn1 shishi_der2asn1_asrep (*Shishi* * `handle`, *const char* *   [Function]
    `der`, *size_t* `derlen`)

    handle: shishi handle as allocated by `shishi_init()`.

    der: input character array with DER encoding.

    derlen: length of input character array with DER encoding.

    Decode DER encoding of AS-REP and create a ASN.1 structure.

    Return value: Returns ASN.1 structure corresponding to DER data.

shishi_der2asn1_tgsrep

Shishi_asn1 shishi_der2asn1_tgsrep (*Shishi* * `handle`, *const char* *   [Function]
    `der`, *size_t* `derlen`)

    handle: shishi handle as allocated by `shishi_init()`.

    der: input character array with DER encoding.

    derlen: length of input character array with DER encoding.

    Decode DER encoding of TGS-REP and create a ASN.1 structure.

    Return value: Returns ASN.1 structure corresponding to DER data.

shishi_der2asn1_kdcrep

Shishi_asn1 shishi_der2asn1_kdcrep (*Shishi* * `handle`, *const char* *   [Function]
    `der`, *size_t* `derlen`)

    handle: shishi handle as allocated by `shishi_init()`.

    der: input character array with DER encoding.

    derlen: length of input character array with DER encoding.

    Decode DER encoding of KDC-REP and create a ASN.1 structure.

    Return value: Returns ASN.1 structure corresponding to DER data.

shishi_der2asn1_encasreppart

`Shishi_asn1 shishi_der2asn1_encasreppart` (*Shishi* `* handle`,   [Function]
    const char `* der`, *size_t* `derlen`)
    handle: shishi handle as allocated by `shishi_init()`.

    der: input character array with DER encoding.

    derlen: length of input character array with DER encoding.

    Decode DER encoding of EncASRepPart and create a ASN.1 structure.

    Return value: Returns ASN.1 structure corresponding to DER data.

shishi_der2asn1_enctgsreppart

`Shishi_asn1 shishi_der2asn1_enctgsreppart` (*Shishi* `* handle`,   [Function]
    const char `* der`, *size_t* `derlen`)
    handle: shishi handle as allocated by `shishi_init()`.

    der: input character array with DER encoding.

    derlen: length of input character array with DER encoding.

    Decode DER encoding of EncTGSRepPart and create a ASN.1 structure.

    Return value: Returns ASN.1 structure corresponding to DER data.

shishi_der2asn1_enckdcreppart

`Shishi_asn1 shishi_der2asn1_enckdcreppart` (*Shishi* `* handle`,   [Function]
    const char `* der`, *size_t* `derlen`)
    handle: shishi handle as allocated by `shishi_init()`.

    der: input character array with DER encoding.

    derlen: length of input character array with DER encoding.

    Decode DER encoding of EncKDCRepPart and create a ASN.1 structure.

    Return value: Returns ASN.1 structure corresponding to DER data.

shishi_der2asn1_authenticator

`Shishi_asn1 shishi_der2asn1_authenticator` (*Shishi* `* handle`,   [Function]
    const char `* der`, *size_t* `derlen`)
    handle: shishi handle as allocated by `shishi_init()`.

    der: input character array with DER encoding.

    derlen: length of input character array with DER encoding.

    Decode DER encoding of Authenticator and create a ASN.1 structure.

    Return value: Returns ASN.1 structure corresponding to DER data.

shishi_der2asn1_krberror

Shishi_asn1 shishi_der2asn1_krberror (*Shishi* * `handle`, *const*   [Function]
    char * `der`, *size_t* `derlen`)

    handle: shishi handle as allocated by `shishi_init()`.

    der: input character array with DER encoding.

    derlen: length of input character array with DER encoding.

    Decode DER encoding of KRB-ERROR and create a ASN.1 structure.

    Return value: Returns ASN.1 structure corresponding to DER data.

shishi_der2asn1_krbsafe

Shishi_asn1 shishi_der2asn1_krbsafe (*Shishi* * `handle`, *const char*   [Function]
    * `der`, *size_t* `derlen`)

    handle: shishi handle as allocated by `shishi_init()`.

    der: input character array with DER encoding.

    derlen: length of input character array with DER encoding.

    Decode DER encoding of KRB-SAFE and create a ASN.1 structure.

    Return value: Returns ASN.1 structure corresponding to DER data.

shishi_der2asn1_priv

Shishi_asn1 shishi_der2asn1_priv (*Shishi* * `handle`, *const char* *   [Function]
    `der`, *size_t* `derlen`)

    handle: shishi handle as allocated by `shishi_init()`.

    der: input character array with DER encoding.

    derlen: length of input character array with DER encoding.

    Decode DER encoding of KRB-PRIV and create a ASN.1 structure.

    Return value: Returns ASN.1 structure corresponding to DER data.

shishi_der2asn1_encprivpart

Shishi_asn1 shishi_der2asn1_encprivpart (*Shishi* * `handle`, *const*   [Function]
    char * `der`, *size_t* `derlen`)

    handle: shishi handle as allocated by `shishi_init()`.

    der: input character array with DER encoding.

    derlen: length of input character array with DER encoding.

    Decode DER encoding of EncKrbPrivPart and create a ASN.1 structure.

    Return value: Returns ASN.1 structure corresponding to DER data.

shishi_der2asn1_apreq

Shishi_asn1 shishi_der2asn1_apreq (*Shishi* * `handle`, *const char* *   [Function]
  der, *size_t* `derlen`)
  handle: shishi handle as allocated by `shishi_init()`.

  der: input character array with DER encoding.

  derlen: length of input character array with DER encoding.

  Decode DER encoding of AP-REQ and create a ASN.1 structure.

  Return value: Returns ASN.1 structure corresponding to DER data.

shishi_der2asn1_aprep

Shishi_asn1 shishi_der2asn1_aprep (*Shishi* * `handle`, *const char* *   [Function]
  der, *size_t* `derlen`)
  handle: shishi handle as allocated by `shishi_init()`.

  der: input character array with DER encoding.

  derlen: length of input character array with DER encoding.

  Decode DER encoding of AP-REP and create a ASN.1 structure.

  Return value: Returns ASN.1 structure corresponding to DER data.

shishi_der2asn1_encappreppart

Shishi_asn1 shishi_der2asn1_encappreppart (*Shishi* * `handle`,   [Function]
  const char * `der`, *size_t* `derlen`)
  handle: shishi handle as allocated by `shishi_init()`.

  der: input character array with DER encoding.

  derlen: length of input character array with DER encoding.

  Decode DER encoding of EncAPRepPart and create a ASN.1 structure.

  Return value: Returns ASN.1 structure corresponding to DER data.

shishi_der2asn1_kdcreq

Shishi_asn1 shishi_der2asn1_kdcreq (*Shishi* * `handle`, *const char* *   [Function]
  der, *size_t* `derlen`)
  handle: shishi handle as allocated by `shishi_init()`.

  der: input character array with DER encoding.

  derlen: length of input character array with DER encoding.

  Decode DER encoding of AS-REQ, TGS-REQ or KDC-REQ and create a ASN.1
  structure.

  Return value: Returns ASN.1 structure corresponding to DER data.

shishi_asn1_print

void **shishi_asn1_print** (*Shishi * **handle**, *Shishi_asn1* **node**, *FILE **   [Function]
     fh)

> *handle*: shishi handle as allocated by **shishi_init()**.
>
> *node*: ASN.1 data that have field to extract.
>
> *fh*: file descriptor to print to, e.g. stdout.
>
> Print ASN.1 structure in human readable form, typically for debugging purposes.

5.17 Error Handling

Most functions in 'Libshishi' are returning an error if they fail. For this reason, the application should always catch the error condition and take appropriate measures, for example by releasing the resources and passing the error up to the caller, or by displaying a descriptive message to the user and cancelling the operation.

Some error values do not indicate a system error or an error in the operation, but the result of an operation that failed properly.

5.17.1 Error Values

Errors are returned as an **int**. Except for the SHISHI_OK case, an application should always use the constants instead of their numeric value. Applications are encouraged to use the constants even for SHISHI_OK as it improves readability. Possible values are:

SHISHI_OK

> This value indicates success. The value of this error is guaranteed to always be 0 so you may use it in boolean constructs.

SHISHI_ASN1_ERROR

> Error in ASN.1 function (corrupt data?)

SHISHI_FOPEN_ERROR

> Could not open file

SHISHI_IO_ERROR

> File input/output error

SHISHI_MALLOC_ERROR

> Memory allocation error in shishi library.

SHISHI_BASE64_ERROR

> Base64 encoding or decoding failed. Data corrupt?

SHISHI_REALM_MISMATCH

> Client realm value differ between request and reply.

SHISHI_CNAME_MISMATCH

> Client name value differ between request and reply.

SHISHI_NONCE_MISMATCH

> Replay protection value (nonce) differ between request and reply.

SHISHI_TGSREP_BAD_KEYTYPE

> Incorrect key type used in TGS reply.

`SHISHI_KDCREP_BAD_KEYTYPE`
>   Incorrect key type used in reply from KDC.

`SHISHI_APREP_BAD_KEYTYPE`
>   Incorrect key type used in AP reply.

`SHISHI_APREP_VERIFY_FAILED`
>   Failed verification of AP reply.

`SHISHI_APREQ_BAD_KEYTYPE`
>   Incorrect key type used in AP request.

`SHISHI_TOO_SMALL_BUFFER`
>   Provided buffer was too small.

`SHISHI_DERIVEDKEY_TOO_SMALL`
>   Derived key material is too short to be applicable.

`SHISHI_KEY_TOO_LARGE`
>   The key is too large to be usable.

`SHISHI_CRYPTO_ERROR`
>   Low-level cryptographic primitive failed. This usually indicates bad password
>   or data corruption.

`SHISHI_CRYPTO_INTERNAL_ERROR`
>   Internal error in low-level crypto routines.

`SHISHI_SOCKET_ERROR`
>   The system call socket() failed. This usually indicates that your system does
>   not support the socket type.

`SHISHI_BIND_ERROR`
>   The system call bind() failed. This usually indicates insufficient permissions.

`SHISHI_SENDTO_ERROR`
>   The system call sendto() failed.

`SHISHI_RECVFROM_ERROR`
>   Error receiving data from server

`SHISHI_CLOSE_ERROR`
>   The system call close() failed.

`SHISHI_KDC_TIMEOUT`
>   Timed out talking to KDC. This usually indicates a network or KDC address
>   problem.

`SHISHI_KDC_NOT_KNOWN_FOR_REALM`
>   No KDC known for given realm.

`SHISHI_TTY_ERROR`
>   No TTY assigned to process.

`SHISHI_GOT_KRBERROR`
>   Server replied to the request with an error message.

`SHISHI_HANDLE_ERROR`
> Failure to use handle. Missing handle, or misconfigured.

`SHISHI_INVALID_TKTS`
> Ticket set not initialized. This usually indicates an internal application error.

`SHISHI_TICKET_BAD_KEYTYPE`
> Key type used to encrypt ticket doesn't match provided key. This usually indicates an internal application error.

`SHISHI_INVALID_KEY`
> Reference to invalid encryption key.

`SHISHI_APREQ_DECRYPT_FAILED`
> Could not decrypt AP-REQ using provided key. This usually indicates an internal application error.

`SHISHI_TICKET_DECRYPT_FAILED`
> Could not decrypt Ticket using provided key. This usually indicates an internal application error.

`SHISHI_INVALID_TICKET`
> Invalid ticked passed in call.

`SHISHI_OUT_OF_RANGE`
> Argument lies outside of valid range.

`SHISHI_ASN1_NO_ELEMENT`
> The ASN.1 structure does not contain the indicated element.

`SHISHI_SAFE_BAD_KEYTYPE`
> Attempted access to non-existent key type.

`SHISHI_SAFE_VERIFY_FAILED`
> Verification failed on either side.

`SHISHI_PKCS5_INVALID_PRF`
> Invalid PKCS5 descriptor.

`SHISHI_PKCS5_INVALID_ITERATION_COUNT`
> Invalid claim of iteration count in PKCS5 descriptor.

`SHISHI_PKCS5_INVALID_DERIVED_KEY_LENGTH`
> Derived key length is incorrect for PKCS5 descriptor.

`SHISHI_PKCS5_DERIVED_KEY_TOO_LONG`
> Derived key is too long for PKCS5 descriptor.

`SHISHI_INVALID_PRINCIPAL_NAME`
> Principal name syntax error.

`SHISHI_INVALID_ARGUMENT`
> Invalid argument passed in call. Wrong or unknown value.

`SHISHI_ASN1_NO_VALUE`
> The indicated ASN.1 element does not carry a value.

SHISHI_CONNECT_ERROR

       Connection attempt failed. Try again, or check availability.

SHISHI_VERIFY_FAILED

       Verification failed on either side.

SHISHI_PRIV_BAD_KEYTYPE

       The private key uses an incompatible encryption type.

SHISHI_FILE_ERROR

       The desired file could not be accessed. Check permissions.

SHISHI_ENCAPREPPART_BAD_KEYTYPE

       The present AP reply specifies an inpermissible key type.

SHISHI_GETTIMEOFDAY_ERROR

       A request for present time of day has failed. This is usually internal, but a valid time is imperative for us.

SHISHI_KEYTAB_ERROR

       Failed to parse keytab file

SHISHI_CCACHE_ERROR

       Failed to parse credential cache file

5.17.2 Error Functions

shishi_strerror

const char * shishi_strerror (*int* **err**)   [Function]

    err: shishi error code.

    Convert return code to human readable string.

    Return value: Returns a pointer to a statically allocated string containing a description of the error with the error value **err**. This string can be used to output a diagnostic message to the user.

shishi_error

const char * shishi_error (*Shishi* * **handle**)   [Function]

    handle: shishi handle as allocated by **shishi_init()**.

    Extract detailed error information string. Note that the memory is managed by the Shishi library, so you must not deallocate the string.

    Return value: Returns pointer to error information string, that must not be deallocate by caller.

shishi_error_clear

void shishi_error_clear (*Shishi* * **handle**)   [Function]

    handle: shishi handle as allocated by **shishi_init()**.

    Clear the detailed error information string. See **shishi_error()** for how to access the error string, and **shishi_error_set()** and **shishi_error_printf()** for how to set the error string. This function is mostly for Shishi internal use, but if you develop an extension of Shishi, it may be useful to use the same error handling infrastructure.

shishi_error_set

void **shishi_error_set** (*Shishi * handle*, *const char * errstr*)   [Function]
    handle: shishi handle as allocated by **shishi_init ()**.

errstr: Zero terminated character array containing error description, or NULL to clear the error description string.

Set the detailed error information string to specified string. The string is copied into the Shishi internal structure, so you can deallocate the string passed to this function after the call. This function is mostly for Shishi internal use, but if you develop an extension of Shishi, it may be useful to use the same error handling infrastructure.

shishi_error_printf

void **shishi_error_printf** (*Shishi * handle*, *const char * format*,   [Function]
    ...)
    handle: shishi handle as allocated by **shishi_init ()**.

format: printf style format string. ...: print style arguments.

Set the detailed error information string to a printf formatted string. This function is mostly for Shishi internal use, but if you develop an extension of Shishi, it may be useful to use the same error handling infrastructure.

shishi_error_outputtype

int **shishi_error_outputtype** (*Shishi * handle*)   [Function]
    handle: shishi handle as allocated by **shishi_init ()**.

Get the current output type for logging messages.

Return value: Return output type (NULL, stderr or syslog) for informational and warning messages.

shishi_error_set_outputtype

void **shishi_error_set_outputtype** (*Shishi * handle*, *int type*)   [Function]
    handle: shishi handle as allocated by **shishi_init ()**.

type: output type.

Set output type (NULL, stderr or syslog) for informational and warning messages.

shishi_info

void **shishi_info** (*Shishi * handle*, *const char * format*, ...)   [Function]
    handle: shishi handle as allocated by **shishi_init ()**.

format: printf style format string. ...: print style arguments.

Print informational message to output as defined in handle.

shishi_warn

void **shishi_warn** (*Shishi * handle*, *const char * format*, *...*)   [Function]
> *handle*: shishi handle as allocated by `shishi_init()`.

> *format*: printf style format string. ...: print style arguments.

> Print a warning to output as defined in handle.

shishi_verbose

void **shishi_verbose** (*Shishi * handle*, *const char * format*, *...*)   [Function]
> *handle*: shishi handle as allocated by `shishi_init()`.

> *format*: printf style format string. ...: print style arguments.

> Print a diagnostic message to output as defined in handle.

5.18 Examples

This section will be extended to contain walk-throughs of example code that demonstrate how 'Shishi' is used to write your own applications that support Kerberos 5. The rest of the current section consists of some crude hints for the example client/server applications that is part of Shishi, taken from an email but saved here for lack of a better place to put it.

There are two programs: 'client' and 'server' in src/.

The client output an AP-REQ, waits for an AP-REP, and then simply reads data from stdin.

The server waits for an AP-REQ, parses it and prints an AP-REP, and then read data from stdin.

Both programs accept a Kerberos server name as the first command line argument. Your KDC must know this server, since the client tries to get a ticket for it (first it gets a ticket granting ticket for the default username), and you must write the key for the server into /usr/local/etc/shishi.keys on the Shishi format, e.g.:

```
-----BEGIN SHISHI KEY-----
Keytype: 16 (des3-cbc-sha1-kd)
Principal: sample/latte.josefsson.org
Realm: JOSEFSSON.ORG

8WOVrQQBpxlACPQEqN91EHxbvFFo2ltt
-----END SHISHI KEY-----
```

You must extract the proper encryption key from the KDC in some way. (This part will be easier when Shishi include a KDC, a basic one isn't far away, give me a week or to.)

The intention is that the data read, after the authentication phase, should be protected using KRB_SAFE (see RFC) but I haven't added this yet.

5.19 Kerberos Database Functions

Shisa is a separate and standalone library from Shishi (see Section 3.1 [Introduction to Shisa], page 18). If you only wish to manipulate the information stored in the Kerberos user database used by Shishi, you do not need to link or use the Shishi library at all. However, you may find it useful to combine the two libraries.

For two real world examples on using the Shisa library, refer to 'src/shisa.c' (Shisa command line tool) and 'src/kdc.c' (part of Shishid server).

Shisa uses two 'struct's to carry information. The first, Shisa_principal, is used to hold information about principals. The struct does not contain pointers to strings etc, so the library assumes the caller is responsible for allocating and deallocating the struct itself. Each such struct is (uniquely) identified by the combination of principal name and realm name.

```
struct Shisa_principal
{
  int isdisabled;
  uint32_t kvno;
  time_t notusedbefore;
  time_t lastinitialtgt;      /* time of last initial request for a TGT */
  time_t lastinitialrequest;  /* time of last initial request */
  time_t lasttgt;             /* time of issue for the newest TGT used */
  time_t lastrenewal;         /* time of the last renewal */
  time_t passwordexpire;      /* time when the password will expire */
  time_t accountexpire;       /* time when the account will expire. */
};
typedef struct Shisa_principal Shisa_principal;
```

The second structure is called Shisa_key and hold information about cryptographic keys. Because the struct contain pointers, and the caller cannot know how many keys a principal have, the Shisa library manages memory for the struct. The library allocate the structs, and the pointers within them. The caller may deallocate them, but it is recommended to use shisa_key_free or shisa_keys_free instead. Note that each principal may have multiple keys.

```
struct Shisa_key
{
  uint32_t kvno;
  int32_t etype;
  int priority;
  char *key;
  size_t keylen;
  char *salt;
  size_t saltlen;
  char *str2keyparam;
  size_t str2keyparamlen;
  char *password;
};
typedef struct Shisa_key Shisa_key;
```

Shisa is typically initialized by calling `shisa_init`, and deinitialized (when the application no longer need to use Shisa, typically when it shuts down) by calling `shisa_done`, but here are the complete (de)initialization interface functions.

shisa

`Shisa * shisa ( void)`   [Function]

> Initializes the Shisa library. If this function fails, it may print diagnostic errors to stderr.
>
> **Return value:** Returns Shisa library handle, or `NULL` on error.

shisa_done

`void shisa_done (Shisa * dbh)`   [Function]

> Deallocates the shisa library handle. The handle must not be used in any calls to shisa functions after this.

shisa_init

`int shisa_init (Shisa ** dbh)`   [Function]

> *dbh*: pointer to library handle to be created.
>
> Create a Shisa library handle, using `shisa()`, and read the system configuration file from their default locations. The paths to the default system configuration file is decided at compile time ($sysconfdir/shisa.conf).
>
> The handle is allocated regardless of return values, except for SHISA_INIT_ERROR which indicates a problem allocating the handle. (The other error conditions comes from reading the files.)
>
> **Return value:** Returns `SHISA_OK` iff successful.

shisa_init_with_paths

`int shisa_init_with_paths (Shisa ** dbh, const char * file)`   [Function]

> *dbh*: pointer to library handle to be created.
>
> *file*: Filename of system configuration, or NULL.
>
> Create a Shisa library handle, using `shisa()`, and read the system configuration file indicated location (or the default location, if `NULL`). The paths to the default system configuration file is decided at compile time ($sysconfdir/shisa.conf).
>
> The handle is allocated regardless of return values, except for SHISA_INIT_ERROR which indicates a problem allocating the handle. (The other error conditions comes from reading the files.)
>
> **Return value:** Returns `SHISA_OK` iff successful.

The default configuration file is typically read automatically by calling `shisa_init`, but if you wish to manually access the Shisa configuration file functions, here is the complete interface.

shisa_cfg_db

int shisa_cfg_db (*Shisa* * *dbh*, *const char* * `value`) [Function]
> *dbh*: Shisa library handle created by `shisa()`.
>
> *value*: string with database definition.
>
> Setup and open a new database. The syntax of the `value` parameter is "TYPE[LOCATION[PARAMETER]]", where TYPE is one of the supported database types (e.g., "file") and LOCATION and PARAMETER are optional strings passed to the database during initialization. Neither TYPE nor LOCATION can contain " " (SPC), but PARAMETER may.
>
> **Return Value:** Returns `SHISA_OK` if database was parsed and open successfully.

shisa_cfg

int shisa_cfg (*Shisa* * *dbh*, *const char* * `option`) [Function]
> *dbh*: Shisa library handle created by `shisa()`.
>
> *option*: string with shisa library option.
>
> Configure shisa library with given option.
>
> **Return Value:** Returns SHISA_OK if option was valid.

shisa_cfg_from_file

int shisa_cfg_from_file (*Shisa* * *dbh*, *const char* * `cfg`) [Function]
> *dbh*: Shisa library handle created by `shisa()`.
>
> *cfg*: filename to read configuration from.
>
> Configure shisa library using configuration file.
>
> **Return Value:** Returns `SHISA_OK` iff successful.

shisa_cfg_default_systemfile

const char * shisa_cfg_default_systemfile (*Shisa* * *dbh*) [Function]
> *dbh*: Shisa library handle created by `shisa()`.
>
> **Return value:** Return system configuration filename.

The core part of the Shisa interface follows. The typical procedure is to use `shisa_principal_find` to verify that a specific principal exists, and to extract some information about it, and then use `shisa_keys_find` to get the cryptographic keys for the principal, usually supplying some hints as to which of all keys you are interested in (e.g., key version number and encryption algorithm number).

shisa_enumerate_realms

int shisa_enumerate_realms (*Shisa* * *dbh*, *char* *** `realms`, *size_t* * [Function]
>   `nrealms`)
> *dbh*: Shisa library handle created by `shisa()`.
>
> *realms*: Pointer to newly allocated array of newly allocated zero-terminated UTF-8 strings indicating name of realm.

nrealms: Pointer to number indicating number of allocated realm strings.

Extract a list of all realm names in backend, as zero-terminated UTF-8 strings. The caller must deallocate the strings.

Return value: Returns SHISA_OK on success, or error code.

shisa_enumerate_principals

int **shisa_enumerate_principals** (*Shisa * dbh*, *const char * realm*,   [Function]
        *char *** principals*, *size_t * nprincipals*)
dbh: Shisa library handle created by **shisa()**.

realm: Name of realm, as zero-terminated UTF-8 string.

nprincipals: Pointer to number indicating number of allocated realm strings.

Extract a list of all principal names in realm in backend, as zero-terminated UTF-8 strings. The caller must deallocate the strings.

Return value: Returns SHISA_OK on success, SHISA_NO_REALM if the specified realm does not exist, or error code.

shisa_principal_find

int **shisa_principal_find** (*Shisa * dbh*, *const char * realm*, *const*   [Function]
        *char * principal*, *Shisa_principal * ph*)
dbh: Shisa library handle created by **shisa()**.

realm: Name of realm the principal belongs in.

principal: Name of principal to get information on.

ph: Pointer to previously allocated principal structure to fill out with information about principal.

Extract information about given PRINCIPALREALM.

Return value: Returns `SHISA_OK` iff successful, `SHISA_NO_REALM` if the indicated realm does not exist, `SHISA_NO_PRINCIPAL` if the indicated principal does not exist, or an error code.

shisa_principal_update

int **shisa_principal_update** (*Shisa * dbh*, *const char * realm*, *const*   [Function]
        *char * principal*, *const Shisa_principal * ph*)
dbh: Shisa library handle created by **shisa()**.

realm: Name of realm the principal belongs in.

principal: Name of principal to get information on.

ph: Pointer to principal structure with information to store in database.

Modify information stored for given PRINCIPALREALM. Note that it is usually a good idea to only set the fields in **ph** that you actually want to update. Specifically, first calling **shisa_principal_find()** to get the current information, then modifying one field, and calling **shisa_principal_update()** is not recommended in general, as this will 1) overwrite any modifications made to other fields between the two calls (by other processes) and 2) will cause all values to be written again, which may generate more overhead.

Return value: Returns SHISA_OK if successful, SHISA_NO_REALM if the indicated realm does not exist, SHISA_NO_PRINCIPAL if the indicated principal does not exist, or an error code.

shisa_principal_add

int shisa_principal_add (*Shisa* * **dbh**, *const char* * **realm**, *const char*   [Function]
     * **principal**, *const Shisa_principal* * **ph**, *const Shisa_key* * **key**)
dbh: Shisa library handle created by shisa().

realm: Name of realm the principal belongs in.

principal: Name of principal to add, may be NULL to indicate that the **realm** should be created, in which case **ph** and **key** are not used.

ph: Pointer to principal structure with information to store in database.

key: Pointer to key structure with information to store in database.

Add given information to database as PRINCIPALREALM.

Return value: Returns SHISA_OK iff successfully added, or an error code.

shisa_principal_remove

int shisa_principal_remove (*Shisa* * **dbh**, *const char* * **realm**, *const*   [Function]
     char * **principal**)
dbh: Shisa library handle created by shisa().

realm: Name of realm the principal belongs in.

principal: Name of principal to remove, may be NULL to indicate that the **realm** itself should be removed (requires that the realm to be empty).

Remove all information stored in the database for given PRINCIPALREALM.

Return value: Returns SHISA_OK if successful, or an error code.

shisa_keys_find

int shisa_keys_find (*Shisa* * **dbh**, *const char* * **realm**, *const char* *   [Function]
     principal, *const Shisa_key* * **hint**, *Shisa_key* *** **keys**, *size_t* * **nkeys**)
dbh: Shisa library handle created by shisa().

realm: Name of realm the principal belongs in.

principal: Name of principal to add key for.

hint: Pointer to Shisa key structure with hints on matching the key to modify, may be NULL to match all keys.

keys: pointer to newly allocated array with Shisa key structures.

nkeys: pointer to number of newly allocated Shisa key structures in **keys**.

Iterate through keys for given PRINCIPALREALM and extract any keys that match **hint**. Not all elements of **hint** need to be filled out, only use the fields you are interested in. For example, if you want to extract all keys with an etype of 3 (DES-CBC-MD5), set the **key->etype** field to 3, and set all other fields to 0.

Return value: Returns SHISA_OK iff successful, or an error code.

shisa_key_add

int shisa_key_add (*Shisa * dbh*, *const char * realm*, *const char *   [Function]
     principal*, *const Shisa_key * key*)

> *dbh*: Shisa library handle created by shisa().
>
> *realm*: Name of realm the principal belongs in.
>
> *principal*: Name of principal to add key for.
>
> *key*: Pointer to Shisa key structure with key to add.
>
> Add key to database for given PRINCIPALREALM.
>
> **Return value:** Returns SHISA_OK iff successful, or an error code.

shisa_key_update

int shisa_key_update (*Shisa * dbh*, *const char * realm*, *const char *   [Function]
     principal*, *const Shisa_key * oldkey*, *const Shisa_key * newkey*)

> *dbh*: Shisa library handle created by shisa().
>
> *realm*: Name of realm the principal belongs in.
>
> *principal*: Name of principal to remove key for.
>
> *oldkey*: Pointer to Shisa key structure with hints on matching the key to modify.
>
> *newkey*: Pointer to Shisa key structure with new values for the key, note that all fields are used (and not just the ones specified by oldkey).
>
> Modify data about a key in the database, for the given PRINCIPALREALM. First the oldkey is used to locate the key to update (similar to shisa_keys_find()), then that key is modified to contain whatever information is stored in newkey. Not all elements of oldkey need to be filled out, only enough as to identify the key uniquely. For example, if you want to modify the information stored for the only key with an etype of 3 (DES-CBC-MD5), set the key->etype field to 3, and set all other fields to 0.
>
> **Return value:** Returns SHISA_OK on success, SHISA_NO_KEY if no key could be identified, and SHISA_MULTIPLE_KEY_MATCH if more than one key matched the given criteria, or an error code.

shisa_key_remove

int shisa_key_remove (*Shisa * dbh*, *const char * realm*, *const char *   [Function]
     principal*, *const Shisa_key * key*)

> *dbh*: Shisa library handle created by shisa().
>
> *realm*: Name of realm the principal belongs in.
>
> *principal*: Name of principal to remove key for.
>
> *key*: Pointer to Shisa key structure with hints on matching the key to remove.
>
> Remove a key, matching the hints in key, from the Shisa database for the user PRINCIPALREALM. Not all elements of key need to be filled out, only those you are interested in. For example, if you want to remove the only key with an etype of 3 (DES-CBC-MD5), set the key->etype field to 3, and set all other fields to 0.

Return value: Returns `SHISA_OK` on success, `SHISA_NO_KEY` if no key could be identified, and `SHISA_MULTIPLE_KEY_MATCH` if more than one key matched the given criteria, or an error code.

shisa_key_free

void `shisa_key_free` (*Shisa* * ***dbh***, *Shisa_key* * ***key***)   [Function]

> *dbh*: Shisa library handle created by `shisa()`.
>
> *key*: Pointer to Shisa key structure to deallocate.
>
> Deallocate the fields of a Shisa key structure, and the structure itself.

shisa_keys_free

void `shisa_keys_free` (*Shisa* * ***dbh***, *Shisa_key* ** ***keys***, *size_t* ***nkeys***)   [Function]

> *dbh*: Shisa library handle created by `shisa()`.
>
> *keys*: Pointer to array with `nkeys` elements of keys.
>
> *nkeys*: Number of key elements in `keys` array.
>
> Deallocate each element of an array with Shisa database keys, using `shisa_key_free()`.

Error handling is similar to that for Shishi in general (see Section 5.17 [Error Handling], page 220), i.e., you invoke `shisa_strerror` on the integer return value received by some function, if the return value is non-zero. Below is the complete interface.

shisa_strerror

const char * `shisa_strerror` (*int* ***err***)   [Function]

> *err*: shisa error code
>
> **Return value:** Returns a pointer to a statically allocated string containing a description of the error with the error value `err`. This string can be used to output a diagnostic message to the user.

shisa_info

void `shisa_info` (*Shisa* * ***dbh***, *const char* * ***format***, ...)   [Function]

> *dbh*: Shisa library handle created by `shisa()`.
>
> *format*: printf style format string. ...: print style arguments.
>
> Print informational message to standard error.

5.20 Generic Security Service

As an alternative to the native Shishi programming API, it is possible to program Shishi through the Generic Security Services (GSS) API. The advantage of using GSS-API in your security application, instead of the native Shishi API, is that it will be easier to port your application between different Kerberos 5 implementations, and even beyond Kerberos 5 to different security systems, that support GSS-API. In the free software world, however, almost the only widely used security system that supports GSS-API is Kerberos 5, so the last advantage is somewhat academic. But if you are porting applications using GSS-API for other Kerberos 5 implementations, or want a more mature and stable API than the native Shishi API, you may find using Shishi's GSS-API interface compelling. Note that GSS-API only offer basic services, for more advanced uses you must use the native API.

Since the GSS-API is not specific to Shishi, it is distributed independently from Shishi. Further information on the GSS project can be found at `http://www.gnu.org/software/gss/`.

6 Acknowledgements

Shishi uses Libtasn1 by Fabio Fiorina, Libgcrypt and Libgpg-error by Werner Koch, Libidn by Simon Josefsson, cvs2cl by Karl Fogel, and gdoc by Michael Zucchi.

Several GNU packages simplified development considerably, those packages include Autoconf, Automake, Libtool, Gnulib, Gettext, Indent, CVS, Texinfo, Help2man and Emacs.

Several people reported bugs, sent patches or suggested improvements, see the file THANKS.

Nicolas Pouvesle wrote the section about the Kerberos rsh/rlogin protocol.

This manual borrows text from the Kerberos 5 specification.

Appendix A Criticism of Kerberos

The intention with this section is to discuss various problems with Kerberos 5, so you can form a conscious decision how to deploy and use Shishi correctly in your organization. Currently the issues below are condensed, and mostly serve as a reminder for the author to elaborate on them.

No encryption scheme with security proof.

No standardized API, and GSS mechanism lack important functionality.

Lack of authorization system. (krb5_kuserok())

Host to realm mapping relies on insecure DNS or static configuration files.

Informational model and user database administration.

Non-formal specification. Unclear on the etype to use for session keys (etype in request or database?). Unclear on how to populate some "evident" fields (e.g., cname in tickets for AS-REQ, or crealm, cname, realm, sname, ctime and cusec in KRB-ERROR). Unclear error code semantics (e.g., logic for when to use S_PRINCIPAL_UNKNOWN absent). Some KRB-ERROR fields are required, but can't be usefully populated in some situations, and no guidance is given on what they should contain.

RFC 1510/1510bis incompatibilities. NULL enctype removed without discussion, and it is still used by some 1964 GSSAPI implementations. KRB_SAFE text (3.4.1) says the checksum is generated using the session or sub-session key, which contradicts itself (compare section 3.2.6) and also RFC 1510, which both allow the application to define the key. Verification of KRB_SAFE now require the key to be compatible with the (sub-)session key, in 1510 the only requirement was that it was collision proof.

Problems with RFC 1510bis. Uses bignum INTEGER for TYPED-DATA and AD-AND-OR.

Problems with crypto specification. It uses the word "random" many times, but there is no discussion on the randomness requirements. Practical experience indicate it is impossible to use true randomness for all "random" fields, and no implementation does this. A post by Don Davis on the ietf-krb-wg list tried to provide insight, but the information was never added to the specification.

Appendix B Protocol Extensions

This appendix specifies the non-standard protocol elements implemented by Shishi. By nature of being non-standard, everything described here is experimental. Comments and feedback is appreciated.

B.1 STARTTLS protected KDC exchanges

Shishi is able to "upgrade" TCP communications with the KDC to use the Transport Layer Security (TLS) protocol. The TLS protocol offers integrity and privacy protected exchanges. TLS also offers authentication using username and passwords, X.509 certificates, or OpenPGP certificates. Kerberos 5 claims to offer some of these features, although it is not as rich as the TLS protocol. An inconclusive list of the motivation for using TLS is given below.

- Server authentication of the KDC to the client. In traditional Kerberos 5, KDC authentication is only proved as a side effect that the KDC knows your encryption key (i.e., your password).

- Client authentication against KDC. Kerberos 5 assume the user knows a key (usually in the form of a password). Sometimes external factors make this hard to fulfill. In some situations, users are equipped with smart cards with a RSA authentication key. In others, users have a OpenPGP client on their desktop, with a public OpenPGP key known to the server. In some situations, the policy may be that password authentication may only be done through SRP.

- Kerberos exchanges are privacy protected. Part of many Kerberos packets are transfered without privacy protection (i.e., encryption). That part contains information, such as the client principal name, the server principal name, the encryption types supported by the client, the lifetime of tickets, etc. Revealing such information is, in some threat models, considered a problem. Thus, this enables "anonymity".

- Prevents downgrade attacks affecting encryption types. The encryption type of the ticket in KDC-REQ are sent in the clear in Kerberos 5. This allows an attacker to replace the encryption type with a compromised mechanisms, e.g. 56-bit DES. Since clients in general cannot know the encryption types other servers support, it is difficult for the client to detect if there was a man-in-the-middle or if the remote server simply did not support a stronger mechanism. Clients may chose to refuse 56-bit DES altogether, but in some environments this leads to operational difficulties.

- TLS is well-proved and the protocol is studied by many parties. This is an advantage in network design, where TLS is often already assumed as part of the solution since it is used to protect HTTP, IMAP, SMTP etc. In some threat models, the designer prefer to reduce the number of protocols that can hurt the overall system security if they are compromised.

Other reasons for using TLS exists.

B.1.1 TCP/IP transport with TLS upgrade (STARTTLS)

RFC 1510bis requires Kerberos servers (KDCs) to accept TCP requests. Each request and response is prefixed by a 4 octet integer in network byte order, indicating the length of the packet. The high bit of the length was reserved for future expansion, and servers that do not understand how to interpret a set high bit must return a `KRB-ERROR` with a `KRB_ERR_FIELD_TOOLONG` and close the TCP stream.

The TCP/IP transport with TLS upgrade (STARTTLS) uses this reserved bit as follows. First we define a new extensible typed hole for Kerberos 5 messages, because we used the only reserved bit. It is thus prudent to offer future extensions on our proposal. Secondly we reserve two values in this new typed hole, and described how they are used to implement STARTTLS.

B.1.2 Extensible typed hole based on reserved high bit

When the high bit is set, the remaining 31 bits of the 4 octets are treated as an extensible typed hole, and thus form a 31 bit integer enumerating various extensions. Each of the values indicate a specific extended operation mode, two of which are used and defined here, and the rest are left for others to use. If the KDC do not understand a requested extension, it MUST return a `KRB-ERROR` with a `KRB_ERR_FIELD_TOOLONG` value (prefixed by the 4 octet length integer, with the high bit clear, as usual) and close the TCP stream.

Meaning of the 31 lower bits in the 4 octet field, when the high bit is set:

```
0                   RESERVED.
1                   STARTTLS requested by client.
2                   STARTTLS request accepted by server.
3...2147483647      AVAILABLE for registration (via bug-shishi@josefsson.org).
2147483648          RESERVED.
```

B.1.3 STARTTLS requested by client (extension mode 1)

When this is sent by the client, the client is requesting the server to start TLS negotiation on the TCP stream. The client MUST NOT start TLS negotiation immediately. Instead, the client wait for either a KRB-ERROR (sent normally, prefixed by a 4 octet length integer) indicating the server do not understand the set high bit, or 4 octet which is to interpreted as an integer in network byte order, where the high bit is set and the remaining 31 bit are interpreted as an integer specifying the "STARTTLS request accepted by server". In the first case, the client infer that the server do not understand (or wish to support) STARTTLS, and can re-try using normal TCP, if unprotected Kerberos 5 exchanges are acceptable to the client policy. In the latter case, it should invoke TLS negotiation on the stream. If any other data is received, the client MUST close the TCP stream.

B.1.4 STARTTLS request accepted by server (extension mode 2)

This 4 octet message should be sent by the server when it has received the previous 4 octet message. The message is an acknowledgment of the client's request to initiate STARTTLS on the channel. The server MUST then invoke a TLS negotiation.

B.1.5 Proceeding after successful TLS negotiation

If the TLS negotiation ended successfully, possibly also considering client or server policies, the exchange within the TLS protected stream is performed like normal UDP Kerberos 5 exchanges, i.e., there is no TCP 4 octet length field before each packet. Instead each Kerberos packet MUST be sent within one TLS record, so the application can use the TLS record length as the Kerberos 5 packet length.

B.1.6 Proceeding after failed TLS negotiation

If the TLS negotiation fails, possibly due to client or server policy (e.g., inadequate support of encryption types in TLS, or lack of client or server authentication) the entity that detect the failure MUST disconnected the connection. It is expected that any error messages that explain the error condition is transfered by TLS.

B.1.7 Interaction with KDC addresses in DNS

Administrators for a KDC may announce the KDC address by placing SRV records in DNS for the realm, as described in 'draft-ietf-krb-wg-krb-dns-locate-03.txt'. That document mention TLS, but do not reference any work that describe how KDCs uses TLS. Until further clarified, consider the TLS field in that document to refer to implementation supporting this STARTTLS protocol.

B.1.8 Using TLS authentication logic in Kerberos

The server MAY consider the authentication performed by the TLS exchange as sufficient to issue Kerberos 5 tickets to the client, without requiring, e.g., pre-authentication. However, it is not an error to require or use pre-authentication as well.

The client may also indicate that it wishes to use TLS both for authentication and data protection by using the 'NULL' encryption type in its request. The server can decide from its local policy whether or not issuing tickets based solely on TLS authentication, and whether 'NULL' encryption within TLS, is acceptable or not. This mode is currently under investigation.

B.1.9 Security considerations

Because the initial token is not protected, it is possible for an active attacker to make it appear to the client that the server do not support this extension. It is up to client configuration to disallow non-TLS connections, if this vulnerability is deemed unacceptable. For interoperability, we suggest the default behaviour should be to allow automatic fallback to TCP or UDP.

The security considerations of both TLS and Kerberos 5 are inherited. Using TLS for authentication and/or data protection together with Kerberos alter the authentication logic fundamentally. Thus, it may be that even if the TLS and Kerberos 5 protocols and implementations were secure, the combination of TLS and Kerberos 5 described here could be insecure.

No channel bindings are provided in the Kerberos messages. It is an open question whether, and how, this should be fixed.

B.2 Telnet encryption with AES-CCM

This appendix describe how Shishi use the Advanced Encryption Standard (AES) encryption algorithm in Counter with CBC-MAC mode (RFC 3610) with the telnet encryption option (RFC 2946).

B.2.1 Command Names and Codes

Encryption Type

```
     AES_CCM                 12
```

Suboption Commands

```
     AES_CCM_INFO            1
     AES_CCM_INFO_OK         2
     AES_CCM_INFO_BAD        3
```

B.2.2 Command Meanings

`IAC SB ENCRYPT IS AES_CCM AES_CCM_INFO <M> <L> <nonce> IAC SE`

The sender of this command select desired M and L parameters, and nonce, as described in RFC 3610, and sends it to the other side of the connection. The parameters and the nonce are sent in clear text. Only the side of the connection that is WILL ENCRYPT may send the AES_CCM_INFO command.

`IAC SB ENCRYPT REPLY AES_CCM AES_CCM_INFO_BAD IAC SE`

The sender of this command reject the parameters received in the AES_CCM_INFO command. Only the side of the connection that is DO ENCRYPT may send the AES_CCM_INFO_BAD command. The command MUST be sent if the nonce field length does not match the selected value for L. The command MAY be sent if the receiver do not accept the parameters for reason such as policy. No capability is provided to negotiate these parameters.

`IAC SB ENCRYPT REPLY AES_CCM AES_CCM_INFO_OK IAC SE`

The sender of this command accepts the parameters received in the AES_CCM_INFO command. Only the side of the connection that is DO ENCRYPT may send the AES_CCM_INFO_BAD command. The command MUST NOT be sent if the nonce field length does not match the selected value for L.

B.2.3 Implementation Rules

Once a AES_CCM_INFO_OK command has been received, the WILL ENCRYPT side of the connection should do keyid negotiation using the ENC_KEYID command. Once the keyid negotiation has successfully identified a common keyid, then START and END commands may be sent by the side of the connection that is WILL ENCRYPT. Data will be encrypted using the AES-CCM algorithm, with the negotiated nonce and parameters M and L. After each successful encryption and decryption, the nonce is treated as an integer in network byte order, and incremented by one.

If encryption (decryption) is turned off and back on again, and the same keyid is used when re-starting the encryption (decryption), the intervening clear text must not change the state of the encryption (decryption) machine. In particular, the AES-CCM nonce must not be re-set.

If a START command is sent (received) with a different keyid, the encryption (decryption) machine must be re-initialized immediately following the end of the START command with the new key and the parameters sent (received) in the last AES_CCM_INFO command.

If a new AES_CCM_INFO command is sent (received), and encryption (decryption) is enabled, the encryption (decryption) machine must be re-initialized immediately following the end of the AES_CCM_INFO command with the new nonce and parameters, and the keyid sent (received) in the last START command.

If encryption (decryption) is not enabled when a AES_CCM_INFO command is sent (received), the encryption (decryption) machine must be re- initialized after the next START command, with the keyid sent (received) in that START command, and the nonce and parameters sent (received) in this AES_CCM_INFO command.

At all times MUST each end make sure that a AES-CCM nonce is not used twice under the same encryption key. The rules above help accomplish this in an interoperable way.

B.2.4 Integration with the AUTHENTICATION telnet option

<<This section is slightly complicated. Can't we simplify this?>>

As noted in the telnet ENCRYPTION option specifications, a keyid value of zero indicates the default encryption key, as might be derived from the telnet AUTHENTICATION option. If the default encryption key negotiated as a result of the telnet AUTHENTICA-TION option contains less than 32 bytes (corresponding to two 128 bit keys), then the AES_CCM option MUST NOT be offered or used as a valid telnet encryption option. Furthermore, depending on policy for key lengths, the AES_CCM option MAY be disabled if the default encryption key contain less than 48 bytes (for two 192 bit keys), or less than 64 bytes (for two 256 bit keys), as well.

The available encrypt key data is divided on two halves, where the first half is used to encrypt data sent from the server (decrypt data received by the client), and the second half is used to encrypt data sent from the client (decrypt data received by the server).

Note that the above algorithm assumes that the AUTHENTICATION mechanism generate keying material suitable for AES-CCM as used in this specification. This is not necessarily true in general, but we specify this behaviour as the default since it is true for most authentication systems in popular use today. New telnet AUTHENTICATION mechanisms may specify alternative methods for determining the keys to be used for this cipher suite in their specification, if the session key negotiated by that authentication mechanism is not a DES key and where this algorithm may not be safely used.

Kerberos 5 authentication clarification: The key used to encrypt data from the client to the server is taken from the sub-session key in the AP-REQ. The key used to decrypt data from the server to the client is taken from the sub-session key in the AP-REP. If mutual authentication is not negotiated, the key used to encrypt data from the client to the server is taken from the session key in the ticket, and the key used to decrypt data from the server to the client is taken from the sub-session key in the AP-REQ. Leaving the AP-REQ sub-key field empty MUST disable the AES_CCM option.

B.2.5 Security Considerations

The protocol must be properly and securely implemented. For example, an implementation should not be vulnerable to various implementation-specific attacks such as buffer overflows or side-channel analysis.

We wish to repeat the suggestion from RFC 2946, to investigate in a STARTTLS approach for Telnet encryption (and also authentication), when the security level provided by this specification is not adequate.

B.2.5.1 Telnet Encryption Protocol Security Considerations

The security consideration of the Telnet encryption protocol are inherited.

It should be noted that the it is up to the authentication protocol used, if any, to bind the authenticity of the peers to a specific session.

The Telnet encryption protocol does not, in general, protect against possibly malicious downgrading to any mutually acceptable, but not preferred, encryption type. This places a requirement on each peer to only accept encryption types it trust fully. In other words, the Telnet encryption protocol do not guarantee that the strongest mutually acceptable encryption type is always selected.

B.2.5.2 AES-CCM Security Considerations

The integrity and privacy claims are inherited from AES-CCM. In particular, the implementation must make sure a nonce is not used more than once together with the same key.

Furthermore, the encryption key is assumed to be random, i.e., it should not be possible to guess it with probability of success higher than guessing any uniformly selected random key. RFC 1750 gives an overview of issues and recommendations related to randomness.

B.2.6 Acknowledgments

This document is based on the various Telnet Encryption RFCs (RFC 2946, RFC 2947, RFC 2948, RFC 2952 and RFC 2953).

B.3 Kerberized rsh and rlogin

This appendix describe the KCMDV0.2 protocol used in shishi patched version of inetutils. The KCMD protocol was developped by the MIT Kerberos team for kerberized rsh an rlogin programs. Differences between rlogin an rsh will be explained, like those between v0.1 and v0.2 of the protocol for compatibility reasons. It is possible that some parts of this document are not in conformity with original KCMD protocol because there is no official specification about it. However, it seems that shishi implementation is compatible with MIT's one.

Warning: If you are seriously considering using Kerberos rsh or rlogin, instead of more robust remote access protocols such as SSH, you may first want to explore `http://www.cs.berkeley.edu/~hildrum/kerberos/` and the full paper at `http://www.cs.berkeley.edu/~hildrum/043.pdf`.

B.3.1 Establish connection

First the client should establish a TCP connection with the server. Default ports are 543 (klogin), 544 (kshell), 2105 (eklogin). eklogin is the same as klogin but with encryption. Their is no longer ekshell port because encrypted and normal connection use the same port (kshell). Kshell need a second connection for stderr. The client should send a null terminated string that represent the port of this second connection. Klogin and eklogin does not use a second connection for stderr so the client must send a null byte to the server. Contrary to classic rsh/rlogin, server must not check if the client port is in the range 0-1023.

B.3.2 Kerberos identification

When connections are established, first thing to do is to indicate kerberos authentication must be used. So the client will send a string to indicate it will used kerberos 5. It will call a length-string "strl" the couple (lenght of the string strl, null terminated string strl). Length of the string is an int32 (32bits int) in MSB order (for the network). So the client send this length-string strl :

```
KRB5_SENDAUTH_V1.0
```

After that the client must indicate which version of the protocol it will used by sending this length-string strl :

```
KCMDV0.2
```

It can be V0.1 for older versions. If indentification from client is good, server will send a null byte (0x00). Else if authentication message is wrong, server send byte 0x01, else if protocol version message is wrong server send byte 0x02.

B.3.3 Kerberos authentication

When client is indentified, kerberos authentication can begin. The client must send an AP-REQ to the server. AP-REQ authenticator must have a subkey (only for KCMDV0.2) and a checksum. Authenticator checksum is created on following string :

```
"serverport:""terminaltype""remoteusername"
```

for example :

```
543:linux/38400user
```

remoteusername corresponds to the identity of the client on remote machine.

AP-REQ is sended in der encoded format. The length (int32) of der encoded AP-REQ is sended in network format (MSB), following by the der encoded AP-REQ. If all is correct, server send a null int32 (MSB format but like it is null it is not important). KCMD protocol use mutual authentication, so server must now send and AP-REP : (in32 lenght in MSB of der encoded AP-REP)(der encoded AP-REP).

Now server and client are partially authenticated.

B.3.4 Extended authentication

Client must now send 3 different null terminated strings (without lenght) :

- remote user name (user identity on remote machine)
- terminal type for rlogin or command for rsh
- local user name (user identity on client machine)

example for rsh :

```
"rname\0"
"cat /usr/local/etc/shishi.conf"
"lname\0"
```

Server must verify that checksum in AP-REQ authenticator is correct by computing a new hash like client has done.

Server must verify that principal (in AP-REQ) has right to log in on the remote user account. For the moment shishi only check if remote user name is equal to principal. A more complex authorization code is planned. Look at the end to know how MIT/Heimdal do to check authorization.

If all is correct server send a null byte, else an error message string (null terminated string) is sent. User read the first byte. If it is equal to zero, authentication is correct and is logged on the remote host. Else user can read the error messsage send by the server.

B.3.5 Window size

For rlogin protocol, when authentication is complete, the server can optionnaly send a message to ask for window terminal size of user. Then the user can respond but it is not an obligation.

In KCMDV0.1 server send an urgent TCP message (MSG_OOB) with one byte :

```
TIOCPKT_WINDOW = 0x80
```

In KCMDV0.2 server does not send an urgent message but write on the socket 5 bytes :

```
'\377', '\377', 'o', 'o', TIOCPKT_WINDOW
```

If encryption is enabled (eklogin) server must send this 5 bytes encrypted.

Client can answer in both protocol version with :

```
'\377', '\377', 's', 's', "struct winsize"
```

The winsize structure is filled with corresponding setting to client's terminal. If encryption is enabled this answer must be send encrypted.

B.3.6 End of authentication

The "classic" rsh/rlogin can be used now.

B.3.7 Encryption

Encryption mode is used when a connection with eklogin is established. Encryption with krsh can be used too. Before, there was a specific port for that (ekshell), but now to indicate that encryption must be used with krsh, client must add "-x " before the command when it send it between remote user name and local user name. When the client compute the checksum for AP-REQ authenticator the "- x" must not be included.

Encryption in KCMDV0.2 is not the same as in KCMDV0.1. KCMDV0.1 uses ticket session key as encryption key, and use standard Kerberos encryption functions. This protocol only supports des-cbc-crc, des-cbc-md4, des-cbc-md5 and does not use initialisation vectors.

For example on each encryption/decryption calls, the following prototype kerberos function should be used :

```
kerberos_encrypt (key, keyusage, in, out)  (or decrypt)
```

KCMDV0.2 can be used with all kerberos encryption modes (des, 3des, aes, arcfour) and use AP-REQ authenticator subkey. In opposite to KCMDV0.1 initialisation vectors are used. All encryptions/descryptions must be made using a cryptographic context (for example to use the updated iv, or sbox) :

```
kerberos_init(ctx, iv, key, keyusage)
kerberos_encrypt (ctx, in, out)
```

For both protocols, keyusage id for des-cbc-md5, des-cbc-md4, des-cbc-crc and des3-cbc-sha1 (for KCMDV0.2) :

```
keyusage = 1026
```

For other KCMDV0.2 modes keyusage is different for each encryption/decryption usage. To understand, eklogin use 1 socket. It encrypts data (output 1) to send and decrypts (input 1) received data. Kshell use 2 sockets (1 for transmit data, 1 for stderr). So there are four modes :

```
transmit  : input   1
            output  1


stderr    : input   2
            output  2
```

There is a keyusage for each modes. The keyusage must correspond on client and server side. For example in klogin client input 1 keyusage will be server output 1 keyusage.

I/O	Client	Server
intput 1	1028	1030
output 1	1030	1028
intput 2	1032	1034
output 2	1034	1032

Those keyusages must be used with AES and ARCFOUR modes.

KCMDV0.2 uses IV (initialisation vector). Like for keyusage, client IV must correspond to server IV. IV size is equal to key type, blocksize. All bytes of IV must be initialised to :

I/O	Client	Server
intput 1	0	1
output 1	1	0
intput 2	2	3
output 2	3	2

ARCFOUR mode does not use IV. However, like it is said before, a context must be used to keep the updated sbox.

Normal message with klogin and kshell are sent like that :

```
(int 32 lenght of message in MSB order)
(message)
```

In encrypted mode it is a bit different :

```
(int 32 length of unencrypted message in MSB order)
(encrypted message)
```

In KCMDV0.2 encrypted message is create like that :

```
encrypt (
(int 32 length of message in MSB order)
(message)
)
```

A check on message size can be made in second version of the protocol.

B.3.8 KCMDV0.3

This part only gives possible ways to extend KCMD protocol. Does not take that as must have in KCMD implementation.

Extensions of KCMV0.2 could be made. For example kshell supposes there are no files with name "-x *". I think the same thing can be supposed with terminal name for klogin. So client could add "-x " to terminal type it sends to server to indicate it will use encryption. Like that there will be only one port for klogin/eklogin : 543.

In encrypted mode kshell send command in clear on the network, this could be considered as insecure as user have decided to use encryption. This is not really a problem for klogin because it just sends terminal type.

In encrypted mode, klogin and kshell clients could only send "-x" as command or terminal type. After that encryption is activated, and the client could send terminal type or command encrypted. The server will send the null byte to say that all is correct, or error message in encrypted form.

B.3.9 MIT/Heimdal authorization

This part describes how MIT/Heimdal version check authorization of the user to log in on the remote machine.

Authorization check is made by looking if the file .k5login exists on the account of the remote user. If this file does not exist, remote user name must be the same as principal in AP-REQ to valid authorization. Else if this file exists, check first verify that remote user or root are the owner of .k5login. If it is not the case, the check fails. If it is good, check reads each line of that file and compare each readed name to principal. If principal is found in .k5login, authorization is valid, else user is not allowed to connect on remote host with the specified remote user name (that can be the same as principal).

So someone (for example user "user1") can remote log into "user2" account if .k5login is present in user2 home dir and this file is owned by user2 or root and user1 name is present in this file.

B.4 Key as initialization vector

The des-cbc-crc algorithm (see Section 1.4 [Cryptographic Overview], page 5) uses the DES key as the initialization vector. This is problematic in general (see below[1]), but may be mitigated in Kerberos by the CRC checksum that is also included.

```
From daw@espresso.CS.Berkeley.EDU Fri Mar  1 13:32:34 PST 1996
Article: 50440 of sci.crypt
Path: agate!daw
From: daw@espresso.CS.Berkeley.EDU (David A Wagner)
Newsgroups: sci.crypt
Subject: Re: DES-CBC and Initialization Vectors
Date: 29 Feb 1996 21:48:16 GMT
Organization: University of California, Berkeley
Lines: 31
Message-ID: <4h56v0$3no@agate.berkeley.edu>
References: <4h39li$33o@gaia.ns.utk.edu>
NNTP-Posting-Host: espresso.cs.berkeley.edu
```

---

[1] The post is copyrighted by David Wagner, included here with permission, the canonical location is http://www.cs.berkeley.edu/~daw/my-posts/key-as-iv-broken

In article <4h39li$33o@gaia.ns.utk.edu>,
Nair Venugopal <venu@mars.utcc.utk.edu> wrote:
> Is there anything wrong in using the key as the I.V. in DES-CBC mode?

Yes, you're open to a chosen-ciphertext attack which recovers the key.

Alice is sending stuff DES-CBC encrypted with key K to Bob. Mary is an
active adversary in the middle. Suppose Alice encrypts some plaintext
blocks P_1, P_2, P_3, ... in DES-CBC mode with K as the IV, and sends off
the resulting ciphertext
        A->B: C_1, C_2, C_3, ...
where each C_j is a 8-byte DES ciphertext block. Mary wants to discover
the key K, but doesn't even know any of the P_j's. She replaces the above
message by
        M->B: C_1, 0, C_1
where 0 is the 8-byte all-zeros block. Bob will decrypt under DES-CBC,
recovering the blocks
        Q_1, Q_2, Q_3
where
        Q_1 = DES-decrypt(K, C_1) xor K = P_1
        Q_2 = DES-decrypt(K, C_2) xor C_1 = (some unimportant junk)
        Q_3 = DES-decrypt(K, C_1) xor 0 = P_1 xor K
Bob gets this garbage-looking message Q_1,Q_2,Q_3 which Mary recovers
(under the chosen-ciphertext assumption: this is like a known-plaintext
attack, which isn't too implausible). Notice that Mary can recover K by
        K = Q_1 xor Q_3;
so after this one simple active attack, Mary gets the key back!

So, if you must use a fixed IV, don't use the key-- use 0 or something
like that. Even better, don't use a fixed IV-- use the DES encryption
of a counter, or something like that.

B.5 The Keytab Binary File Format

The keytab file format is described in the file 'keytab.txt', included in verbatim below.

The Kerberos Keytab Binary File Format
Copyright (C) 2006 Michael B Allen <mba2000 ioplex.com>
http://www.ioplex.com/utilities/keytab.txt
Last updated: Fri May 5 13:39:40 EDT 2006

The MIT keytab binary format is not a standard format, nor is it
documented anywhere in detail. The format has evolved and may continue
to. It is however understood by several Kerberos implementations including
Heimdal and of course MIT and keytab files are created by the ktpass.exe
utility from Windows. So it has established itself as the defacto format
for storing Kerberos keys.

The following C-like structure definitions illustrate the MIT keytab
file format. All values are in network byte order. All text is ASCII.

```
keytab {
    uint16_t file_format_version;                    /* 0x502 */
    keytab_entry entries[*];
};

keytab_entry {
    int32_t size;
    uint16_t num_components;    /* sub 1 if version 0x501 */
    counted_octet_string realm;
    counted_octet_string components[num_components];
    uint32_t name_type;   /* not present if version 0x501 */
    uint32_t timestamp;
    uint8_t vno8;
    keyblock key;
    uint32_t vno; /* only present if >= 4 bytes left in entry */
};

counted_octet_string {
    uint16_t length;
    uint8_t data[length];
};

keyblock {
    uint16_t type;
    counted_octet_string;
};
```

The keytab file format begins with the 16 bit file_format_version which
at the time this document was authored is 0x502. The format of older
keytabs is described at the end of this document.

The file_format_version is immediately followed by an array of
keytab_entry structures which are prefixed with a 32 bit size indicating
the number of bytes that follow in the entry. Note that the size should be
evaluated as signed. This is because a negative value indicates that the
entry is in fact empty (e.g. it has been deleted) and that the negative
value of that negative value (which is of course a positive value) is
the offset to the next keytab_entry. Based on these size values alone
the entire keytab file can be traversed.

The size is followed by a 16 bit num_components field indicating the
number of counted_octet_string components in the components array.

The num_components field is followed by a counted_octet_string
representing the realm of the principal.

A counted_octet_string is simply an array of bytes prefixed with a 16
bit length. For the realm and name components, the counted_octet_string
bytes are ASCII encoded text with no zero terminator.

Following the realm is the components array that represents the name of
the principal. The text of these components may be joined with slashs
to construct the typical SPN representation. For example, the service
principal HTTP/www.foo.net@FOO.NET would consist of name components
"HTTP" followed by "www.foo.net".

Following the components array is the 32 bit name_type (e.g. 1 is
KRB5_NT_PRINCIPAL, 2 is KRB5_NT_SRV_INST, 5 is KRB5_NT_UID, etc). In
practice the name_type is almost certainly 1 meaning KRB5_NT_PRINCIPAL.

The 32 bit timestamp indicates the time the key was established for that
principal. The value represents the number of seconds since Jan 1, 1970.

The 8 bit vno8 field is the version number of the key. This value is
overridden by the 32 bit vno field if it is present.

The keyblock structure consists of a 16 bit value indicating the keytype
(e.g. 3 is des-cbc-md5, 23 is arcfour-hmac-md5, 16 is des3-cbc-sha1,
etc). This is followed by a counted_octet_string containing the key.

The last field of the keytab_entry structure is optional. If the size of
the keytab_entry indicates that there are at least 4 bytes remaining,
a 32 bit value representing the key version number is present. This
value supersedes the 8 bit vno8 value preceeding the keyblock.

Older keytabs with a file_format_version of 0x501 are different in
three ways:

  1) All integers are in host byte order [1].
  2) The num_components field is 1 too large (i.e. after decoding,
     decrement by 1).
  3) The 32 bit name_type field is not present.

[1] The file_format_version field should really be treated as two
    separate 8 bit quantities representing the major and minor version
    number respectively.

Permission to copy, modify, and distribute this document, with or
without modification, for any purpose and without fee or royalty is
hereby granted, provided that you include this copyright notice in ALL

copies of the document or portions thereof, including modifications.

B.6 The Credential Cache Binary File Format

The credential cache file format is described in the file 'keytab.txt', included in verbatim below.

```
The Kerberos Credential Cache Binary File Format
Copyright (C) 2006-2013 Simon Josefsson <simon josefsson.org>
http://josefsson.org/shishi/ccache.txt
Last updated: Sat Sep 23 12:04:11 CEST 2006


Like the MIT keytab binary format (see Michael B Allen's reverse
engineered description in keytab.txt), the credential cache format is
not standard nor documented anywhere.


In C style notation, the MIT credential cache file format is as
follows.  All values are in network byte order.  All text is ASCII.


ccache {
        uint16_t file_format_version; /* 0x0504 */
        uint16_t headerlen;           /* only if version is 0x0504 */
        header headers[];             /* only if version is 0x0504 */
        principal primary_principal;
        credential credentials[*];
};


header {
      uint16_t tag;                     /* 1 = DeltaTime */
      uint16_t taglen;
      uint8_t tagdata[taglen]
};


The ccache.taglen and ccache.tags fields are only present in 0x0504
versions, not in earlier.  Both MIT and Heimdal appear to correctly
ignore unknown tags, so it appears safe to add them (although there is
no central place to "register" tags).


Currently only one tag is widely implemented, DeltaTime (0x0001).  Its
taglen is always 8, and tagdata will contain:


DeltaTime {
      uint32_t time_offset;
      uint32_t usec_offset;
};


After reading the file_format_version, header tags, and default
principal, a list of credentials follow.  You deduce from the file
```

length when there are no more credentials.

```
credential {
        principal client;
        principal server;
        keyblock key;
        times    time;
        uint8_t  is_skey;              /* 1 if skey, 0 otherwise */
        uint32_t tktflags;             /* stored in reversed byte order */
        uint32_t num_address;
        address  addrs[num_address];
        uint32_t num_authdata;
        authdata authdata[num_authdata];
        countet_octet_string ticket;
        countet_octet_string second_ticket;
};

keyblock {
        uint16_t keytype;
        uint16_t etype;                /* only present if version 0x0503 */
        uint16_t keylen;
        uint8_t keyvalue[keylen];
};

times {
      uint32_t  authtime;
      uint32_t  starttime;
      uint32_t  endtime;
      uint32_t  renew_till;
};

address {
        uint16_t addrtype;
        counted_octet_string addrdata;
};

authdata {
        uint16_t authtype;
        counted_octet_string authdata;
};

principal {
        uint32_t name_type;            /* not present if version 0x0501 */
        uint32_t num_components;       /* sub 1 if version 0x501 */
        counted_octet_string realm;
        counted_octet_string components[num_components];
};
```

```
counted_octet_string {
    uint32_t length;
    uint8_t data[length];
};
```

Permission to copy, modify, and distribute this document, with or
without modification, for any purpose and without fee or royalty is
hereby granted, provided that you include this copyright notice in ALL
copies of the document or portions thereof, including modifications.

Appendix C Copying Information

C.1 GNU Free Documentation License

Version 1.3, 3 November 2008

Copyright © 2000, 2001, 2002, 2007, 2008 Free Software Foundation, Inc.
`http://fsf.org/`

Everyone is permitted to copy and distribute verbatim copies
of this license document, but changing it is not allowed.

0. PREAMBLE

The purpose of this License is to make a manual, textbook, or other functional and useful document *free* in the sense of freedom: to assure everyone the effective freedom to copy and redistribute it, with or without modifying it, either commercially or non-commercially. Secondarily, this License preserves for the author and publisher a way to get credit for their work, while not being considered responsible for modifications made by others.

This License is a kind of "copyleft", which means that derivative works of the document must themselves be free in the same sense. It complements the GNU General Public License, which is a copyleft license designed for free software.

We have designed this License in order to use it for manuals for free software, because free software needs free documentation: a free program should come with manuals providing the same freedoms that the software does. But this License is not limited to software manuals; it can be used for any textual work, regardless of subject matter or whether it is published as a printed book. We recommend this License principally for works whose purpose is instruction or reference.

1. APPLICABILITY AND DEFINITIONS

This License applies to any manual or other work, in any medium, that contains a notice placed by the copyright holder saying it can be distributed under the terms of this License. Such a notice grants a world-wide, royalty-free license, unlimited in duration, to use that work under the conditions stated herein. The "Document", below, refers to any such manual or work. Any member of the public is a licensee, and is addressed as "you". You accept the license if you copy, modify or distribute the work in a way requiring permission under copyright law.

A "Modified Version" of the Document means any work containing the Document or a portion of it, either copied verbatim, or with modifications and/or translated into another language.

A "Secondary Section" is a named appendix or a front-matter section of the Document that deals exclusively with the relationship of the publishers or authors of the Document to the Document's overall subject (or to related matters) and contains nothing that could fall directly within that overall subject. (Thus, if the Document is in part a textbook of mathematics, a Secondary Section may not explain any mathematics.) The relationship could be a matter of historical connection with the subject or with related matters, or of legal, commercial, philosophical, ethical or political position regarding them.

The "Invariant Sections" are certain Secondary Sections whose titles are designated, as being those of Invariant Sections, in the notice that says that the Document is released under this License. If a section does not fit the above definition of Secondary then it is not allowed to be designated as Invariant. The Document may contain zero Invariant Sections. If the Document does not identify any Invariant Sections then there are none.

The "Cover Texts" are certain short passages of text that are listed, as Front-Cover Texts or Back-Cover Texts, in the notice that says that the Document is released under this License. A Front-Cover Text may be at most 5 words, and a Back-Cover Text may be at most 25 words.

A "Transparent" copy of the Document means a machine-readable copy, represented in a format whose specification is available to the general public, that is suitable for revising the document straightforwardly with generic text editors or (for images composed of pixels) generic paint programs or (for drawings) some widely available drawing editor, and that is suitable for input to text formatters or for automatic translation to a variety of formats suitable for input to text formatters. A copy made in an otherwise Transparent file format whose markup, or absence of markup, has been arranged to thwart or discourage subsequent modification by readers is not Transparent. An image format is not Transparent if used for any substantial amount of text. A copy that is not "Transparent" is called "Opaque".

Examples of suitable formats for Transparent copies include plain ASCII without markup, Texinfo input format, LaTeX input format, SGML or XML using a publicly available DTD, and standard-conforming simple HTML, PostScript or PDF designed for human modification. Examples of transparent image formats include PNG, XCF and JPG. Opaque formats include proprietary formats that can be read and edited only by proprietary word processors, SGML or XML for which the DTD and/or processing tools are not generally available, and the machine-generated HTML, PostScript or PDF produced by some word processors for output purposes only.

The "Title Page" means, for a printed book, the title page itself, plus such following pages as are needed to hold, legibly, the material this License requires to appear in the title page. For works in formats which do not have any title page as such, "Title Page" means the text near the most prominent appearance of the work's title, preceding the beginning of the body of the text.

The "publisher" means any person or entity that distributes copies of the Document to the public.

A section "Entitled XYZ" means a named subunit of the Document whose title either is precisely XYZ or contains XYZ in parentheses following text that translates XYZ in another language. (Here XYZ stands for a specific section name mentioned below, such as "Acknowledgements", "Dedications", "Endorsements", or "History".) To "Preserve the Title" of such a section when you modify the Document means that it remains a section "Entitled XYZ" according to this definition.

The Document may include Warranty Disclaimers next to the notice which states that this License applies to the Document. These Warranty Disclaimers are considered to be included by reference in this License, but only as regards disclaiming warranties: any other implication that these Warranty Disclaimers may have is void and has no effect on the meaning of this License.

2. VERBATIM COPYING

You may copy and distribute the Document in any medium, either commercially or noncommercially, provided that this License, the copyright notices, and the license notice saying this License applies to the Document are reproduced in all copies, and that you add no other conditions whatsoever to those of this License. You may not use technical measures to obstruct or control the reading or further copying of the copies you make or distribute. However, you may accept compensation in exchange for copies. If you distribute a large enough number of copies you must also follow the conditions in section 3.

You may also lend copies, under the same conditions stated above, and you may publicly display copies.

3. COPYING IN QUANTITY

If you publish printed copies (or copies in media that commonly have printed covers) of the Document, numbering more than 100, and the Document's license notice requires Cover Texts, you must enclose the copies in covers that carry, clearly and legibly, all these Cover Texts: Front-Cover Texts on the front cover, and Back-Cover Texts on the back cover. Both covers must also clearly and legibly identify you as the publisher of these copies. The front cover must present the full title with all words of the title equally prominent and visible. You may add other material on the covers in addition. Copying with changes limited to the covers, as long as they preserve the title of the Document and satisfy these conditions, can be treated as verbatim copying in other respects.

If the required texts for either cover are too voluminous to fit legibly, you should put the first ones listed (as many as fit reasonably) on the actual cover, and continue the rest onto adjacent pages.

If you publish or distribute Opaque copies of the Document numbering more than 100, you must either include a machine-readable Transparent copy along with each Opaque copy, or state in or with each Opaque copy a computer-network location from which the general network-using public has access to download using public-standard network protocols a complete Transparent copy of the Document, free of added material. If you use the latter option, you must take reasonably prudent steps, when you begin distribution of Opaque copies in quantity, to ensure that this Transparent copy will remain thus accessible at the stated location until at least one year after the last time you distribute an Opaque copy (directly or through your agents or retailers) of that edition to the public.

It is requested, but not required, that you contact the authors of the Document well before redistributing any large number of copies, to give them a chance to provide you with an updated version of the Document.

4. MODIFICATIONS

You may copy and distribute a Modified Version of the Document under the conditions of sections 2 and 3 above, provided that you release the Modified Version under precisely this License, with the Modified Version filling the role of the Document, thus licensing distribution and modification of the Modified Version to whoever possesses a copy of it. In addition, you must do these things in the Modified Version:

A. Use in the Title Page (and on the covers, if any) a title distinct from that of the Document, and from those of previous versions (which should, if there were any, be listed in the History section of the Document). You may use the same title as a previous version if the original publisher of that version gives permission.

B. List on the Title Page, as authors, one or more persons or entities responsible for authorship of the modifications in the Modified Version, together with at least five of the principal authors of the Document (all of its principal authors, if it has fewer than five), unless they release you from this requirement.

C. State on the Title page the name of the publisher of the Modified Version, as the publisher.

D. Preserve all the copyright notices of the Document.

E. Add an appropriate copyright notice for your modifications adjacent to the other copyright notices.

F. Include, immediately after the copyright notices, a license notice giving the public permission to use the Modified Version under the terms of this License, in the form shown in the Addendum below.

G. Preserve in that license notice the full lists of Invariant Sections and required Cover Texts given in the Document's license notice.

H. Include an unaltered copy of this License.

I. Preserve the section Entitled "History", Preserve its Title, and add to it an item stating at least the title, year, new authors, and publisher of the Modified Version as given on the Title Page. If there is no section Entitled "History" in the Document, create one stating the title, year, authors, and publisher of the Document as given on its Title Page, then add an item describing the Modified Version as stated in the previous sentence.

J. Preserve the network location, if any, given in the Document for public access to a Transparent copy of the Document, and likewise the network locations given in the Document for previous versions it was based on. These may be placed in the "History" section. You may omit a network location for a work that was published at least four years before the Document itself, or if the original publisher of the version it refers to gives permission.

K. For any section Entitled "Acknowledgements" or "Dedications", Preserve the Title of the section, and preserve in the section all the substance and tone of each of the contributor acknowledgements and/or dedications given therein.

L. Preserve all the Invariant Sections of the Document, unaltered in their text and in their titles. Section numbers or the equivalent are not considered part of the section titles.

M. Delete any section Entitled "Endorsements". Such a section may not be included in the Modified Version.

N. Do not retitle any existing section to be Entitled "Endorsements" or to conflict in title with any Invariant Section.

O. Preserve any Warranty Disclaimers.

If the Modified Version includes new front-matter sections or appendices that qualify as Secondary Sections and contain no material copied from the Document, you may at your option designate some or all of these sections as invariant. To do this, add their titles to the list of Invariant Sections in the Modified Version's license notice. These titles must be distinct from any other section titles.

You may add a section Entitled "Endorsements", provided it contains nothing but endorsements of your Modified Version by various parties—for example, statements of peer review or that the text has been approved by an organization as the authoritative definition of a standard.

You may add a passage of up to five words as a Front-Cover Text, and a passage of up to 25 words as a Back-Cover Text, to the end of the list of Cover Texts in the Modified Version. Only one passage of Front-Cover Text and one of Back-Cover Text may be added by (or through arrangements made by) any one entity. If the Document already includes a cover text for the same cover, previously added by you or by arrangement made by the same entity you are acting on behalf of, you may not add another; but you may replace the old one, on explicit permission from the previous publisher that added the old one.

The author(s) and publisher(s) of the Document do not by this License give permission to use their names for publicity for or to assert or imply endorsement of any Modified Version.

5. COMBINING DOCUMENTS

You may combine the Document with other documents released under this License, under the terms defined in section 4 above for modified versions, provided that you include in the combination all of the Invariant Sections of all of the original documents, unmodified, and list them all as Invariant Sections of your combined work in its license notice, and that you preserve all their Warranty Disclaimers.

The combined work need only contain one copy of this License, and multiple identical Invariant Sections may be replaced with a single copy. If there are multiple Invariant Sections with the same name but different contents, make the title of each such section unique by adding at the end of it, in parentheses, the name of the original author or publisher of that section if known, or else a unique number. Make the same adjustment to the section titles in the list of Invariant Sections in the license notice of the combined work.

In the combination, you must combine any sections Entitled "History" in the various original documents, forming one section Entitled "History"; likewise combine any sections Entitled "Acknowledgements", and any sections Entitled "Dedications". You must delete all sections Entitled "Endorsements."

6. COLLECTIONS OF DOCUMENTS

You may make a collection consisting of the Document and other documents released under this License, and replace the individual copies of this License in the various documents with a single copy that is included in the collection, provided that you follow the rules of this License for verbatim copying of each of the documents in all other respects.

You may extract a single document from such a collection, and distribute it individually under this License, provided you insert a copy of this License into the extracted document, and follow this License in all other respects regarding verbatim copying of that document.

7. AGGREGATION WITH INDEPENDENT WORKS

A compilation of the Document or its derivatives with other separate and independent documents or works, in or on a volume of a storage or distribution medium, is called an "aggregate" if the copyright resulting from the compilation is not used to limit the legal rights of the compilation's users beyond what the individual works permit. When the Document is included in an aggregate, this License does not apply to the other works in the aggregate which are not themselves derivative works of the Document.

If the Cover Text requirement of section 3 is applicable to these copies of the Document, then if the Document is less than one half of the entire aggregate, the Document's Cover Texts may be placed on covers that bracket the Document within the aggregate, or the electronic equivalent of covers if the Document is in electronic form. Otherwise they must appear on printed covers that bracket the whole aggregate.

8. TRANSLATION

Translation is considered a kind of modification, so you may distribute translations of the Document under the terms of section 4. Replacing Invariant Sections with translations requires special permission from their copyright holders, but you may include translations of some or all Invariant Sections in addition to the original versions of these Invariant Sections. You may include a translation of this License, and all the license notices in the Document, and any Warranty Disclaimers, provided that you also include the original English version of this License and the original versions of those notices and disclaimers. In case of a disagreement between the translation and the original version of this License or a notice or disclaimer, the original version will prevail.

If a section in the Document is Entitled "Acknowledgements", "Dedications", or "History", the requirement (section 4) to Preserve its Title (section 1) will typically require changing the actual title.

9. TERMINATION

You may not copy, modify, sublicense, or distribute the Document except as expressly provided under this License. Any attempt otherwise to copy, modify, sublicense, or distribute it is void, and will automatically terminate your rights under this License.

However, if you cease all violation of this License, then your license from a particular copyright holder is reinstated (a) provisionally, unless and until the copyright holder explicitly and finally terminates your license, and (b) permanently, if the copyright holder fails to notify you of the violation by some reasonable means prior to 60 days after the cessation.

Moreover, your license from a particular copyright holder is reinstated permanently if the copyright holder notifies you of the violation by some reasonable means, this is the first time you have received notice of violation of this License (for any work) from that copyright holder, and you cure the violation prior to 30 days after your receipt of the notice.

Termination of your rights under this section does not terminate the licenses of parties who have received copies or rights from you under this License. If your rights have been terminated and not permanently reinstated, receipt of a copy of some or all of the same material does not give you any rights to use it.

10. FUTURE REVISIONS OF THIS LICENSE

The Free Software Foundation may publish new, revised versions of the GNU Free Documentation License from time to time. Such new versions will be similar in spirit to the present version, but may differ in detail to address new problems or concerns. See http://www.gnu.org/copyleft/.

Each version of the License is given a distinguishing version number. If the Document specifies that a particular numbered version of this License "or any later version" applies to it, you have the option of following the terms and conditions either of that specified version or of any later version that has been published (not as a draft) by the Free Software Foundation. If the Document does not specify a version number of this License, you may choose any version ever published (not as a draft) by the Free Software Foundation. If the Document specifies that a proxy can decide which future versions of this License can be used, that proxy's public statement of acceptance of a version permanently authorizes you to choose that version for the Document.

11. RELICENSING

"Massive Multiauthor Collaboration Site" (or "MMC Site") means any World Wide Web server that publishes copyrightable works and also provides prominent facilities for anybody to edit those works. A public wiki that anybody can edit is an example of such a server. A "Massive Multiauthor Collaboration" (or "MMC") contained in the site means any set of copyrightable works thus published on the MMC site.

"CC-BY-SA" means the Creative Commons Attribution-Share Alike 3.0 license published by Creative Commons Corporation, a not-for-profit corporation with a principal place of business in San Francisco, California, as well as future copyleft versions of that license published by that same organization.

"Incorporate" means to publish or republish a Document, in whole or in part, as part of another Document.

An MMC is "eligible for relicensing" if it is licensed under this License, and if all works that were first published under this License somewhere other than this MMC, and subsequently incorporated in whole or in part into the MMC, (1) had no cover texts or invariant sections, and (2) were thus incorporated prior to November 1, 2008.

The operator of an MMC Site may republish an MMC contained in the site under CC-BY-SA on the same site at any time before August 1, 2009, provided the MMC is eligible for relicensing.

ADDENDUM: How to use this License for your documents

To use this License in a document you have written, include a copy of the License in the document and put the following copyright and license notices just after the title page:

```
Copyright (C)  year  your name.
Permission is granted to copy, distribute and/or modify this document
under the terms of the GNU Free Documentation License, Version 1.3
or any later version published by the Free Software Foundation;
with no Invariant Sections, no Front-Cover Texts, and no Back-Cover
Texts.  A copy of the license is included in the section entitled ``GNU
Free Documentation License''.
```

If you have Invariant Sections, Front-Cover Texts and Back-Cover Texts, replace the "with...Texts." line with this:

```
with the Invariant Sections being list their titles, with
the Front-Cover Texts being list, and with the Back-Cover Texts
being list.
```

If you have Invariant Sections without Cover Texts, or some other combination of the three, merge those two alternatives to suit the situation.

If your document contains nontrivial examples of program code, we recommend releasing these examples in parallel under your choice of free software license, such as the GNU General Public License, to permit their use in free software.

Function and Data Index

Concept Index

Short Contents

Table of Contents

www.ingramcontent.com/pod-product-compliance
Lightning Source LLC
LaVergne TN
LVHW060138070326
832902LV00018B/2837